# *Karen Brown*

# Italy

## *Charming Inns & Itineraries*

Written by

CLARE BROWN

Illustrations by Barbara Tapp
Cover Painting by Jann Pollard

Karen Brown's Guides, San Mateo, California

# Karen Brown Titles

Austria: Charming Inns & Itineraries

California: Charming Inns & Itineraries

England: Charming Bed & Breakfasts

England, Wales & Scotland: Charming Hotels & Itineraries

France: Charming Bed & Breakfasts

France: Charming Inns & Itineraries

Germany: Charming Inns & Itineraries

Ireland: Charming Inns & Itineraries

Italy: Charming Bed & Breakfasts

Italy: Charming Inns & Itineraries

New England: Charming Inns & Itineraries

Portugal: Charming Inns & Itineraries

Spain: Charming Inns & Itineraries

Switzerland: Charming Inns & Itineraries

*With Love*
*to*
*My Best Friend, Bill*
*With Love and Gratitude for*
*Many Miles of Memories*

**The painting on the front cover is of the town of Bellagio on Lake Como**

*Editors: Karen Brown, June Brown, Clare Brown, Kim Brown Holmsen, Iris Sandilands, Nicole Franchini, Lorena Aburto, Cathy Knight.*

*Technical support: William H. Brown III; Webmistress: Lynn Upthagrove.*

*Illustrations: Barbara Tapp; Cover painting: Jann Pollard.*

*Maps: Susanne Lau Alloway—Greenleaf Design & Graphics; Inside cover photo: W. Russell Ohlson.*

*Distributed by Fodor's Travel Publications, Inc., 280 Park Avenue, New York, NY 10017, USA.*

*Distributed in the United Kingdom by Random House UK, 20 Vauxhall Bridge Road, London, SW1V 2SA, England, phone: 44 20 7849 4000, fax: 44 20 7840 8406.*

*Distributed in Canada by Random House of Canada Limited, 2775 Matheson Blvd. East, Mississanga, Ontario L4W 4P7, Canada, phone: 905 624 0673, fax: 905 624 6217.*

*Distributed in Australia by Random House Australia, 20 Alfred Street, Milsons Point, Sydney NSW 2061, Australia, 2066, phone: 61 2 9954 9966, fax: 61 2 9954 4562.*

*Distributed in New Zealand by Random House New Zealand, 18 Poland Road, Glenfield, Auckland, New Zealand, phone: 64 9 444 7197, fax: 64 9 444 7524.*

*Distributed in South Africa by Random House South Africa, Endulani, East Wing, 5A Jubilee Road, Parktown 2193, South Africa, phone: 27 11 484 3538, fax: 27 11 484 6180.*

*A catalog record for this book is available from the British Library.*

### Library of Congress Cataloging-in-Publication Data

Brown, Clare.
   Karen Brown's Italy ; charming inns & itineraries / written by Clare Brown ;
illustrations by Barbara Tapp ; cover painting by Jann Pollard.
     p. cm. -- (Karen Brown's country inn series)
   ISBN 0-928901-13-1
   1.  Bed and breakfast accommodations--Italy--Guidebooks.  2.
Hotels--Italy--Guidebooks.  3. Italy--Guidebooks. I. Title: Italy. II. Brown, Karen, 1956-
III Title.IV.  Series

TX907.5.I8 B76 2001
647.9445'01--dc21

                                               00-039734

# Contents

 *Introduction*

Of all the countries in the world, there is none more magical than Italy: it is truly a tourist's paradise—a traveler's dream destination. No one could be so blasé, that within Italy's narrow boot there would not be something to tantalize his fancy. For the archaeologist, there are some of the most fascinating and perfectly preserved ancient monuments existing today, just begging to be explored. For the gourmet, there is the finest food in the world. For the outdoors enthusiast, there are towering mountains to conquer and magnificent ski slopes to enjoy. For the lover of art, the museums are bursting with the genius of Italy's sons such as Michelangelo, Leonardo da Vinci, and Raphael. For the architect, Italy is a school of design—you are surrounded by the ancient buildings whose perfection still inspires the styles of today. For the history buff, Italy is a joy of wonders—her cities are veritable living museums. For the wine connoisseur, Italy produces an unbelievable selection of wine whose quality is unsurpassed. For the adventurer, Italy has intriguing medieval walled villages tucked away in every part of the country. For the beach buff, Italy's coastline and lakes hold the promise of some of the most elegant resorts in the world. For the religious pilgrim, Italy is the cradle of the Christian faith and home of some to the world's most famous saints. The miracle of Italy is that all these treasures come packaged in a gorgeous country of majestic mountains, misty lakes, idyllic islands, wonderful walled villages, and gorgeous cities. In addition, the climate is ideal and the people warm and gracious. Italy is truly a perfect destination.

# About This Guide

This guide is written with two main objectives: to describe the most romantic hotels throughout Italy and to tie these hotels together with itineraries that include enough details so that you can plan your own holiday. This introduction explains how to use the guide and also touches upon what to expect while traveling. After the introduction the main part of the guide is divided into three sections: itineraries, hotel descriptions, and maps. The itinerary section outlines itineraries with sightseeing suggestions along the way; the hotel description section gives a comprehensive list of recommended lodgings (appearing alphabetically by town); the map section has 14 maps to help you pinpoint each town where we suggest a place to stay. The pertinent regional map number is given at the right on the *top line* of each hotel's description. To make it easier for you, we have divided each location map into a grid of four parts, a, b, c, and d, as indicated on each map's key.

We have personally inspected each place that we recommend and describe its ambiance and merits in our write-up, which is followed by an illustration and practical information such as address, telephone and fax numbers, rates, etc. Our choices are strictly based on hotels we think you would most enjoy. Frequently we hear, "I don't care where I stay—I'm rarely in my room except to sleep." If this is your true philosophy, then this book is *not* for you. To our way of thinking, where you stay weaves the very fabric of your trip and your choice of hotels is of absolutely prime importance. Not that the hotel needs to be expensive: a moonlit dinner on the terrace of a simple inn can be as memorable as dining at a fancy hotel—sometimes even more so because the owner is there to pamper you. The recommendations in our guide vary tremendously: some are grand hotels—fit for a king and priced accordingly; others are simple, inexpensively priced hotels tucked away in remote hamlets. We include them all if they have personality, romantic charm, and antique ambiance.

# *About Itineraries*

In the itinerary section of this guide you'll be able to find an itinerary, or portion of an itinerary, that can be easily tailored to fit your exact time frame and suit your own particular interests. If your time is limited, you can certainly follow just a segment of an itinerary. In the itineraries we have not specified the number of nights at each destination, since to do so seemed much too confining. Some travelers like to see as much as possible in a short period of time. For others, just the thought of packing and unpacking each night makes them shudder in horror and they would never stop for less than three or four nights at any destination. A third type of tourist doesn't like to travel at all—the destination is the focus and he uses this guide to find the perfect place from which he never wanders except for daytime excursions. So, use this guide as a reference to plan your personalized trip.

Our advice is not to rush. Part of the joy of traveling is to settle in at a hotel that you like and use it as a hub from which to take side trips to explore the countryside. When you dash too quickly from place to place, you never have the opportunity to get to know the owners of the hotels and to become friends with other guests. Look at the maps in the back of this guide to find the places to stay in the areas where you want to travel. Read about each hotel in the hotel description section of this book and decide which sound most suited to your taste and budget, then choose a base for each area you want to visit.

## MAPS

Each itinerary is preceded by a map showing the route and each hotel listing is referenced on its top line to a map at the back of the book. To make it easier for you, hotel location maps are divided into a grid of four parts—a, b, c, and d—as indicated on each map's key. All maps are an artist's renderings and are not intended to replace detailed commercial maps. We use the *Michelin Tourist and Motoring Atlas of Italy,* a book of maps with a scale of 1:300,000 (1 cm = 3 km). We also find the regional Michelin maps very useful and we state which Michelin 400-series map each hotel's town is found on in the hotel description. To outline your visit to Italy you might want to consider the one-page map of Italy, Michelin map 988. Italy hotel maps in this book can be cross-referenced with those in our companion guide, *Italy: Charming Bed & Breakfasts*. We sell Michelin country maps, city maps, and regional green guides in our website store at *www.karenbrown.com*.

## SIGHTSEEING

Ideas on what to see and do are suggested throughout the six itineraries. However, we just touch upon some of the sightseeing highlights. There is a wealth of wonders to see in Italy, plus, of course, many local festivals and events. Before you leave, check with the tourist office for further information targeted at exactly where you plan to travel. And, once on the road, make it a habit to always make your first stop the local tourist office to pick up maps, schedules of special events, and sightseeing information. Even more important, before you drive out of your way to see a particular museum or place of interest, check when it is open. As a general guideline, most museums are closed on Mondays and for a couple of hours in the middle of the day. Small museums are usually open only in the morning. Outdoor museums usually open at 9 am and close about an hour before sunset. Most monuments and museums close on national holidays—see "Holidays" on page 15. *NOTE*: To save waiting in line for hours to buy entrance tickets, buy tickets for major museums in advance from travel agencies, hotels, or tobacco shops.

# About Hotels

## BASIS FOR SELECTION

This guide does not try to appeal to everyone. It is definitely prejudiced: each hotel included is one we have seen and liked. We visit hundreds of hotels and choose only those we think are special. It might be a splendid villa elegantly positioned overlooking one of Italy's romantic lakes or a simple little chalet snuggled high in a mountain meadow. But there is a common denominator—they all have charm. Therefore, if you too prefer to travel spending your nights in romantic old villas, appealing chalets, dramatic medieval castles, ancient monasteries, converted stone cottages, and gorgeous palaces, we are kindred souls.

For some of you, cost will not be a factor if the hotel is outstanding. For others, a budget guides your choice. The appeal of a simple little inn with rustic wooden furniture beckons some, while the glamour of ornate ballrooms dressed with crystal chandeliers and gilded mirrors appeals to others. What we have tried to do is to indicate what each hotel has to offer and describe the setting, so that you can make the choice to suit your own preferences and holiday. We feel if you know what to expect, you won't be disappointed, so we have tried to be candid and honest in our appraisals.

## CREDIT CARDS

Most hotels in this guide accept credit cards. Those hotels that do accept plastic payment are indicated in the hotel description section using the following abbreviations: AX–American Express, MC–MasterCard, VS–Visa, or simply, all major. *NOTE:* When calculating how much cash you will need, be aware that some hotels will accept a credit card to guarantee the reservation, but will not let you pay your bill by credit card. Always ask in advance if you can pay by credit card when you check out.

## DECOR

It is difficult to find hotels in Italy furnished in a simple style. Italian hotels frequently reflect a rather formal opulence and tend toward a rather fussy decor. There are some exceptions. In a few instances (which we note in the hotel descriptions) the hotels are decorated with a more rustic ambiance using country antiques, but this is not the norm. When antiques are used, they are very often the fancy, gilded variety.

## GROUPS & AFFILIATIONS

There are two well-known groups of hotels to which many of the hotels in this guide belong. The *Romantik Hotels* group is an affiliation of charming small hotels that are managed by the owner and are usually located in a historic building. You can recognize the hotels that belong to this group because they have the word *Romantik* preceding their name. The *Relais & Châteaux* group is an affiliation of luxurious small hotels that are very expensive, with extremely high standards of excellence. You can tell which of the hotels in our guide belong to this group because we have indicated "Relais & Châteaux" in the hotel's bottom information.

## RATES

In the hotel section in the back of the book each listing shows a rate range that reflects the approximate 2001 nightly cost, high season, in lire for a room for two persons including tax, service, and Continental breakfast. There are a few hotels where breakfast and one other meal (either lunch or dinner) are included in the rate and, if so, this too is noted. Please use the rates given only as a general guide because each hotel has such a wide range of price possibilities that it is impossible to project with complete accuracy. Be sure to ask at the time of booking exactly what the price is and what it includes (breakfast, parking, etc.) so that you won't be in for any unpleasant surprises—sometimes rates increase after this book goes to print. When you plan your holiday, check the current exchange rate with your bank.

HOW TO ECONOMIZE: The price for a room in Italy has soared in the last few years. However, if you study carefully the rates given in the back of this guide, you can still find a few bargains available and can plan your trip using one of the less expensive hotels as your hub from which to venture out each day. We also publish *Karen Brown's Italy: Charming Bed & Breakfasts*, which makes an ideal companion to this guide. The maps in both are similar, making it easy to choose a place to stay from either book. Not only can you save money by sometimes choosing a bed and breakfast for a night's accommodation, but you can also enjoy the experience of staying where you have the opportunity to know your host and fellow guests. We highly recommend choosing a combination of places to stay from both books.

For those of you who want to squeeze the most value out of each night's stay, we have several other suggestions:

1) Travel off season—spring and fall are usually lovely in Italy and the hotels often have less expensive rates.

2) Ask for a room without a private bathroom—some hotels have very nice rooms, usually with a washbasin in the room, but with a shared bathroom down the hall.

3) Ask if there is a weekly rate—frequently hotels offer a price break for guests staying a week or more. If traveling with children, ask if there is a special family suite at a lesser price than separate rooms.

4) Ask about rates with meals included. For a stay of three days or longer, many hotels offer a special rate including meals: MAP (Modified American Plan) means two meals a day are included; AP (American Plan) means three meals a day are included.

5) Last, but not least, is the most important way to save money: stay in the countryside instead of in the cities. We cannot stress enough how much more value you receive when you avoid the cities—especially the tourist centers such as Rome, Florence, Milan, and Venice. Of course stay right in the heart of town if you are not watching your budget, but if you are trying to squeeze the greatest value from your lire, choose hotels in the countryside and take side trips to visit the more-pricey tourist centers.

## RESERVATIONS

People frequently ask, "Do I need a hotel reservation?" The answer really depends on how flexible you want to be, how tight your time schedule is, in which season you are traveling, and how disappointed you would be if your first choice is unavailable.

It is not unusual for the major tourist cities to be completely sold out during the peak season of June through September. Be forewarned: hotel space in Rome, Florence, Milan, and Venice is really at a premium and unless you don't mind taking your chances on a last-minute cancellation or staying on the outskirts of town, make a reservation as far in advance as possible. Space in the countryside is a little easier. However, if you have your heart set on some special little hotel, you certainly should reserve as soon as your travel dates are firm. Reservations are confining. Most hotels want a deposit to hold your room and frequently you cannot get a refund if you change your plans. So it is a double bind: making reservations locks you into a solid framework, but without reservations you might be stuck with accommodations you do not like. During the height of the tourist season, some small hotels accept reservations only for a minimum of three or more nights. However, do not give up, because almost all of the hotels that have this policy take a last-minute booking for a shorter period of time if you call along the way and there is space available. For those who like the security blanket of having each night pre-planned so that once you leave home you do not have to worry about where to rest your head, several options for making reservations are listed on the following pages.

When making your reservations, be sure to identify yourself as a "Karen Brown traveler." The hotels appreciate your visit, value their inclusion in our guide, and

*Introduction–About Hotels*

frequently tell us they take special care of our readers. We hear over and over again that the people who use our guides are such wonderful guests!

E-MAIL: This is our preferred way of making a reservation. If the hotel is on our website, we have included their e-mail address in the listing details and added a direct link on their Karen Brown web page. Clearly state the following: number of people in your party; how many rooms you desire; whether you want a private bathroom; date of arrival and date of departure; ask the rate per night and if a deposit is needed. When you receive a reply, send the deposit requested and ask for a receipt and a map showing directions to their hotel. *NOTE:* When corresponding with Italy, be sure to spell out the month. Do not use numbers since in Europe they reverse the American system—e.g. 6/9 means September 6, not June 9.

FAX: If you have access to a fax machine, this is a super-efficient way to reach a hotel. The majority of hotels in Italy have fax numbers, which we have noted in the back of the book under each hotel listing. Do not forget to include your fax number for their response. Although most hotels can understand a letter written in English, at the end of this introduction we provide a letter written in Italian with an English translation. Photocopy it and use it when you fax your reservation request. See comments under "E-mail" above, and the "Telephone" paragraph below for instructions on how to fax.

LETTER: If you start early, you can write directly to the hotels and request exactly what you need. Again, be sure to be specific as to your arrival and departure dates, number in your party, and what type of room you want. For convenience, use photocopies of the sample reservation-request letter on page 25. See comments under "E-mail" above. Allow six weeks for an answer—mail to and from Italy is *very* slow.

TELEPHONE: Another way to make a reservation is to telephone. You can have your answer immediately, and if space is not available, you can then decide on an alternative. The cost is minimal if you dial direct —ask your local operator when to call for the lowest rates. Also consider what time it is in Italy when you call (even the most gracious of owners are sometimes a bit grouchy when awakened at 3 am). If you are dialing from the United States, the system is to dial 011 (the international code), then 39 (Italy code), then the city code (do *not* drop the 0 in front of the city code), and then the telephone number. Almost all of the hotels have someone who speaks English. The best chance for finding the owner or manager who speaks English is to call when it is late afternoon in Italy (Italy is six hours ahead of New York). Be aware that Italy's telephone numbers are constantly changing, so if you cannot reach a hotel, ask for operator assistance.

TRAVEL AGENT: A travel agent can be of great assistance, particularly if your own time is limited. A proficient agent can expertly handle all the details of your holiday and tie them together for you in a neat package—including hotel reservations, airline tickets, boat tickets, train reservations, ferry schedules, and theater tickets. For your airline tickets there is usually no service fee (unless you are using some kind of discount coupon), but the majority of travel agencies do charge for their other services. Talk with your agent about fees and be frank about how much you want to spend. If your travel agent is not familiar with all the small places in this guide (many are so tiny that they appear in no other major publications), you can loan him or her your book.

UNITED STATES REPRESENTATIVE: In the back of the book there is a page giving information on KB Travel Service, a company that specializes in Karen-Brown-recommended hotels and "mini-tours." Also in the back of the book there is information on Hidden Treasures of Italy (HTI), a company that can arrange reservations for any hotel in this book. Telephone numbers are given for both companies. If you are interested, call to check on the services offered and the fees.

# *About Italy*

## CURRENCY

Italy's unit of currency is the lire. However, in January 1999, 11 European countries (Austria, Belgium, Finland, France, Germany, Ireland, Italy, Luxembourg, Netherlands, Portugal, and Spain) had their currencies fixed to the new unit of European Monetary Union (EMU) currency, the euro. No bills or coins were issued immediately. For the first three years the euro will be the internationally traded currency, though local currencies will remain in circulation, then, during a six-month period beginning January 1, 2002, the euro will be phased in and local currencies will be phased out. Both types of currency will be valid during this period. Finally, on July 1, 2002, local currencies will be removed from circulation.

## DRIVING

CAR RENTAL: Readers frequently ask our advice on car rental companies. For many years for our personal use, we have chosen Auto Europe, a car rental broker that works with the major car rental companies to find the lowest possible price. They also offer a variety of other rentals and services besides cars, such as motor homes and chauffeur services. Auto Europe's toll-free phone service from every European country connects you to their US-based, 24-hour reservation center (ask for the card with European phone numbers to be sent to you). Auto Europe offers our readers a 5% discount, and occasionally free upgrades. Be sure to use the Karen Brown ID number 99006187 to receive your discount and any special offers. You can make your own reservations via our website, *www.karenbrown.com* (select Auto Europe from the home page under Travel Center), or by phone (800-223-5555).

DISTANCES: Distances are indicated in kilometers (one kilometer equals 0.621 mile). As you drive through the countryside, you will be astonished at how dramatically the scenery can change in just an hour's drive.

DRIVER'S LICENSE: A current license from your home country is valid for driving throughout Italy if you are on holiday. However, when renting a car, certain age limits apply. Please check on the age limit policy with the car rental company.

GASOLINE: Gasoline (petrol) is expensive. Budget this as part of the cost of your trip if you are driving. Most gas stations now accept Visa credit cards, and the ERG stations accept American Express. Be aware that service stations off the expressways close in the afternoon for several hours and are frequently closed on Sundays, so plan accordingly.

ROADS: The Italian roads are nothing short of spectacular, including some of the finest highways in the world. In fact, the Italians are absolute geniuses when it comes to their engineering feats (which actually is not such a surprising fact when you consider what a fantastic road system the Romans built 2,000 years ago). Nothing seems to daunt the Italian engineers: you would think the mountains are made of clay instead of solid rock, the way the roads tunnel through them. Sometimes a roadway seems endlessly suspended in mid-air as it bridges a mountain crevasse.

ROAD SIGNS: Before starting on the road prepare yourself by learning the international driving signs so that you can obey all the rules. There are several basic sign shapes: triangular signs warn that there is danger ahead; circular signs indicate compulsory rules and information; square signs give information concerning telephones, parking, camping, etc. Yellow signs are for tourists and indicate a site of historical or cultural interest, hotels, and restaurants.

TOLL ROADS: Italy has a network of super expressways that makes any spot in the country an easy destination by car. Once you are on the toll roads, you can go quickly from almost any area of Italy to another, but be forewarned—these toll roads are expensive. However, every cent is well spent when you consider the alternative of creeping along within a maze of trucks and buzzing motorcycles, taking forever to go only a few kilometers. Use the toll roads for the major distances you need to cover, and then choose the small roads when you wish to meander leisurely through the countryside. Toll roads are mystifying until you learn the system—even then it is confusing because just when you think you have the operation down pat, you find it varies slightly. This is the most common routine: first follow the green expressway signs toward the toll road. Sometimes these signs begin many kilometers from the expressway, so be patient and continue the game of follow-the-sign. Each entrance to the expressway handles traffic going in both directions. As you enter into the tollgate, there is usually a red button you push and a card pops out of a slot. After going through the toll station you choose the direction you want to go. As you leave the expressway, there is a toll station where your ticket is collected and you pay according to how many kilometers you traveled. For convenience, a *Viacard*, or magnetic reusable card for tolls, is available in all tollway gas stations for 50,000 or 100,000 lire, or a MasterCard or Visa card can now be used in specified lanes.

## ELECTRICAL CURRENT

If you are taking any electrical appliances made for use in the United States, you will need a transformer plus a two-pin adapter. A voltage of 220 AC current at 50 cycles per second is almost countrywide, though in remote areas you may encounter 120V. The voltage is often displayed on the socket. Even though we recommend that you purchase appliances with dual-voltage options whenever possible, it will still be necessary to have the appropriate socket adapter. Also, be especially careful with expensive equipment such as computers—verify with the manufacturer the adapter/converter capabilities and requirements.

## FOOD & DRINK

It is almost impossible to get a bad meal in Italy. Italians themselves love to eat and dining is a social occasion to be with family and friends. Restaurants are bustling not only with tourists, but also with the Italians who dawdle at the tables long after the meal is over, chatting and laughing with perhaps a glass of wine or a last cup of coffee.

You soon get in the spirit of the game of deciding which kind of restaurant to choose for your next meal. The selection is immense, all the way from the simple family trattoria where mama is cooking in the kitchen to the most elegant of gourmet restaurants with world-renowned chefs. Whichever you choose, you won't be disappointed. The Italians are artists when it comes to pasta, seen on every menu and prepared in endless, fascinating ways. Some restaurants offer a set-price tourist menu *(menu turistico)* that includes soup or pasta, a meat dish with vegetable, dessert, and mineral water or wine. A tip is usually included in the price, but it is customary to leave some small change.

Wine, of course, is offered with every meal. You rarely see an Italian family eating without their bottle of wine on the table. Unless you are a true wine connoisseur, we suggest the regional wines and if you ask your waiter to assist you with the choice, you flatter him and discover many superb wines.

Some of the most popular wines that you see on the Italian menus are: Chianti, a well-known wine produced in the Tuscany area south of Florence; Marsala, a golden sweet wine from Sicily (a favorite of Lord Nelson); Soave, a superb light white wine produced near Venice; Orvieto, a semi-sweet wine from the Umbria region near Assisi, and Est Est Est, a beautiful semi-sweet wine produced near Rome. The story that we heard about Est Est Est is lots of fun and perhaps even true. It seems that many years ago a wealthy nobleman was traveling south. Being a true gourmet both of food and drink, he sent his servant before him to pick out all the best places to eat and drink along the way. When the servant neared Rome he discovered such a divine wine that all he could relay back to his master was "Est, est, est," meaning "Yes, yes, yes." Today you will think the same about most of the wines you enjoy in Italy—the answer is still "Yes, yes, yes!"

## HOLIDAYS

It is very important to know Italian holidays because most museums, shops, and offices are closed. National holidays are listed below:

New Year's Day (January 1)                    Assumption Day (August 15)
Epiphany (January 6)                          All Saints' Day (November 1)
Easter (and the following Monday)             Christmas (December 25)
Liberation Day (April 25)                     Santo Stefano (December 26)
Labor Day (May 1)

In addition to the national holidays, each town has its own special holiday to honor its patron saint. Some of the major ones are listed below:

Bologna–St. Petronio (October 4)              Palermo–Santa Rosalia (July 15)
Florence–St. John the Baptist (June 24)       Rome–St. Peter (June 29)
Milan–St. Ambrose (December 7)                Venice–St. Mark (April 25)

The Vatican in Rome has its own schedule. The museums are closed every Sunday, except the last Sunday of each month when admission is free.

# INFORMATION SOURCES

If you have questions not answered in this guide or need special guidance for a particular destination, the Italian Government Travel Offices can assist you. If you have access to the Internet, check out the Italian Tourist Board's websites: *www.italiantourism.com* or *www.enit.it*. The offices listed below are usually open from 9 am–5 pm, Monday through Friday.

UNITED STATES

*Chicago*: Italian Government Travel Office, 500 N. Michigan Ave., Suite 2240, Chicago, IL 60611 USA; tel: (312) 644-0996, fax: (312) 644-3019. (Mail, fax, or phone only.)

*Los Angeles*: Italian Government Tourist Board, 12400 Wilshire Blvd., Suite 550, Los Angeles, CA 90025, USA; tel: (310) 820-1898, fax: (310) 820-6357.

*New York*: Italian Government Travel Office, 630 5th Ave., Suite 1565, New York, NY 10111, USA; tel: (212) 245-4822, fax: (212) 586-9249.

CANADA

*Montreal*: Italian Government Travel Office, 1 Place Ville Marie, Suite 1914, Montreal, Quebec H3B 2C3, Canada; tel: (514) 866-7667, fax: (514) 392-1429.

GREAT BRITAIN

*London*: Italian State Tourist Board, 1 Princes Street, London W1R 9AY1, England; tel: (020) 7355-1557, fax: (020) 7493-6695.

ITALY

*Rome:* ENTE Nazionale Italiano per il Turismo (Italian Government Travel Office), Via Marghera, 2, Rome 00185, Italy; tel: (06) 49 711, fax: (06) 44 633 79.

AUSTRALIA

*Sydney:* Italian Government Travel Office, Level 26, 44 Market Street, Sydney NSW 2000, Australia; tel: (61292) 621.666, fax: (61292) 625.677.

# PROVINCES

Italy is divided into Provinces, which appear in abbreviated form in addresses. Some of the provinces you are likely to see and their abbreviated codes are as follows:

| | | | | | | | |
|---|---|---|---|---|---|---|---|
| AG | *Agrigento* | AL | *Alessandria* | AN | *Ancona* | AO | *Aosta* |
| AR | *Arezzo* | AP | *Ascoli Picino* | AT | *Asti* | AV | *Avellino* |
| BA | *Bari* | BL | *Belluno* | BG | *Bergamo* | BN | *Benevento* |
| BO | *Bologna* | BZ | *Bolzano* | BS | *Brescia* | BR | *Brindisi* |
| CA | *Cagliari* | CE | *Caserta* | CH | *Chieti* | CZ | *Catanzaro* |
| CO | *Como* | CS | *Cosenza* | CR | *Cremona* | CT | *Catania* |
| CB | *Campobasso* | EN | *Enna* | FE | *Ferrara* | FG | *Froggia* |
| FI | *Firenze* | FO | *Forli* | GE | *Genova* | GO | *Gorizia* |
| GR | *Grosseto* | IM | *Imperia* | IS | *Isernia* | LA | *Latina* |
| LE | *Lecce* | LI | *Livorno* | LT | *Latino* | LU | *Lucca* |
| MS | *Massa* | MN | *Mantova* | MI | *Milano* | MO | *Modena* |
| ME | *Messina* | M | *Macerata* | MT | *Matera* | NA | *Napoli* |
| NO | *Novara* | NU | *Nuoro* | OR | *Oristano* | PA | *Palermo* |
| PC | *Piacunga* | PE | *Pescara* | PD | *Padova* | PR | *Parma* |
| PV | *Pavia* | PG | *Perugia* | PS | *Pesaro* | PI | *Pisa* |
| PT | *Pistoia* | PZ | *Potenza* | RA | *Ravenna* | RI | *Rieti* |
| RM | *Roma* | RN | *Rimini* | RO | *Ravigo* | SA | *Salerno* |
| SI | *Siena* | SO | *Sondrio* | SP | *La Spezia* | SR | *Siracusa* |
| SV | *Savona* | TA | *Taranto* | TE | *Teramo* | TR | *Terni* |
| TO | *Torino* | TS | *Trieste* | TN | *Trento* | TV | *Treviso* |
| VE | *Venezia* | VC | *Vercelli* | VR | *Verona* | VI | *Vicenza* |
| VT | *Viterbo* | | | | | | |

# REGIONS

Italy is divided into 20 regions. A map showing the location of each region is found in the back of the book in the map section. Below is a list of the regions and their capital cities.

| REGION | CAPITAL CITY | REGION | CAPITAL CITY |
|---|---|---|---|
| Abruzzo | *L'Aquila* | Marches | *Ancona* |
| Apulia | *Bari* | Molise | *Campobasso* |
| Basilicata | *Potenza* | Piedmont | *Torino* |
| Calabria | *Catanzaro* | Sardinia | *Cagliari* |
| Campania | *Naples* | Sicily | *Palermo* |
| Emila-Romagna | *Bologna* | Tuscany | *Florence* |
| Friuli-Venezia Giulia | *Trieste* | Trentino-Alto Adige | *Trento & Bolzano* |
| Lazio | *Rome* | Umbria | *Perugia* |
| Liguria | *Genova* | Valle d'Aosta | *Aosta* |
| Lombardy | *Milan* | Veneto | *Venice* |

# SECURITY WHILE TRAVELING

The Italians are wonderful hosts. It seems every Italian has a brother or cousin in the United States, and so the warmth of camaraderie is further enhanced. In spite of the overall graciousness of the Italians, there are instances where cars are pilfered or purses snatched, but this happens all over the world. Just be cautious. Watch your purse. Don't let your wallet stand out like a red light in your back pocket. Lock your valuables in the hotel safe. Don't leave valuables temptingly exposed in your car. Never set down luggage in train stations or airports, even for a minute. In other words, use common sense. *NOTE:* Whenever you travel to any country, it is wise to make a photocopy of the pages of your passport showing your picture, passport number, date, and where issued. With this photocopy in hand it is much easier to get a replacement passport.

## SHOPPING

Italy is definitely a shopper's paradise. Not only are the stores brimming with tempting merchandise, but their displays are beautiful, from the tiniest fruit market to the most chic boutique. Each region has its specialty. In Venice items made from blown glass and handmade laces are very popular. Milan is famous for its clothing and silk wear (gorgeous scarves, ties, and blouses). Florence is a paradise for leather goods (purses, shoes, wallets, gloves, suitcases) and also for gold jewelry (you can buy gold jewelry by weight). Rome is a fashion center—you can stroll the pedestrian shopping streets browsing in some of the world's most elegant, sophisticated boutiques. You can buy the very latest designer creations and, of course, religious items are available, especially near St. Peter's. Naples and the surrounding regions (Capri, Ravello, Positano) offer delightful coral jewelry and also a wonderful selection of ceramics.

For purchases over 300,000 lire an immediate cash refund of the tax amount is offered by the Italian government to non-residents of the EU. Goods must be purchased at an affiliated retail outlet with the "tax-free for tourists" sign. Ask for the store receipt **plus** the tax-free shopping receipt. At the airport go first to the customs office where they will examine the items purchased and stamp both receipts, and then to the "tax-free cash refund" point after passport control. There are also tax-free refund facilities available at some road border crossings. You can also mail your tax-free receipt back to Italy in a pre-addressed envelope no later than 60 days from the date of purchase.

## TELEPHONES—HOW TO MAKE CALLS

CALLING HOME: Calling overseas is very expensive from Italy. In addition, hotels usually add a hefty surcharge to telephone calls charged to your room. The best bet is to use one of the many available international telephone cards. With these you can make a local call within Italy and be connected with your home operator. When you arrive home, the cost appears on your telephone bill. Ask your local telephone company what access number to use. In the United States all of the long-distance phone companies, including AT&T, MCI, and Sprint, offer this option.

CALLING WITHIN ITALY: Most telephones in Italy take either 100- or 200-lire coins. Becoming more common are the telephones that take a telephone credit card called a *scheda*. These credit cards can be purchased at tobacco stores or telephone offices. You choose a card costing 5,000 or 10,000 lire and use it until the credit is used up by the calls you made. It is very simple and the telephones have instructions demonstrating how to use them. There are a few telephones still remaining that take only special tokens. These can usually be purchased at a vending machine near the telephone.

Dial 113 for emergencies of all kinds—24-hour service nationwide.
Dial 116 for Automobile Club for urgent breakdown assistance on the road.

## TRANSPORTATION

BOATS: Italy has gorgeous islands dotting her shorelines, a glorious string of lakes gracing her mountains to the north, and romantic canals in Venice. Luckily for the tourist, the country's boat system is excellent.

All of Italy's islands are linked to the mainland by a wonderful maritime network. The many outlying islands sometimes have overnight ferries that offer sleeping accommodations and facilities for cars. The closer islands usually offer a choice—the hydrofoil that zips quickly across the water or the regular ferry that is slower. Italy also offers you an enchanting selection of lakes. One of the true highlights of traveling in Italy is to explore these wondrous lakes by hopping on one of the nostalgic ferry boats that glide romantically between little villages clustered along the shorelines. Again, there is usually a choice of either the

*Introduction–About Italy*

hydrofoil that darts between the hamlets, or the ferry that glides leisurely across the water and usually offers beverage and food service on board. The boat schedules are posted at each pier, or you can request a timetable from the Italian tourist office. *NOTE:* These little boats are punctual, to the minute. Be right at the pier with your ticket in hand so you can jump on board during the brief interlude that the boat stops at the shore. If at all possible, try to squeeze in at least one boat excursion—it is a treat you will long remember.

TRAINS: Italy has an excellent network of trains. The major express trains are usually a quick, reliable way to whip between the major cities. In contrast, the local trains stop at every little town, take much longer, and are frequently delayed. Each train station is well organized. There is almost always an information desk where someone speaks English who will answer any questions and advise you as to the best schedule. There is another counter where you purchase your tickets. Still a third counter is where seat reservations are made. We strongly recommend purchasing your train tickets in advance: it is quite time-consuming to stand in two lines at each train station, only to find—particularly in summer—that the train you want is already sold out. You can purchase open tickets in the United States. However, it is almost impossible to purchase seat reservations in advance (except for major European routes). Go ahead and buy the open tickets, and then you can either purchase your seat reservations locally, or else pay the concierge at your hotel to handle this transaction for you. Seat reservations cannot be made just before getting on the train—it is best to make them as far in advance as possible. *NOTE:* Your ticket must be stamped with the time and date **before** you board the train; otherwise, you will be issued a 40,000 lire fine. Tickets are stamped at small and not very obvious yellow machines near the exits to the tracks.

The Eurailpass, which allows travel for varying periods of time on most trains throughout Europe, is valid in Italy. However, if you are going to travel exclusively in Italy, buy instead an Italian Rail Pass. These bargain passes which must be purchased outside of Italy include the *Tourist Pass* and the *Flexi Pass*. The *Tourist Pass* is available for unlimited travel for a period of 8, 15, 21, or 30 consecutive days. The *Flexi Pass* allows you to choose the number of days you want to travel within a month. You can buy the *Flexi Pass* for 4 days, 8 days, or 12 days of travel. All of the Italian passes can be bought for either first- or second-class travel. You can purchase these passes through your local travel agent or, in the United States, from the Italian State Railways (CIT Rail), 15 West 44th St., 10th Floor, New York, NY 10036, telephone: (800) 248-7245 or (212) 730-2400, fax: (212) 730-4300. *NOTE:* In the summer when rail traffic is very heavy, unless you make dining car reservations in advance, you might not be able to have the fun of eating your meal en route. If you have not made these reservations, as soon as you board the train, stroll down to the dining car and ask to reserve a table.

TRANSFERS INTO CITIES: Travelers from abroad normally arrive by plane in Milan, Florence, Rome, or Venice and often pick up their rental car at the airport. However, if your first destination is the city and you plan on picking up your car after your stay, approximate transfer rates are as follows:

MILAN

| | |
|---|---|
| From Malpensa to city by taxi (70 min) | Lire 145,000 |
| From Malpensa to Cadorna station by train (every 30 min) | Lire 15,000 |
| From Malpensa to Central Station by bus (every 20 min) | Lire 13,000–22,000 |
| From Linate to city by taxi (20 min) | Lire 50,000 |
| From Linate to city by bus (every 20 min) | Lire 4,000 |

FLORENCE

| | |
|---|---|
| From airport to city by taxi (30 min) | Lire 40,000 |

ROME

| | |
|---|---|
| From Da Vinci to city by train (every 30 min) | Lire 16,000 |
| From Da Vinci to city by taxi (45 min) | Lire 90,000–120,000 |

VENICE

| | |
|---|---|
| From airport to city by waterbus (1 hour) | Lire 17,000 |
| From airport to city by private waterbus | Lire 140,000 |
| From station to city by waterbus (15 min) | Lire 8,000 |
| From station to city by private waterbus | Lire 140,000 |

## WEATHER

Italy is blessed with lovely weather. However, unless you are a ski enthusiast following the promise of what the majestic mountains have to offer in the winter, or must travel in summer due to school holidays, we highly recommend traveling in spring or fall. Travel at either of these times has two dramatic advantages: you miss the rush of the summer tourist season when all of Italy is packed and you are more likely to have beautiful weather. In spring the meadows are painted with wildflowers. In fall the forests are a riot of color and the vineyards are mellow in shades of red and gold. Although the mountains of Italy are delightfully cool in summer, the rest of the country can be very hot, especially in the cities. *NOTE:* Many hotels are not air-conditioned. Those that are sometimes charge extra for it.

## WEBSITE

Please supplement this book by looking at our website (*www.karenbrown.com*). We have the world's best web mistress who is daily improving our website with the aim of providing an enhanced extension of our guides and supplying you with even more in-depth information on the properties and destinations that we recommend. Most of our favorite hotels are featured on our website—their web addresses are detailed on the description pages. In 2001 we will continue to add color photos, maps, and direct links to the hotels' individual websites for additional photos and even more information. On the hotel's web page, you can usually link to their e-mail so that making a reservation is a breeze. Our site also features comments, feedback, and discoveries from you, our readers, information of our latest finds, current updates, drawings for free books, changes in phone or fax numbers, lists of hotels that have closed since the book went to press, and any current specials we are offering. Look at our site also for promotions that "our" hotels are advertising. In addition, we sell the Michelin maps that will assist you in locating the hotels and sightseeing we recommend. We want our website to serve as a valuable and added dimension to our guides. Remember: *www.karenbrown.com.*

## WHAT TO WEAR

During the day informal wear is most appropriate, including comfortable slacks for women. In the evening, if you are at a sidewalk café or a simple pizzeria, women do not need to dress up nor men to wear coats and ties. However, Italy does have some elegant restaurants where a dress and coat and tie are definitely the proper attire. A basic principle is to dress as you would in any city at home. There are perhaps a few special situations: the churches are still very conservative—shorts are definitely inappropriate, as are low-cut dresses. Some of the cathedrals still insist that women have their arms covered. It is rare that a scarf on the head is required, but to wear one is a respectful gesture. If you have an audience with the Pope, then the dress code is even more conservative. The layered effect is ideal. Italy's climate runs the gamut from usually cool in the mountains to frequently very hot in the south. The most efficient wardrobe is one where light blouses and shirts can be reinforced by layers of sweaters that can be added or peeled off as the day demands.

*Introduction–About Italy*

# HOTEL RESERVATION REQUEST LETTER IN ITALIAN

HOTEL NAME & ADDRESS—clearly printed or typed

Vi richiediamo la sequente prenotazione:
*We would like to request the following reservation:*

Numero delle camere con bagno o doccia privata     _____
*Number of rooms with private bath or shower*

Numero delle camere senza bagno o doccia     _____
*Number of rooms without private bath or shower*

Data di arrivo _____   Data di partenza _____
*Date of arrival*                    *Date of departure*

Vi prego inoltre de fornirmi le seguenti informazioni:
*Please let me know as soon as possible the following:*

Potete riservare le camere richieste? Si / No
*Can you reserve the space requested? Yes / No*

I pasti sono compresi nel prezzo?   Si / No
*Are meals included in your rate?*    *Yes / No*

E necessario un deposito?   Si / No
*Do you need a deposit?*    *Yes / No*

Prezzo giornaliero     _____
*Price per night*

Quanto e necessario come deposito?   _____
*How much deposit do you need?*

Ringraziando anticipatamente per la gentile conferma, porgo cordiali saluti,
*We thank you in advance for your confirmation,*

YOUR NAME & ADDRESS—clearly printed or typed (your fax number if pertinent)

*Florence*

# ITINERARY SECTION

*Highlights by Boat & Train-or Car*

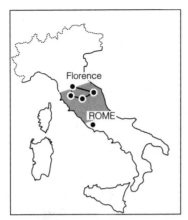

*Romantic Hilltowns of Tuscany & Umbria*

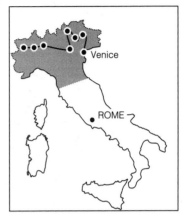

*Mountain & Lake Adventures*

*Rome to Milan via the Italian Riviera*

*Highlights of Southern Italy*

*Exploring the Wonders of Sicily*

27

*Colosseum, Rome*

# Italian Highlights by Train & Boat – or Car

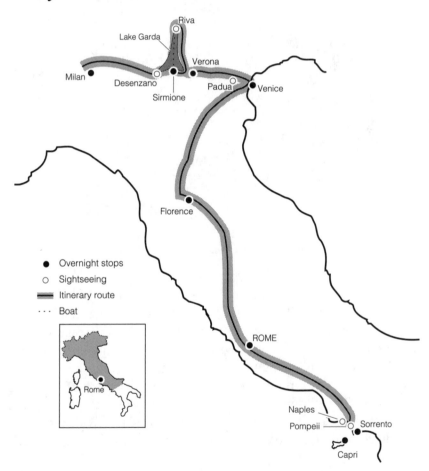

Riva

Lake Garda

Verona

Milan

Desenzano

Sirmione

Padua

Venice

Florence

ROME

Naples

Pompeii

Sorrento

Capri

Rome

● Overnight stops

○ Sightseeing

▬ Itinerary route

··· Boat

# Italian Highlights by Train & Boat—or Car

*Island of Burano, near Venice*

If you delight in the freedom of following a whim to explore a back road, this itinerary can easily be duplicated by car. However, the thought of Italian expressways sometimes intimidates even the bravest breed of tourist, so we have given you the formula to see the highlights of Italy either way—by public transportation or by car. An aversion to driving does not mean that your *only* alternative is the confining structure of a package tour. Italy can be seen splendidly by train and boat. This is a glorious way to travel and has many advantages: everyone can watch the scenery instead of the road, you can enjoy a glass of wine with lunch, and you arrive rested and ready to enjoy the sights. Perhaps the best advantage of all is that while using public transportation, you make friends. Perhaps there is just a smile at first, then maybe the sharing of a piece of fruit, and later comes the admiration of each other's family photographs. Somehow barriers break down on a long journey and the universal warmth of friendliness—at this the Italians are masters—spans any language barriers. Please be aware however that if you choose to travel this way, you must travel lightly—when burdened by heavy suitcases, the charm of public transportation quickly diminishes!

This itinerary covers some of the most famous destinations within Italy. For a short holiday it is impossible to include all the places of interest. However, following this pathway easily provides you with a glimpse of some of the highlights of Italy and will tempt you to return quickly to delve more deeply into the wonders that Italy has to offer. This itinerary is woven around towns that are conveniently linked by public transportation. Of course, if your time is extremely limited, this itinerary lends itself well to segmentation. If you cannot travel with us all the way, then choose what fits into your schedule and what most appeals to you.

In the following itinerary approximate train and boat times have been included. Please note that these are given only as a reference to show you how the pieces of this itinerary tie together. Schedules are constantly changing, so these must be verified. Also, many boats and some trains are seasonal, so be very meticulous in making your plans.

## ORIGINATING CITY               MILAN

This highlight tour begins in **Milan**, a most convenient city since it is the hub of airline flights from many parts of Europe and has non-stop air service from the eastern and western United States. Also, Milan is strategically located for trains arriving from all over Europe—trains rush into its busy station via the Gotthard, Simplon, and Bernina passes. However, it is not location alone that makes Milan an ideal starting point—although frequently bypassed as an enormous industrial city of little tourist interest, Milan has, at its core, a truly charming old section. Be forewarned: not only is this a major city, but it also hosts many merchandise fairs, so hotel space is often limited and rates are very expensive. After being a pedestrian center for many years, the heart of Milan is now open to cars. The city is divided into four quadrants and you cannot drive from one quadrant to another without backtracking to the central ring road. If you are arriving by car, it is very important that you know where your hotel is located and discuss with the hotel staff how to approach the city.

*Duomo, Milan*

While in Milan you must not miss visiting the **Duomo**, the third-largest cathedral in the world. There is no denying the beauty of the interior but best of all is the exterior, so take an elevator or the stairs to the roof where you can admire the view and examine at close hand the statues that adorn this gingerbread fantasy.

Facing the Duomo is one of the world's most beautiful arcades, the forerunner of the modern shopping mall, but with far more style. Even if you are not a shopper, be sure to just browse and have a cup of tea in the **Galleria Vittorio Emanuele**. In this Victorian-era fantasy creation, there are two main intersecting wings, both completely domed with intricately patterned glass. Along the pedestrian-only arcades are boutiques and beautiful little restaurants with outside tables for people-watching.

After more than two decades of controversial restoration, Leonardo da Vinci's famous mural, **The Last Supper**, is once again on view in the church of **Santa Maria delle**

**Grazie.** The mural, which covers an entire wall of the church, has been a problem for many years mainly because Leonardo experimented with painting onto drywall rather than employing the more usual fresco technique of applying paint to wet plaster. In an effort to prevent further damage, air filters, special lights, and dust-absorbing carpets have been installed, and the small groups of visitors are limited to a stay of 15 minutes. It is vital that you make an appointment in advance: from the USA call 011-39 (Europe, 00-39) 0289-421146; from within Italy, 199-19.91.00. The unilingual Italian-speaking reservationist will make you an appointment and give you a confirmation number. Arrive at the church about 15 minutes before your appointment, confirmation number in hand, and pay cash for your ticket.

Milan's other great claim to fame is **La Scala**, one of the world's most renowned opera houses. In addition to wonderful opera, other types of performances are given here. If it is opera season, try your best to go to a performance; if not, try to get tickets for whatever is playing. It is such fun to watch the lights go down and the curtains go up in this fairy-tale-like theater with row upon row of balconies rising like layers on a wedding cake. Tickets are sold in the ticket office located around the left-hand side of the theater.

## DESTINATION I                    SIRMIONE

Sirmione is located on Lake Garda. The station where you need to disembark is in the town of Desenzano, which is on the main rail route between Milan and Venice. There are many trains each day between Milan and Venice, but not all stop in Desenzano. One we suggest runs as follows:

>  1:10 pm depart Milan Central Station by train
>  2:21 pm arrive Desenzano

When the train arrives in the ancient port of **Desenzano**, you can take a taxi to the pier where hydrofoils, steamers, and buses leave regularly for Sirmione. However, although it is more expensive, we suggest you splurge and take a taxi directly to Sirmione (only about 10 kilometers away). This is definitely the most convenient means of transportation since you are taken directly to your hotel.

**Sirmione** is a walled medieval village fabulously located on a tiny peninsula jutting out into **Lake Garda**. This peninsula seems more like an island because it is connected to the mainland by just a thread of land. To enter the ancient town, you first cross over a moat, and then enter through massive medieval gates. Unless you are one of the lucky ones with a hotel confirmed for the night, you cannot take your automobile inside the town walls, since only pedestrians are allowed through the entrance. But if you have hotel reservations, stop near the entrance at the information office where you are given a pass to enter in your car or taxi.

There are several hotels in the heart of Sirmione, but the most glamorous choice, the **Villa Cortine Palace Hotel** (formerly a private home) is located in a parklike estate on the outskirts of town. The entrance is absolutely Hollywood. You ring a bell at the impressive gates which then slowly swing open, allowing you to wind your way up through the truly beautiful park to the hotel crowning the small hill. For those looking for an inexpensive place to stay, the **Hotel Grifone** is an excellent choice and although the rooms are simply decorated, they are spotlessly clean and the restaurant is extremely charming. A good choice in the moderate price range is the **Albergo Sirmione**, which is conveniently located next to the pier where the boats dock.

From any of the above hotels it is an easy walk to the dock in the center of town where you can study the posted schedule to decide which boat you want to take for your day's excursion. You can glide around the lake all day and have a snack on board, or get off in some small jewel of a town and enjoy lunch at a lakefront café. There is a choice of transportation: either the romantic ferry boats or the faster hydrofoils.

There are some **Roman ruins** on the very tip of the Sirmione peninsula which can be reached either on foot, or, if you prefer, by a miniature motorized train that shuttles back and forth between the ruins and the village.

*NOTE FOR TRAVELERS BY CAR:* Sirmione is an excellent choice for a place to stay if you are traveling by public transportation. However, if you are traveling by car, consider staying in **Gargnano**, **Gardone**, or **San Vigilio**—these towns are also located on Lake Garda and offer a rich selection of places to stay.

## DESTINATION II                    VERONA

There are trains almost every hour that cover the half-hour journey between Desenzano and Verona. But if it is a beautiful day, it is much more romantic to incorporate sightseeing into your transportation and take a boat and bus instead of the train. If this appeals to you, the following gives an idea of how this can be done.

   10:20 am  depart Sirmione by ferry
    2:20 pm  arrive Riva

You can have lunch on board the ferry or else you can wait until you reach the medieval town of **Riva**, located on the northern shore of Lake Garda. The outdoor terrace overlooking the lake at the **Hotel Sole** (just across from where the ferry docks) provides a serene luncheon setting. The interesting ancient core of Riva is small, so it doesn't take long to stroll through the old city.

After lunch and a walk through the old part of town, leave Riva by bus for Verona (buses run every 15 minutes in summer), tracing a scenic route along the eastern shore of the lake.

When you arrive in **Verona,** you are in for a treat. This is a town that is all too frequently bypassed by the tourist, but what a prize it is. This medieval gem is the perfect city to explore on foot. Buy a detailed map and be on your way.

Definitely not to be missed is the **Roman amphitheater**, one of the largest in Italy. This dramatic arena, dating from the 1st century, has perfect acoustics and hosts operatic performances in summer. As you continue to wander through Verona's enchanting streets, you discover many delights, including the **Piazza delle Erbe** (Square of Herbs), which is the old Roman forum where chariot races used to take place. Follow your map to nearby 23 Via Cappello to find the 13th-century **Capulets' Palace** and the balcony where Juliet rendezvoused with Romeo. Another colorful square, the **Piazza dei Signori,** features a stature of Dante in its center and 12th- and 13th-century buildings. The **Castelvecchio** (Old Castle), built by Congrande I Scaligerbuthe in the 14th century, houses an art museum with paintings, sculptures, jewelry, and armaments. The 14th-century **Ponte Scaligero** (Scaliger Bridge) links the Castelvecchio with the opposite side of the river. The **cathedral**, dating from the 12th century, is well worth a visit to see its fine red marble columns and richly adorned interior. Just across the river from the heart of the old city, visit the old **Roman theater** where performances are still held in summer.

Verona has several good hotels to complement her marvelous sights. A favorite in the heart of the city is the **Hotel Gabbia d'Oro**, which is brimming with charm and conveniently located near all the places of interest. If you are traveling by car, you have the option of choosing a hotel in the countryside outside of Verona where you get more value for your money. Hotels we suggest in the area are in **Pedemonte** and **Gargagnago**.

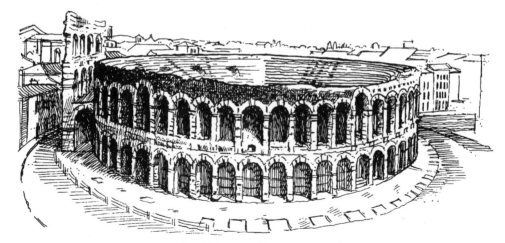

*Amphitheater, Verona*

When you are ready to leave Verona, there is frequent train service to **Venice** so the following departure time is just a suggestion. *NOTE:* As you approach Venice, be sure not to get off the train at the Venice Mestre station, but instead wait for the next stop, the Santa Lucia station (about ten minutes further).

> 2:33 pm  depart Verona Porto Nuova station by train
> 3:55 pm  arrive Venice, Santa Lucia station

As you come out of the front door of the train station, you find that the station is directly on the **Grand Canal**. It is a few short steps down to where you can board a boat to take you to your hotel. The **vaporetti** are the most popular means of transportation and are a very inexpensive means of getting about the city. They are like boat buses that constantly shuttle back and forth from the train station to St. Mark's Square. If you have a lot of luggage you might want to consider a watertaxi. The **motoscafi** (watertaxis) cost about 90,000 lire but deliver you right to the door of your hotel, provided there is a motorboat dock (noted on the hotel description). The third choice of transportation is the

*St. Mark's Square, Venice*

**gondola**, but these are much slower and very expensive, so save your gondola ride for a romantic interlude rather than a train connection. If you arrive in Venice by car, keep in mind that some hotels offer a special rate at the Tronchetto garage. Check with the hotel about parking and transfers when making your reservation.

Venice has many hotels in every price range. If you want to splurge, consider the very expensive, very sumptuous, **Gritti Palace**, a former home of the immensely wealthy Doge Andrea Gritti. If you are on a more limited budget, one of our favorites is the intimate, family-operated **Hotel Flora**. It is superbly located and a gem in its moderately priced category. These and other excellent choices of places to stay in Venice are described in detail in the back of this guide. The closest boat stop to each hotel is given in the bottom details so that you know where to disembark if you come by canal from the train station. *NOTE*: For a few of the hotels, you need to change boats at the San Marco boat stop.

*Glass Blowing, Island of Murano*

Venice has so many sights—marvelous restaurants, beautiful boutiques, and fascinating little alleyways to explore—that you could happily stay for weeks.

Of course, you must savor the incomparable ambiance of **Piazza San Marco** (St. Mark's Square). Late afternoon is especially romantic as music wafts across the enormous square, courtesy of the tiny orchestras entertaining visitors as they enjoy an aperitif. A colonnaded walkway encloses the square on three sides, forming a protected path for window-shoppers at the beautiful boutiques and fancy cafés. The fourth side of the square is dominated by the **Basilica di San Marco** (St. Mark's Cathedral), richly endowed with gold and mosaics. The church dates back to the 12th century when it was built to house the remains of St. Mark. Next to the church rises the 99-meter-tall **campanile** (bell tower) where in the 15th century priests were suspended in a cage to repent their sins. If you are in the plaza on the hour, watch the two Moors strike the hour with their huge bronze hammers as they have for 500 years. To the right of the basilica is the **Palazzo Ducale** (Doge's Palace), a sumptuous fantasy of pink and white marble—open now as a museum. The Palazzo Ducale faces on to the **Piazzetta**, a wide square opening onto the Grand Canal. The square's nickname used to be the *Piazzetta Il Broglio* (Intrigue) because in days of yore, only nobles were allowed in the square between 10 am and noon, at which time the area buzzed with plots of intrigue. Adorning the center of the square are two granite columns, one topped by the Lion of St. Mark and the other by a statue of St. Theodore.

There is no better way to get into the mood of Venice than to join the crowd at St. Mark's pier as they climb aboard one of the ferries that ply the city's waterways. It is a real bargain to board the vaporetto and enjoy the many wonderful palaces bordering the Grand Canal. In addition to exploring the canals that lace Venice, you can take ferries to the outlying islands. Go either on your own or on a tour to the three islands: **Murano** (famous for its hand-blown glass), **Burano** (famous for its colorfully painted fishermen's cottages and lace making), and **Torcello** (once an important city but now just a small village with only its lovely large church to remind you of its past glories).

Another all-day outing by boat is to take the **Il Burchiello**, named for a famous 17th-century Venetian boat. From March to November, this boat departs Tuesdays, Thursdays, and Saturdays at 8:45 am from the Pontile Giardinetti pier near St. Mark's Square and travels the network of rivers and canals linking Venice and Padua. (The schedule might change, so verify dates and times.) This little boat, with an English-speaking guide on board, stops at several of the exquisite palaces en route. Lunch is served and there is time for sightseeing in **Padua** before returning to Venice by bus. Reservation office: Siamic Express, Via Trieste 42, 35121 Padua, Italy, tel: (049) 66 09 44, fax: (049) 66 28 30.

A favorite pastime in Venice is wandering—just anywhere—exploring the maze of twisting canals and criss-crossing back and forth over some of the 400 whimsical bridges. One of the most famous, the **Rialto Bridge**, arching high over the canal, is especially colorful because it is lined by shops. Also much-photographed is the **Bridge of Sighs**, so named because this was the bridge prisoners passed over before their execution.

Although all of Venice is virtually an open-air museum, it also has many indoor museums. Two excellent ones are both easy to find near the Accademia boat stop. The **Galleria dell'Accademia** abounds with 14th- to 18th-century Venetian paintings. Within walking distance of the Galleria dell'Accademia is the **Peggy Guggenheim Museum**, featuring 20th-century art. The paintings and statues were the gift of the now-deceased wealthy American heiress, Peggy Guggenheim. The lovely museum was her canal-front home.

## DESTINATION IV                    FLORENCE

There are several direct trains each day from Venice to Florence: however, in summer, space is at a real premium, so be sure to reserve a seat in advance. Some of the express trains must have prior seat reservations and require a supplemental fee. *NOTE:* During the busy season, if you want to dine on the train, it is necessary to make advance reservations when you buy your ticket.

*Ponte Vecchio, Florence*

11:45 am  depart Venice, Santa Lucia station (reservations obligatory)
2:42 pm  arrive Florence

When you arrive in **Florence**, take a taxi to your hotel. There are outstanding places to stay in every price range either in the heart of Florence or in the nearby countryside. Study the hotel descriptions in the back of the guide and you are sure to find accommodations to suite your personality and budget. Be aware that during tourist season hotel space is very tight, so to avoid disappointment, make your reservation as far in advance as possible.

Be generous with your time and do not rush Florence—there is too much to see. You must, of course, pay a visit to **Michelangelo's David** in the **Galleria dell'Accademia** located just off the **Piazza San Marco**. During your explorations of Florence, you will cross many times through the **Piazza della Signoria**, located in the heart of the old city. Facing this characterful medieval square is the 13th-century **Palazzo Vecchio**, a stern stone structure topped by a crenellated gallery and dominated by a tall bell tower. It was here that the *signoria* (Florence's powerful aristocratic ruling administrators) met for two months each year while attending to government business. During this period they were forbidden to leave the palace (except for funerals)so that there could not

*Palazzo Vecchio, Piazza della Signoria, Florence*

be a hint of suspicion of intrigue or bribery. Of course, you cannot miss one of Florence's landmarks, the **Ponte Vecchio.** Spanning the Arno in the heart of Florence, this colorful bridge is lined with quaint shops just as it has been since the 14th century.

Don't miss the fantastic museums and cathedrals—the world will probably never again see a city that has produced such artistic genius. Florence's **Duomo** is one of the largest in the world. The cathedral's incredible dome (over 100 meters high) was designed by Brunelleschi. Climb the 464 steps to the top of the dome for a superb view of Florence. The **baptistry** has beautiful mosaics and its bronze doors by Ghiberti were said by Michelangelo to be worthy of serving as the gates to paradise. The main door shows scenes from the life of John the Baptist, the north door shows the life of Jesus, and the east door shows stories from the prophets of the Old Testament. The **Uffizi Museum** (housed in a 16th-century palace) is undoubtedly one of the finest museums in the world. You can make advance reservations at the Uffizi Museum but you must prepay for the tickets by postal wire in lire (tel: 055-29.48.83) or call Hidden Treasures (888) 419-6700. Also, do not miss the **Pitti Palace** with its fabulous art collection, including paintings by Titian and Raphael. *NOTE:* In addition to regular hours, museums stay open during June, July, August, and September until 11 pm.

Be sure to buy a guidebook and city map at one of the many magazine stalls and study what you want to see. We just touch on the many highlights. Florence is best appreciated by wandering the historic ancient streets: poke into small boutiques; stop in churches that catch your eye—they all abound with masterpieces; sit and enjoy a cappuccino in one of the little sidewalk cafés and people-watch; stroll through the piazzas and watch the artists at their craft—many of them incredibly clever—as they paint portraits and do sculptures for a small fee. End your day by finding the perfect small restaurant for delicious pasta made by mama in the back kitchen.

There is an excellent train service from Florence to Rome. It is probably best to take one of the midday trains—this allows you to enjoy lunch as you soak in the beauty of the Tuscany hills flowing by your window. Remember that you need both seat and dining reservations.

    12:01 pm  depart Florence via train
    1:55 pm  arrive Rome, Termini station

As the train pulls into **Rome**, you feel overwhelmed by its size and confusion of traffic, but once you settle into your hotel, you realize that Rome is really not as cumbersome as it looks. The ancient part of the city is manageable on foot—a fabulous city for walking with its maze of streets and captivating boutiques just begging to be explored. We recommend many places to stay in this expensive city. The super-deluxe **Hotel Hassler**, just at the top of the Spanish Steps, is a very popular choice. If you prefer to be at the bottom of the Spanish Steps, another fabulous choice is **The Inn at the Spanish Steps**. But you do not need to splurge—there are many less expensive places to stay recommended in the hotel description section that are excellent and equally well located (such as **La Residenza** and the **Hotel Gregoriana**).

*"She Wolf" with Romulus and Remus*

According to legend, Rome was founded in 753 B.C. by Romulus, who, along with his twin brother, Remus (whom he later conveniently "did in"), were suckled by a "she wolf." Although a far less colorful story, historians concur that it was the Etruscans who first settled here and gave the city its name. By the time Christ was born, Rome controlled the entire Italian peninsula plus many areas around the Mediterranean.

Rome is bursting with a wealth of fantastic museums, ancient monuments, spectacular cathedrals, gourmet restaurants, beautiful boutiques, colorful piazzas, whimsical fountains, inspiring statues, theater, and opera—the city itself is virtually a museum. You cannot possibly savor it all. Either before you leave home or once you arrive in Italy, purchase a comprehensive guidebook and decide what is top priority for your special interests. There are many stalls along the streets as well as bookstores throughout Rome

*Vatican–Swiss Guard*

where guidebooks are available and every hotel has brochures that tell about sightseeing tours. If there are several in your party, a private guide might be money well spent since he will custom-tailor your sightseeing—with a private guide you squeeze much more sightseeing into a short period of time.

To even begin to do justice to Rome's many wonders, this entire book would need to be devoted to its sightseeing possibilities. However, we cannot resist mentioning a few places you must see.

You must see the **Vatican City** which includes in its complex **St. Peter's Basilica**, the largest church in the world. The original construction was begun in the 4th century by Emperor Constantine over the site of St. Peter's tomb. In 1506 Pope Julius II began plans for the new cathedral, which took over 100 years to build. It is no wonder the complex is so utterly breathtaking—all of Italy's greatest Renaissance artists were called upon to add their talents—Bramante, Raphael, Sangallo, and Michelangelo, to name just a few.

The Vatican is a miniature nation tucked within the city of Rome. It is ruled by the Pope, has its own flags, issues its own postage stamps, has its own anthem, mints its own coins, and even has its own police force—the Swiss Guard who still wear the uniform designed by Michelangelo.

Fronting the cathedral is the **Piazza San Pietro,** a breathtaking square designed by Bernini. It is so large that it can hold 400,000 people (making the square a favorite place for the Pope to address large audiences). A double semicircle of columns encloses the square, so perfectly designed that the columns fade into each other, giving the illusion that there is a single row. In the center of the square is a towering ancient Egyptian obelisk—adorned, of course, by a Christian cross. As you stand at a distance, the Piazza San Pietro forms a visual frame for the cathedral.

To fully appreciate all the Vatican City has to offer, you could easily spend two days, one in St. Peter's Basilica and one day in the **Vatican museums**. The Basilica is like a museum. Not only is the structure magnificent, but the vast collection of works of art inside are almost unbelievable: imagine gazing at such masterpieces as the **Pietà** (the ethereal sculpture of Mary holding Jesus in her arms after the crucifixion, carved by Michelangelo when he was only 25) and the **Baldaccchino**, the bronze canopy over the papal altar created by another master, Bernini. Also, be aware when you gaze up at the double-columned dome, that this too was designed by Michelangelo.

*St. Peter's Basilica, Rome*

The **Sistine Chapel** alone is well worth a trip to Rome. Savor the breathtaking beauty of its ceiling painted by Michelangelo. In addition to St. Peter's Basilica and the Vatican museums, the gardens and the rest of the Vatican can be visited, but only on guided tours. If you are interested, inquire at the *Ufficio Informazioni Pellegrini et Turisti* in St. Peter's Square. *NOTE:* The Vatican museums are closed on Sundays, except for the last Sunday of the month when they are open free of charge.

The Vatican City, as spectacular as it is, is just one small part of what Rome has to offer. You must see the gigantic **Colosseum**, the entertainment center for the citizens of ancient Rome. Here 50,000 people gathered to be entertained by flamboyant spectacles that included gladiatorial contests, races, games, and contests where Christian martyrs fought against wild beasts.

Another landmark is the **Forum**. It is difficult to make out much of this site because it is mostly in ruins, but at one time this was the heart of Rome. Once filled with elegant palaces, government buildings, and shops, it teemed with people from throughout the known world.

My favorite building in Rome is the **Pantheon**. It is difficult to imagine that this perfectly preserved jewel of a temple dates back to 27 B.C. Step beyond the heavy bronze doors which open into a relatively small, beautifully proportioned room lit only by light streaming in from an opening in the top of the dome.

No trip to Rome would be complete without a stroll down the **Via Veneto**, lined by fancy hotels and luxury boutiques. There are also many outdoor restaurants where a cup of coffee costs almost as much as a meal in a simple trattoria. However, along with your coffee, you are paying the price for the fun of people-watching along one of Rome's most elite avenues.

While walking the back streets of Rome, you find many picturesque squares, usually enhanced by a fountain adorned with magnificent sculptures. Especially popular is the **Trevi Fountain** where tourists go to throw a coin—assuring that they will return to Rome.

Rome has many festivals including the **Festa de Noantri** (Our Festival) that starts on the third Sunday in July. It takes place in Trastevere, which is transformed into the venue of a village fair with stalls, open-air taverns, band music, and theatrical shows throughout the neighborhood. The event is wrapped up with fireworks over the River Tiber.

The **Spanish Steps** are definitely a landmark of Rome. Topped by the twin spires of the Church of the Trinity of the Mountains, the wide avenue of steps leads down to the **Piazza di Spagna** (Spanish Square). This large square is highlighted by the **Fountain of Baraccia** (Fountain of the Boat), a masterpiece by Bernini. The steps are usually crowded both with tourists who come to capture the moment on film and vendors who lay out their wares to sell.

*Spanish Steps, Rome*

Leading from the Piazza di Spagna, the **Via Condotti** is an avenue lined by shops and boutiques selling the finest of merchandise. Branching off the Via Condotti are the narrow lanes of **Old Rome**, again featuring exquisite small boutiques.

When you are ready to relax, walk to the **Villa Borghese**, a splendid large park in the center of Rome that originated in the 17th century as the private gardens of the Borghese family. Stroll through the park watching the children at play. If you are not saturated with sightseeing, there are many museums to see in the park. One of the loveliest is the **Museo di Villa Giulia,** a museum in a pretty villa that features artifacts from the Etruscan era.

## DESTINATION VI　　　　SORRENTO

You could spend weeks discovering the museum that is Rome, but if you have time to add a few more highlights, venture farther south to include Sorrento and Capri. There is frequent train service from Rome to Naples and from there it is a short hydrofoil ride to Capri. However, for the adventurous it is fun to include Pompeii and Sorrento en route to Capri. Please note that this makes a long day of travel and takes some manipulating of schedules, but the rewards are great.

You need an early start to accomplish a tour of Pompeii on your way to Sorrento, but this is a must. How could you be so close without visiting this intriguing city of the Romans that was destroyed, yet preserved forever by the ashes of Vesuvius?

　9:15 am  depart Rome, Termini station
11:58 am  arrive Pompeii, Main station

You arrive in **Pompeii** at the Main station, but you depart from Pompeii at the Villa d'Misteri station, located just across from the main entrance to the archaeological site. Since it's no fun to lug your suitcases around while you do your sightseeing, take a cab from the Main station to the Villa d'Misteri station where there is a place to check luggage, then just walk across the street to the main gate of Pompeii. There is a nice terrace restaurant by the entrance and also a café inside. If you want to do your own touring, you can buy a guidebook in English from a stall, or else you can negotiate with one of the licensed guides for a personal tour. You may have heard that the earthquake of 1980 destroyed much of Pompeii. It is true that many of the sites were damaged, but now almost everything has been reconstructed.

An aura of mystery lingers in the air as you wander the streets of Pompeii. All visitors are touched by this ancient city of an estimated 25,000 inhabitants, which in one day became frozen for all time. Probably there is nowhere else in the world where you can so vividly step back in time. Much of what you see today has been reproduced, but the reality is pure. Plaster was poured into molds formed by the lava that demolished the buildings and buried so many families that fateful day. Thus it became possible for latter-day archaeologists to reconstruct houses and make reproductions of people and pets. Walk through the town along the sunken streets crossed by high stepping-stones, strategically placed so that pedestrians did not get their feet wet on rainy days. Be sure not to miss some of the reconstructed villas that allow you a glimpse into the daily life of long ago. The **Casa del Fauna**, a fine example of how the wealthy lived, has two inner courtyards and several dining rooms. The **Casa del Poeta Tragico**, a more modest home, has a sign in mosaic saying *Cave Canem* (beware of the dog). At the **Villa di Giulia Felice** you see the example of an entrepreneur—in addition to using it as a private villa, the owner rented out rooms, had shops on the ground floor, and operated an adjacent bathhouse. If traveling with children, you might want to go alone into the **Lupanare** (Pompeii's brothel) where there are erotic paintings on the walls. At the **Terme Stabiane** you see a sophisticated underground water-heating system.

There are many more places to visit than those listed above. As you explore Pompeii, there is no need to watch the time. There is a narrow-gauge train departing from the Pompeii Villa d' Misteri station about every 20 minutes for the half-hour scenic journey to Sorrento.

When you arrive in **Sorrento**, stay at the **Grand Hotel Excelsior Vittoria**, a romantic old villa at the center of town in a prime cliff location overlooking the harbor. The hotel's once-perfect grandeur is perhaps a bit faded, but as you sit on the terrace in the evening and watch the sun turning the bay to shades of red and gold, the atmosphere is perfect. There is also a pool for relaxing and sunning. Sorrento, a medieval town with a maze of narrow streets, sits on a bluff overlooking the sea. From the center of town, a road twists down to the harbor from where ferries ply the Amalfi coast and go to Capri.

When it is time to leave Sorrento, there is excellent service by either hydrofoil or ferry to Capri. The following schedule is a suggestion:

3:45 pm  depart Sorrento by hydrofoil
4:10 pm  arrive Capri

Your hydrofoil arrives at the **Marina Grande**, a small harbor filled with colorful boats and edged by brightly painted shops. When the boat docks, you find hotel porters on the pier along with carrier services that go to all of the hotels. They relieve you of your luggage and take it directly to the hotel of your choice, freeing you to take either a mini-bus or the funicular to the main town of Capri, which is located on a flat saddle of land high above the sea.

There are many charming places to stay on **Capri**. Since this is a very popular tourist destination, the hotels are generally expensive, but the ones we recommend are all very special. Some are located in the heart of town, others a short stroll away—read our descriptions and choose one that suits you.

Capri has many wonders. The most famous is its submerged cave, the **Blue Grotto**, which can be accessed by boat when the seas are calm. Large boats begin leaving the harbor every day at 9 am for the short ride to the entrance to the grotto, where you are transferred into tiny rowboats. The earlier you go the better since the seas are calmer in the morning. The excursion is an adventure in itself. As you approach the tiny cave opening, it seems impossible that there is adequate room for a boat to enter, but suddenly the sea surges forward and in you squeeze. Like magic, you see it—the mysterious, stunning blue light reflecting from some hidden source that illuminates the grotto. The cost isn't great, but be aware of the system: You pay for a ticket for the motorboat that takes you to the cave, and then you pay again, on site, to the oarsman who skillfully maneuvers his little rowboat through the hole and into the grotto. It is appropriate to tip

*Marina Grande, Capri*

your boatman—he will do his best to make your short ride memorable, plus, frequently serenade you within the cave.

Capri is a superb island for walking. As you stroll the trails, all your senses are treated by the fragrant flowers, the gorgeous vistas of the brilliant blue waters, and the sound of birds luring you ever onward. There are many spectacular walks. Follow the trail winding down the cliffs to the small harbor **Marina Piccola**, located on the opposite side of the island from the ferry dock.

At the Marina Piccola there are lovely views of the shimmering aqua waters as you make your way to the small beach where you can enjoy a swim before your return. Instead of walking back up the hill, take the little bus that delivers you quickly back to the main square.

Another absolutely spectacular walk—although a long one of at least 45 minutes each way—is to Emperor Tiberius's Palace, **Villa Jovis**, perched high among the trees on the cliffs on the western tip of the island. This is the grandest of the palaces left by Tiberius. Although it is mostly in ruins, you can easily appreciate its former magnificence as you climb about exploring the ruins of the terraced rooms. From the palace there are stunning panoramic vistas: you have an overview of the whole island and can watch the ferries shuttling back and forth to the mainland. A much shorter walk, but one equally as beautiful, is to the **Cannone Belvedere**. This path guides you near delightful private villas hidden behind high walls (you get glimpses through the gates) and on to a promontory overlooking the sea.

Another excursion is to **Anacapri**, the only other town on the island, to visit the **Villa San Michel**, a lovely villa overlooking the sea that was the home of the Swedish scientist Axel Munthe. His residence is now open as a museum. Anacapri is a bit too far to walk easily but buses leave regularly from the main square in town.

During the day, Capri is swarming with tourists on package tours who descend like a swarm of locusts from the constant stream of hydrofoils and ferries. You might surmise that in the evening the activity subsides, but it isn't so. The tour groups leave at dusk but then a new group of people emerges from the secreted villas and fancy hotels. Guests in chic clothes and fancy jewelry stroll the streets—both to see and be seen.

When the real world calls and you must leave Capri, there is frequent ferry or hydrofoil service back to Naples. From Naples, you can take a train to Rome or a plane to your next destination.

# *Romantic Hilltowns of Tuscany and Umbria*

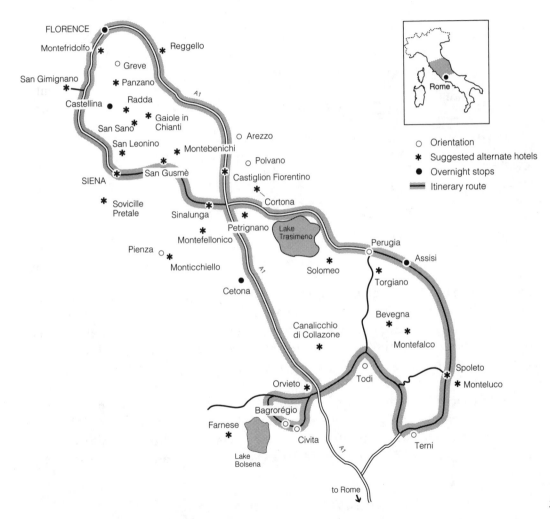

FLORENCE

Montefridolfo ✳

Reggello ✳

○ Greve

San Gimignano

✳ Panzano

Castellina ●

Radda
✳

A1

✳ Gaiole in
Chianti

San Sano ✳

San Leonino
✳

✳ Montebenichi

○ Arezzo

SIENA

San Gusmè
✳

○ Polvano

✳

Castiglion Fiorentino

✳ Sovicille
Pretale

Sinalunga
✳

Cortona

○ Orientation
✳ Suggested alternate hotels
● Overnight stops
▬▬ Itinerary route

Petrignano
✳

Lake
Trasimeno

Perugia ○

Assisi ●

Montefellonico
✳

Solomeo
✳

✳ Torgiano

Pienza ○
✳

Monticchiello

Cetona ●

Bevegna
✳

Canalicchio
di Collazone
✳

Montefalco

Todi ○

Spoleto
✳

✳ Monteluco

Orvieto
✳

Bagrorégio
○ ○

Farnese
✳

Civita

A1

Terni ○

Lake
Bolsena

to Rome
↓

Rome

53

# *Romantic Hilltowns of Tuscany & Umbria*

*Assisi*

Nothing can surpass the exquisite beauty of the countryside near Florence—it is breathtaking. If you meander into the hilltowns of Tuscany and Umbria any time of the year, all your senses are rewarded with the splendors that this enchanting area of Italy has to offer. Almost every hillock is crowned with a picture-perfect walled town; fields are brilliant with vibrant red poppies; vineyards in all their glory and promise lace the fields; olive trees dress the hillsides in a frock of dusky gray-green; pine forests unexpectedly appear to highlight the landscape. As if these attributes were not enough, tucked into the colorful villages is a treasure-trove of some of the finest small hotels in all the world. If this is still not sufficient to tempt you away from the normal tourist route, remember that the food and wines of Tuscany and Umbria are unsurpassed.

When planning your trip to Italy, allow time to treat yourself to a unique adventure. Save at least a few days to slip away from the cities and into the country. Perhaps you won't have time to follow this entire itinerary, but at least sneak in a few days in Umbria and Tuscany. You will be well rewarded with a wealth of memories that will linger long after you return home. The following itinerary makes a southern loop from Florence. Along the way are three suggested stops—one in Umbria, one in the southern region of Tuscany, and one in the northern region of Tuscany. If possible, stay several days in each of these hubs and make excursions into the countryside.

## ORIGINATING CITY        FLORENCE

Your journey begins in **Florence**. Allow enough time to savor this marvelous city but, if you are reluctant to leave, be consoled: there are many treats in store for you in the delightful hilltowns that surround it. Magnificent art is not confined to the city limits of Florence and you will see impressive cathedrals and beautiful works of art throughout the neighboring areas. On pages 40–42 we offer sightseeing suggestions for Florence.

## DESTINATION I        ASSISI

The traffic around Florence is congested. Follow signs in town that lead to the expressway A1 to Rome which you take as far as the turnoff for **Arezzo**, located about 10 kilometers east of the highway. If your time is short, you might want to bypass Arezzo since, although it has a rich history dating back to the Etruscan era, it is a large city and not as quaint as some of its smaller neighbors.

Following the main road 71 south from Arezzo, you soon arrive at **Cortona**. This is a beautifully situated walled town climbing up a steep hillside covered with olive trees. Stop to enjoy the atmosphere of this medieval town: its narrow twisting streets, jumble of small squares, and colorful buildings are delightful. A mighty castle majestically stands guard over the town.

*St. Francis of Assisi*

Leaving Cortona, continue driving south toward **Lake Trasimeno**. Just before you reach the lake, take the four-lane expressway that skirts the lake's northern shore heading east to **Perugia**, a large medieval city surrounded by ramparts. An important Umbrian city since Etruscan days, the heart of the old city is the **Piazza IV Novembre**, a beautiful square with an appealing fountain, the **Fontana Maggiore**, built in the late 13th century. It is only a short drive farther east from Perugia to **Assisi**. Built up the steep slopes of Mount Subasio, this magical city is a tribute to St. Francis. Although he was born into a family of wealth, after several visions in which Christ appeared to him, St. Francis left his privileged life. Obviously a person with a deeply poetic soul, his tender teachings of reverence for the beauties of nature and kindness to all animals and birds still appeal to us today.

Even if it were not for the lingering memory of the gentle St. Francis, Assisi would be a "must see" for it is one of the most spectacular hilltowns in Umbria. Perhaps there are a few too many souvenir shops, but this is a small price to pay for such a very special place. The town walls begin on the valley floor and completely enclose the city as climbs the steep hillside, climaxing in an enormous castle. Assisi with its maze of tiny streets is a marvelous town for walking (you must wear sturdy shoes). It is great fun as you come across intriguing little lanes opening into small squares. When you stop to rest, there are marvelous vistas of the breathtaking Umbrian fields stretching out below.

To truly appreciate the beauty of Umbria, it is best to spend several nights in the area. Luckily, there are good hotel choices—not only in Assisi, but also in nearby towns (see

Map 9 for other towns with recommended hotels). If you prefer to stay in the heart of Assisi, look in the back of the guide and choose a hotel that appeals to you. We recommend quite a few places to stay, each special in its own way.

Along with many other historic buildings, Assisi's most famous monument, **St. Francis's Basilica,** was severely damaged by an earthquake in September 1997. However, most of the repairs had now been completed and the town looks remarkably "back to normal." The basilica, which also houses a monastery, faces onto a large square bound by columns forming vaulted covered walkways. In addition to the monastery, there are two basilicas—upper and lower. Both are adorned with excellent frescoes that were unfortunately damaged by the earthquake. Also while in Assisi, visit **Santa Chiara** (St. Clara's Church). Clara, a close friend of St. Francis, founded the Order of St. Clares. Go into the church to view the lovely frescoes of Santa Clara and her sisters. Part of the enjoyment of Assisi is just to stroll through its narrow cobbled streets—the whole town is like a living museum. If you have time, hike up to the **Rocca Medioevale**, an enormous 14th-century fortress perched on the hillside overlooking the city. From here you have a magnificent bird's-eye view of Assisi and beyond to the enchanting Umbrian countryside sweeping out to the distant hills.

While staying at Assisi, take a side trip to nearby **Torgiano** where there is a splendid wine museum. You would never dream that such a tiny town could boast such a stunning museum, but it is not a coincidence: the Lungarotti family owns the vineyards for many kilometers in every direction. Signore Lungarotti furnished the museum with artifacts pertaining to every aspect of the production of wine from the earliest days. The collection is interesting and beautifully displayed, worthy of a detour by anyone interested in wines. The family also owns a delightful hotel in the center of town, **Le Tre Vaselle**. A charming spot for lunch or an overnight stay, Le Tre Vaselle has the ambiance of a lovely country manor house plus an outstanding restaurant.

Get an early start this morning because it is going to be difficult to squeeze in all of the enchanting hilltop towns en route. Driving south on the 3 from Assisi, you soon come to **Spoleto**, an intriguing town. Not only is medieval Spoleto dramatically perched atop a hill, but it also has an almost unbelievable bridge dating from Roman times. This **Ponte delle Torri**, spanning the deep ravine between Spoleto and the adjoining mountain, was built over an aqueduct existing in the 14th century. This incredible engineering wonder is 230 meters long and soars 81 meters high. It is supported by a series of ten Gothic arches and has a fort at the far end as well as a balcony in the center. The 12th-century **cathedral** in Spoleto is also so lovely that it alone would make a stop in this charming town worth a detour. The exterior of this very old cathedral, with its beautiful rose window and intricate mosaics, is truly charming. Within the town of Spoleto, we recommend both the **Hotel Gattapone**, strategically perched on the side of the cliff overlooking the Ponte delle Torri, and the **Hotel San Luca**, built within a 19th-century building that was completely renovated and reopened as a lovely hotel in 1995.

A third choice for a place to stay near Spoleto is **Eremo delle Grazie**, a gorgeous villa nestled in a dense wooded area on the side of a mountain called Monteluco, overlooking Spoleto. The Eremo delle Grazie has the added bonus of a beautiful swimming pool built on a terrace with a view of the valley far below. The summit of Monteluco was one of the favorite retreats of quiet and beauty where St. Francis went to meditate.

From Spoleto you can take either the 418, a short cut that twists west over the hills to the BIS 3, or the longer route that loops south toward **Terni**. About 4 kilometers past Terni, take the BIS 3 north. Watch carefully for the turnoff to the west to **Todi**, located just off the main road. Take time to park and explore this truly picture-perfect hilltop walled village. Stop for a cappuccino in one of the sidewalk cafés. However, do not linger too long in Todi because the next town, Orvieto, is the real prize.

Whereas Todi is a tiny, easily managed village, **Orvieto** is a city spread across the top of a hill that drops down on every side in steep volcanic cliffs. You wonder how the town could ever have been built. Drive as far as you can up to the city, park your car, and proceed on foot. Have a good map handy because you pass so many churches and squares that it is difficult to orient yourself. Continue on to Orvieto's center where a glorious **Duomo** dominates the immense piazza.

You may think you have seen sufficient stunning cathedrals to last a lifetime, but just wait—Orvieto's is truly special. It is brilliantly embellished with intricate mosaic designs and accented by lacy slender spires stretching gracefully into the sky.

*Duomo, Orvieto*

Also of interest in Orvieto is **St. Patrick's Well**, hewn out of solid volcanic rock. Pope Clement VII took refuge in Orvieto in 1527 and to ensure the town's water supply in case of siege, he ordered the digging of this 62-meter-deep well. What makes it unusual are the 70 windows that illuminate it and the two spiral staircases that wind up and down without meeting.

If you are a photographer and into picturesque walled villages, none in Tuscany can surpass the little-known hamlet of **Civita di Bagnorégio,** located to the west of Orvieto. If you have time for this round-trip excursion from Orvieto, you will find it well worth your effort. Take the N71, which twists west from Orvieto toward Lake Bolsena. Stay on N71 for about 20 kilometers and then turn left, heading to Bagnorégio. Go into town and follow signs to Civita, which crowns the top of a steep, circular-shaped, rocky outcrop. There is no road into the village—the only access is to walk over a long, narrow footpath that bridges a deep ravine. Once you arrive, you will find a few shops, some Etruscan artifacts, a church, and a restaurant. However, the main focus is the town itself with its narrow arcaded alleyways and a dramatic 180-degree view of the desolate, rocky canyons which stretch out in a haunting beauty around the town.

Return to Orvieto and head directly north on the A1 for about 40 kilometers to the turnoff for your night's destination, **Cetona.** As you exit the freeway, follow the signs that wind circuitously into Cetona. Go through the village and follow signs for **Convento San Francesco**, the convent where **La Frateria di Padre Eligio** is located in a 16-hectare forest. After spending time in Assisi, it is most appropriate to stay in a 13th-century convent founded by St. Francis. This idyllic hideaway is well suited as a base from which to explore the wealth of places to see in this lower region of Tuscany.

From Cetona make daily forays into the beautiful countryside. One day visit **Pienza**—a jewel of a tiny walled village crowning a hilltop. Stop for lunch here and then continue taking the back roads for about 35 kilometers to **Abbazia di Monte Oliveto Maggiore**, serenely situated among the cypress forest. Of special interest in this abbey are the beautiful terra cottas adorning the entrance (created by the famous artist, Luca della Robbia) and the charming frescoes in the cloisters portraying the life of St. Benedict.

Take an all-day excursion from Cetona to **Siena**, another of the strategically built walled hilltowns. This is an entrancing city and deserves many hours to savor all its attributes. The ramparts are perfectly preserved with a series of massive gates guarding a meticulously maintained medieval stronghold. Drive as close as you can to the main square, park your car, and set out to explore on foot. The giant **Piazza del Campo** is a sight in itself: it is immense and, instead of being square, is fan shaped. Eleven streets surrounding the square converge into it like spokes of a massive wheel. It is in this gigantic piazza that the colorful **Palio delle Contrade** (dating back to the 11th century) takes place twice a year, on July 2 and August 16. The horse race is only a part of a colorful spectacle of medieval costumes, impressive banners, and parades. The festivities extend beyond the actual date of the races. Monopolizing one side of the Piazza del Campo is the 13th-century Gothic **Palazzo Pubblico** (Town Hall) whose graceful arches are embellished with Siena's coat of arms. The Palazzo Pubblico is open as a museum where you can stroll through the governor's living quarters. Also visit Siena's 12th-century **Duomo**, facing the Piazza del Duomo, just a short walk from the Piazza del Campo. Save time to visit the interior of this fabulous cathedral with its bold patterns of black and white marble because within is an excellent museum of antique religious art and sculptures. *NOTE:* While Cetona is suggested as the hub from which to explore this southern portion of Tuscany, look at Map 9 in the back of this guide to see other choices nearby. There is a rich selection of marvelous places to stay in this region, any one of which would make an excellent base for your explorations.

## DESTINATION III    CASTELLINA IN CHIANTI

Your next destination is **Castellina**, in the heart of Tuscany's Chianti wine region. Here you find the **Tenuta di Ricavo**, a cluster of charming stone cottages deep in the pine forest. The entire village has been converted into a romantic small hotel with tastefully decorated rooms. For a choice of other towns in the Chianti area where we suggest places to stay, study Map 8. Any one of the recommended hotels would make an ideal hub for exploring this part of Tuscany.

Of all the beautiful areas of Tuscany, picture-perfect Chianti is the most special. It lives up to every dream—hills crowned by walled villages, straight rows of towering cypresses, romantic villas, ancient stone farmhouses, vast fields of brilliant poppies, forests of pine trees, vineyards stretching to the horizon. In Chianti the sightseeing is mostly just meandering through the countryside, stopping at quaint hamlets, wandering through perched villages. Do not be too structured. Take a detailed map so that if you get lost, you can find your way home, but otherwise, just explore. Enjoy the freedom to discover your own *perfect village*, your own favorite restaurant.

During your adventures, the one town you must not miss is **San Gimignano**. What is so dramatic about San Gimignano is that at one time this walled town was surrounded by 72

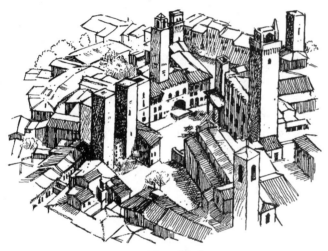

*San Gimignano*

towers. During the Middle Ages it was a status symbol for noble families to build personal towers for their protection—the higher the tower, the greater the image of wealth and importance. It is amazing that 14 of the original towers are still standing. They make a striking silhouette, soaring like skyscrapers. On a clear day you can see them on the horizon from far away. San Gimignano is truly a jewel—plan to spend at least a day here. There are many shops and marvelous restaurants tucked along the maze

of streets. *NOTE:* If you want to spend the night, we highly recommended the **L'Antico Pozzo**, a charming hotel in the center of town. **La Cisterna** on the main square and **La Mangiatoia** near L'Antico Pozzo both serve excellent food.

When it is time to complete your loop, Florence is about an hour's drive away.

# Mountain & Lake Adventures

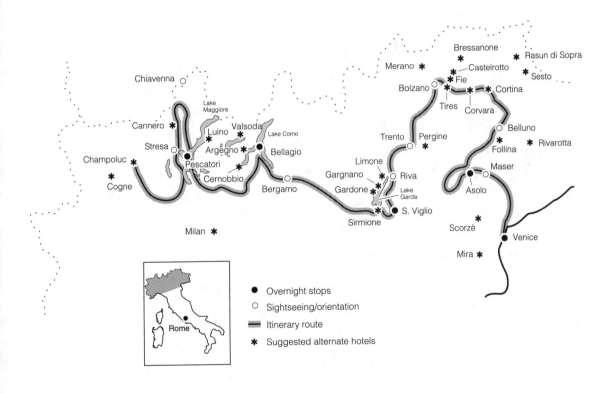

Chiavenna

Lake Maggiore

Cannero ✳

Luino ✳
Valsoda ✳

Lake Como

Stresa ○
Pescatori ●
Argegno ✳
Bellagio ●

Champoluc
✳
Cogne

Cernobbio

Bergamo ○

Milan ✳

Merano ✳
Bressanone ✳
Castelrotto ✳
Rasun di Sopra ✳
Fie ✳
Sesto ✳
Bolzano ○
Tires ✳
Cortina ✳
Corvara ✳

Trento ○
Pergine ✳
Belluno ○
Rivarotta ✳
Follina ✳
Maser ○

Limone ✳
Gargnano ✳
Riva ○
Asolo ●
Gardone ✳
Lake Garda
Scorzè ✳
Sirmione ●
S. Viglio ●
Venice ●
Mira ✳

- ● Overnight stops
- ○ Sightseeing/orientation
- ▨ Itinerary route
- ✳ Suggested alternate hotels

Rome

63

# Mountain & Lake Adventures

*Santa Maria Rezzónico, Lake Como*

For the traveler who wants to combine the magic of seeing some of the world's most splendid mountains with the joy of visiting Italy's scenic northern lakes, this itinerary is ideal. Contrasts will heighten the impact of visual delights as you meander through lovely mountain passes. Along the way you pass lush green meadows splashed with wildflowers and giant mountains piercing the sky with their jagged granite peaks. Farther on you come to lazy blue lakes whose steep shorelines are decorated with villages wrapped in misty cloaks of siennas and ochres. This itinerary can stand alone. However, it is also perfect for the traveler arriving in or departing from neighboring countries. We show detours for the tourist who will be leaving for or entering from Austria, Switzerland, or France. All too often the tourist thinks he has finished Italy when his tour ends in Venice, and he rushes north into Austria or Switzerland. What a waste—a very picturesque region still remains. Please linger to enjoy the mountains and lakes that truly are some of Italy's greatest natural treasures.

## ORIGINATING CITY            VENICE

This itinerary begins in **Venice**, one of the most romantic cities in the world. Her many narrow waterways are criss-crossed by storybook bridges and shadowed by majestic palaces whose soft hues reflect warmly in the shimmering water. Black gondolas quietly glide through the narrow canals as the gondolier in his red-and-white-striped shirt softly serenades his passengers with an operatic selection.

Venice is not a traditional city with streets and automobile traffic, but rather an archipelago of 117 islands glued together by 400 bridges. There is a wealth of things to do here: pick up a guidebook at one of the tourist stalls to give you an idea of what you want to see. On pages 37–40 we give brief sightseeing suggestions.

## DESTINATION I            ASOLO

You need not rush your departure this morning. Venice is a city that should be enjoyed slowly and since your journey today is short, you can certainly have the luxury of a last leisurely breakfast before embarking on your countryside adventure.

Since all the "streets" in Venice are canals, you will need to take a boat to your car. It will probably be at the **Piazzale Roma** where most of the car rental companies are located. Also in the Piazzale Roma there are overnight car parks for storing your car if you drive into Venice. The choice of conveyance will depend upon your budget and your inclination. The **vaporetti** are the most reasonable: similar to river buses. They leave regularly from St. Mark's Square for the approximately half-hour ride to the Piazzale Roma. The **motoscafi** are motorboats that duck through the back canals and usually take about 15 minutes to the Piazzale Roma. The motoscafi are like private cabs and are much more expensive than the "bus," but can be very convenient, especially if your hotel has a private motorboat landing. The most deluxe mode of transportation is by private **gondola**: however, these are very expensive and usually take about an hour to reach the Piazzale Roma.

Once you have retrieved your car from the parking garage, head north from Venice toward **Treviso**, about an hour's drive. If time allows, stop here. Stroll through this picturesque city spider-webbed with canals and surrounded by 15th-century ramparts—perhaps have a cup of coffee or a bite of lunch. Treviso is famous for its arcaded streets, churches lavishly decorated with frescoes, and painted houses. You might want to climb the ramparts for a view of the Alps beckoning you on.

From Treviso it is approximately another hour north to Asolo. However, just a few kilometers before you reach Asolo you see signs for the town of **Maser** where the **Villa di Maser** (some of your books might use the name of **Villa Bararo**) is located. This is a splendid villa designed by Palladio and fabulously decorated with frescoes by Paolo Veronese. It also has a very interesting museum of old carriages and antique cars. This elegant villa has erratic days and hours when it is open to the public—usually in late afternoons on Tuesdays, Saturdays, and Sundays. However, it is only about 1½ kilometers out of your way, so it is well worth a detour to investigate.

Your prize tonight is **Asolo**, a gem of a medieval village snuggled on the side of a hill with exquisite views of the countryside. As you drive toward Asolo, the terrain does not seem to hold much promise—just modern towns and industry. Then a side road winds up a lovely hillside and into the intimate little town. Although definitely a tourist destination, Asolo maintains the atmosphere of a *real* town with colorful fruit stands, candy shops, and the neighborhood grocer for those lucky few who live here. In addition, there are boutiques with exquisite merchandise for the tourist. Of course, a castle adorns the hill above the village—mostly in ruins but setting the proper stage. Naturally, there is a wonderful cathedral dominating the square, just as it should. You will find all this plus vineyards and olive trees on the hillsides and the scent of roses in the air.

No wonder Robert Browning fell in love with Asolo and chose it as his home. It might not be possible for everyone to live here, but at least you have the marvelous option of staying at the **Villa Cipriani**, an enchanting villa that was once Browning's home. Here you can dream on the peaceful terrace in the evening and watch the soft lights paint the distant villa-dotted hills in mellow shades of gold. *NOTE:* We also highly recommend two less expensive hotels in Asolo, the **Hotel Duse** and the **Albergo al Sole**.

*Villa Cipriani, Asolo*

There are a couple of towns that are worth seeing while you are in the Asolo area. If brandy holds a special interest for you, visit **Bassano del Grappa**, an old town famous for its production of grappa (or brandy). The town is also a pottery center. However, it is rather large and, in our estimation, much less interesting than **Marostica**, a tiny town just a few kilometers farther on. If you are in this area in September, check your calendar and consider a stop in Marostica. Here, during the first part of September (in alternate years) the central square is transformed into a giant chess board and local citizens become the human chess pieces. Even if it isn't the year of the chess game, you will enjoy this picturesque little medieval town encircled by ramparts, its pretty central square enclosed by colorful buildings and castle walls. There is also a second castle guarding the town from the top of the hill.

Quite frankly, we think one of the most stunning regions of Italy is the **Dolomites**—truly breathtaking mountains! Look at Map 2 (a and b) in the back of this guide to find the locations of our recommended places to stay—any one of them would make a good base for walking and soaking in the beauty of these soaring, saw-toothed mountain peaks. It is important to have a very detailed map of the region because this is a confusing area for driving. Adding to the confusion of finding your way is the fact that most of the towns have two names: one Italian and one Austrian. Before World War I this section of Italy belonged to the Austrian Empire, and most of the towns have retained their original names along with their new ones. The food is a mixture of Italian and German—strudel is the favorite dessert and ravioli stuffed with meat, vegetables, and cream cheese is called either r*avioletti* or *schulpfkrapfeln*.

*The Dolomites*

There are various routes for driving north into the Dolomites. The major highway heads north through **Feltre** and **Belluno** and then goes on to Cortina d'Ampezzo. However, if the day is nice and your spirit of adventure high, there is really nothing more fun than taking the back roads through the mountains. Journey through tiny hamlets and gorgeous mountain valleys far from the normal tourist path—always keeping a map accessible so that you don't wind up hopelessly lost.

You might want to travel casually and stop in a village that captures your heart as you drive through the picturesque Dolomite valleys. A good base for exploring the region is **Corvara**, a small village ringed by breathtaking mountains. Another excellent choice where we recommend several hotels is **Cortina d'Ampezzo**, a larger tourist center due to its excellent skiing facilities. Its location is truly breathtaking—the town spreads across a sunny meadow ringed by gigantic granite peaks. Although the true allure of Cortina is its beauty, there are a few other attractions—the lovely frescoes in the Romanesque **Church of SS Filippo e Giacomo**; the **stadium** where the 1956 Olympic ice-skating competition was held; and the **Museo Ciasa de Ra Regoles** with its geological display and contemporary art exhibition.

This is a mountain lovers' area where the roads are slow and winding. The scenery is beautiful, with green valleys dominated by the stark mountain walls, but the driving is hard, with lots of hairpin bends. Many routes are spectacular. The 48 and 241 from Cortina to Bolzano form the stupendous **Great Dolomite Road** (*Grande Strada delle Dolomiti*). Another lovely route runs through the **Alpe di Siusi,** high Alpine meadowlands beneath towering mountains. (From the Verona-Brennero autostrada exit at Bolzano Nord and follow a route through Völs [Fiè allo Sciliar], Siusi, and Castelrotto.) It continues on into the **Val Gardena** (Grödner Tal) to **Ortisei** (Sankt Ulrich) and up to the **Sella Pass**. We enjoyed a sensational 50-kilometer drive over four mountain passes that ring the **Gruppo Sella** mountain group—from Corvara we took the Gardena Pass, the Sella Pass, the Podoi Pass, and the Campolongo Pass, which returned us to Corvara.

The only relaxing (albeit strenuous) way to truly appreciate the Dolomites is to get out of your car and walk the well-marked trails that feather out into the hills. Cable cars and ski lifts run in summer and are excellent ways to assist the walker to higher altitudes. At gift shops or tourist offices you can purchase detailed hiking maps that show every little path.

## DESTINATION III          LAKE GARDA

It is a short drive south from Merano to Bolzano. Here you again join the expressway (E7), but this time heading south toward Trent. **Trent** is best known as the town where the Catholic Council met in the 16th century to establish important articles of faith that emphasized the authority of the Catholic church.

*Northern Italian Lake District*

Leave the freeway at Trent and head west on 45 toward the small, but lovely, green **Lake Toblino** which is enhanced by a superb castle on its north shore where you can stop for lunch. From Toblino head south on the pretty country road, lined with fruit trees and vineyards, heading directly south toward Lake Garda, Italy's largest lake. When you come to Arco, the road splits. Take the road to the left and continue south to Lake Garda and then follow the 249 as it curves along the eastern shore of the lake.

Allow several nights in the **Lake Garda** area so that you can enjoy at a leisurely pace several excursions on the lake and a side trip to nearby **Verona**. On Map 3 you can find many towns where we recommend places to stay in every price range that are on or close to the lake. However, we cannot resist sharing with you one or our favorites, **Locanda San Vigilio**.

As you follow the 249 which traces the eastern shore of Lake Garda, continue about 4 kilometers beyond the town of Torri d'Benaco. Turn right when you see San Vigilio signposted. There is a gate

*Locanda San Vigilio, Lake Garda*

where you will be stopped by an attendant who will want you to pay for parking **(San Vigilio** is also a park). Say you are a guest at the hotel and you will be allowed to pass. Drive as far as you can and then park your car. Walk down the path, turn left at the stately villa (glimpsed through tall gates), and follow the lane until it dead-ends at the Locanda San Vigilio, a 16th-century stone building, so close to the water's edge that waves lap beneath the windows. With such a setting, it is not surprising that Winston Churchill used to come here to paint. Inside, you will not be disappointed. The rooms are tastefully decorated with country antiques complemented by color-coordinated fabrics. If you want to splurge, ask for a suite overlooking the lake, but no matter which room you choose, they are all most appealing. There is a romantic dining room where you can eat in your own little niche by a window overlooking the lake.

When you are ready to sightsee, drive a few kilometers farther south along the lake to **Garda**. Park your car and take one of the ferries or hydrofoils that ply the lake. If you have the time, choose a different destination each day—perhaps planning to have a bite of lunch at an enticing little lakeside café. If you have time for only one adventure, visit **Sirmione.** This is a wonderful walled village at the south end of Lake Garda positioned at the end of a miniature peninsula. During the summer this town is absolutely bursting with tourists, but you can easily understand why: this is another one of Italy's "stage setting" villages, almost too perfect to be true. If you take the ferry or hydrofoil to Sirmione, your boat will dock in the center of the town. From here you can stroll through the little boutiques, perhaps have lunch at one of the beautiful terrace cafés overlooking the lake, and explore the tiny island-like village. If you want to go to the tip of the peninsula, there are small motorized trams that take you there.

If time permits, take the ferry to **Riva** on the northern shore of the lake. Although much of the town is of new construction, it has at its medieval core the **Piazza III Novembre** and 13th-century **Tower of Apponale**. A good place to eat lunch is on the terrace of the **Hotel Sole**, located directly across from the boat dock.

Another excursion is by car to **Gardone Riviera** (on the western shore of the lake) to see a nearby museum, the **Vittoriale**, once the home of Gabriele d'Annunzio, the celebrated Italian poet. (For those of us who love stories of romance, **d'Annunzio** is also famous for his love affair with Eleanora Duse.) While there, if you enjoy gourmet food, try the pink and white **Villa Fiordaliso**, a well-known restaurant located right on the lake. The Villa Fiordaliso also has a tidbit of historical romance—this was once the hideaway of Mussolini and his mistress, Claretta. For a simpler meal, just a few kilometers farther north along the lake at **Gargnano-Villa**, you can enjoy a wonderful seafood lunch on the sun-drenched deck of the **Baia d'Oro**.

It might be easier to leave the Lake Garda knowing that beautiful Lake Como awaits your arrival.

*Bergamo*

On your way from Lake Garda to Lake Como, stop at **Bergamo**, about an hour's drive west on the A4. As you approach Bergamo, the congested city doesn't appear to be worth a stop—but it is. The shell of the city is deceiving because it hides a lovely kernel, the **Cita Alta**, or high city. The lower part of Bergamo is modern and a bit dreary, but the old medieval city snuggled on the top of the hill holds such treasures as the **Piazza Vecchia**, the **Colleoni Chapel**, and the **Church of St. Mary Major**. Should you want to time your stop in Bergamo with lunch, there are several excellent restaurants. One suggestion would be the **Agnello d'Oro**, a cozy, charming, 17th-century inn in the Cita Alta.

From Bergamo it is a short drive on to **Bellagio**, a medieval fishing village located at the tip of a peninsula. This peninsula divides the lower section of Lake Como into two lakes, Lake Como on the west and Lake Lecco on the east. Bellagio makes an excellent base for exploring beautiful Lake Como. In the hotel description section we list three hotel suggestions in various price ranges. The **Grand Hotel Villa Serbelloni**, found behind gates opening onto the main square of Bellagio, is a large, imposing, old-world palace. It offers everything you could wish for in a lakeside interlude—tennis, swimming pool, boat excursions, private beach, and more. It is very ornate, still retaining its glory of bygone days with soaring, intricately painted ceilings, heavy chandeliers, and a fabulous sweeping staircase. The setting of the Villa Serbelloni is superb and overshadows what might be perceived as the slightly faded elegance of the hotel's decor. Just outside the gates of the Villa Serbelloni, with a prime location across from the lake, the **Hotel Florence** is also very highly recommended. This moderately priced small hotel is more intimate than the Villa Serbelloni and offers the warmth of welcome found only at family-run hotels.

*Bellagio, Lake Como*

Bellagio is a delightful town. Not only can you meander through its quaint medieval streets, but you can walk to the pier for one of the boats that will take you to all corners of the lake. **Lake Como** is absolutely beautiful—especially the lower eastern branch of the lake called **Lake Lecco** where cliffs enclose the shorelines like gorgeous walls and

*Mountain & Lake Adventures*

give a fjord-like beauty to the area. There are numerous romantic steamers that glide in and out of the picturesque, softly hued little hamlets dotting the lake shore. You can settle onto a steamer equipped with bar and restaurant and from your armchair lazily enjoy the constantly changing, but always intriguing shoreline as the boat maneuvers in and out of the colorful little harbors, past elegant private villas, by postcard-pretty villages. From Bellagio you can also step on board one of the swift hydrofoils that will whisk you about the lake or put your car right on the ferry to either **Varenna** on the eastern shore or **Cadenabbia** on the western shore to visit the **Villa Carlotta**, a fairy-tale-like 18th-century palace—worthy of the Prussian Princess Carlotta for whom it was named. You reach the villa, which is encircled by its own gorgeous park of terraced gardens, by a short drive from the ferry landing along the beautiful tree-lined Via del Paradiso.

## DESTINATION V ISOLA DEI PESCATORI

Continuing on toward Lake Maggiore, take advantage of the expressways to make your drive as easy as possible because there is usually heavy traffic in this part of Italy. It is best to head directly south from Bellagio to pick up the freeway in the direction of Milan. Keep on the bypass which skirts the north of Milan and follow the freeway northwest to **Lake Maggiore**. When you reach the lake, continue along the western shore to Stresa. It seems only suitable that for a "mountain and lake adventure" one of your hotels should be located on an island in a lake—so we have chosen for you one of the **Borromean Islands, Isola dei Pescatori** (Fisherman's Island), in Lake Maggiore. This is an enchanting little island with twisting, narrow, alley-like streets and colorful fishermen's cottages. As the name implies, this is still an active fishing village. During the tourist season the island teems with people and the streets are lined with souvenir shops, but it is hard to dull the charm of this quaint town.

Isola dei Pescatori can be reached by ferry from Stresa, Baveno, or Pallanza, but the most convenient of these is **Stresa** from where there are frequent scheduled departures to the island. Be sure to take one of the scheduled public ferries—these are very reasonable in contrast to the very expensive private speedboats whose captains will attempt to take you to the island. Your best choice for a place to stay here is the **Hotel Verbano.** This is not a deluxe hotel, but its setting is superb, and over the years (since our first visit) the decor

*Isola Bella, Lake Maggiore*

of this most romantic hotel has improved enormously. The bedrooms are pleasantly decorated, but lovely vistas are their most enchanting feature. The view from the terrace, where guests enjoy dining while overlooking the lake, is also outstanding. The food is delicious, and the service of the Zacchera family, who own and manage the Verbano, is warm and gracious. How smug you will feel as you settle into your room then sip a drink on the lovely terrace while watching the last of the tourists hustle onto the boat for shore, leaving you to enjoy the sunset.

This tiny archipelago consisting of Isola Bella (Beautiful Island), Isola dei Pescatori, and Isola Madre (Mother Island) is world famous for its dramatic palaces and spectacular, fragrant gardens. **Isola Bella** is the closest island to dei Pescatori—be sure to allow enough time to visit its sumptuous palace and glorious terraced gardens before returning to the mainland.

*NOTE:* If your next destination is Switzerland, then it is time to leave Italy by heading north in the direction of Domodossolo. You used to be able to drive your car onto a train and ride through the Simplon Tunnel. However, the trains no longer carry cars—so you need to drive over the Simplon Pass and on into Brig, Switzerland.

From Isola Bella, take the ferry back to pick up your car and drive south to the main freeway and head west toward Turin. Before reaching Turin watch for the signs and take the branch of the expressway heading toward Aosta. When you come to Verres, leave the highway and take the small road north to Champoluc, an hour's drive. The road follows

*Villa Anna Maria, Champoluc*

the Evancon River as it cuts its path through the mountains. At first the valley is quite steep and narrow and then opens up into wide meadows lazily stretching out on both sides of the river. In early summer the meadows are truly lovely, blanketed in brilliantly colored wildflowers.

Just before the road leaves **Champoluc,** you see a marker for the Anna Maria. At this sign turn to the right and follow the road for a very short drive up the hill until you see the hotel. It is beautifully located amid pine trees and has views in every direction of the spectacular mountains. The **Villa Anna Maria** is a small chalet-style inn. Its dining room is cozy and inviting with gay red-checked curtains at the windows and rustic Alpine-style carved wooden chairs. The bedrooms, although small, all have private bathrooms and are very appealing with paneled walls and a country flavor.

When it is time to leave Champoluc, if you want to travel into Switzerland you must drive back to the main expressway and head west. In about a half-hour you will come to Aosta at which point you can leave the expressway for the road leading north to the **San Bernardino Tunnel** and into Switzerland's Rhône Valley. Or, by continuing on the expressway west through the village of Courmayeur, you arrive at the **Mont Blanc Tunnel**, which delivers you briefly into France and then on to Geneva via the main highway. Note: A fire in March 1999 closed the Mont Blanc Tunnel. As we went to press for our 2001 guide, we checked with the tourist office and heard that the tunnel is still closed, but due to open soon. Surely it will be ready by the time you travel, but best check in case of further delays in the reconstruction.

Of course, by taking the short drive to Milan you can easily tie in with another Italian holiday suggested in this guide.

# *Rome to Milan via the Italian Riviera*

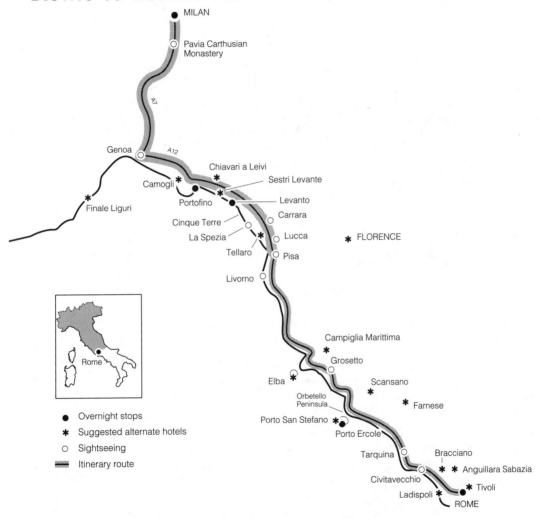

MILAN

Pavia Carthusian Monastery

A7

Genoa

A12

Chiavari a Leivi

Camogli

Sestri Levante

Portofino

Levanto

Cinque Terre

Carrara

La Spezia

Lucca

Tellaro

Pisa

Livorno

FLORENCE

Finale Liguri

Rome

Campiglia Marittima

Grosetto

Elba

Scansano

Orbetello Peninsula

Farnese

Porto San Stefano

Porto Ercole

Bracciano

Tarquina

Anguillara Sabazia

Civitavecchio

Tivoli

Ladispoli

ROME

- ● Overnight stops
- * Suggested alternate hotels
- ○ Sightseeing
- ▨ Itinerary route

79

# Rome to Milan via the Italian Riviera

*Vernazza, Cinque Terre*

This itinerary traces the western coast of Italy as far as Genoa before heading north for the final stretch to Milan. To break the journey, the first stop is Orbetello, a picturesque peninsula-like island joined to the coast by three spits of land. The next destination is Cinque Terre—a string of five tiny peninsulas along the coast that have not yet fallen prey to a great influx of tourists. As you follow the highway up the coast, it becomes a masterpiece of engineering—bridging deep ravines and tunneling in and out of the cliffs, which rise steeply from the sea. Along the way you pass picturesque small towns snuggled into small coves. Then it's on to Portofino—one of the Italy's most treasured jewels—before the final destination of Milan.

This itinerary begins in **Rome**, a perfect introduction to Italy. The joy of Rome is that every place you walk you are immersed in history. The whole of the city is a virtual museum—buildings over 2,000 years old, ancient fountains designed by the world's greatest masters, the Vatican, Renaissance paintings that have never been surpassed in beauty. On pages 43–48 we give just a few suggestions of places you must not miss, but we only touch on the wealth of sightseeing possibilities. Buy a guidebook at one of the many bookstores or magazine stands to plan what you most want to see and do. Also buy a detailed city map and mark each day's excursion. Most places are within walking distance—if not, consider taking the subway which stretches to most of the major points of interest.

Rome has a rich selection of places to stay. We suggest that you browse through the hotel section in the back of this guide where we describe hotels we think are especially appealing. Make a reservation in advance because space is very tight—particularly during the busy summer season. Plan to stay in Rome for several days. When you are saturated with the overwhelming number of sights and are ready to continue your journey, ask at the hotel desk to mark your map for the best route out of town.

## DESTINATION I         ORBETELLO–PORTO ERCOLE

From Rome follow the well-marked signs for the expressway heading west toward the Leonardo da Vinci airport. About 5 kilometers before you arrive at the airport, head north on A12 in the direction of **Civitavecchia**.

About 13 kilometers beyond the Civitavecchia Nord exit, turn right (east) on S1 BIS in the direction of Viterbo. Continue a bit more than 3 kilometers and turn left toward **Tarquinia**, an Etruscan city that historians date back to the 12th century B.C. Even if it is not quite that old, archaeologists have established that people were living here as early as 600 years before Christ. Before you reach Tarquinia, you will see on your right an open-air **museum**—an open field dotted with Etruscan tombs. The site is not well-marked, but your clue will be tour buses lining the road. Park your car, buy a ticket at the gate, and explore the fascinating tombs. There are over a thousand tombs stretching over 5 kilometers, but only a small select group are open to the public. You can wander at leisure. Each tomb has a sign describing what drawings are found within. You will find a rich treasure trove of paintings depicting the life of the ancient Etruscans, including scenes of hunting, dining, fishing, drinking, and frolicking. All of the burial sites are underground. To access a tomb, you have to climb down a narrow flight of steps and when you reach the bottom, everything is semi-dark. However, when you push a button, the tomb is magically illuminated behind a glass window. Each tomb is individually decorated with paintings that offer a poignant glimpse of life over a thousand years ago. There is no way you can visit all the burial chambers, but one of the most popular is the **Tomb of the Leopards** where there is a well-preserved banquet scene.

After viewing the tombs, ask the attendant at the gate for directions to the **Museo Nazionale Tarquiniese**, which is located in the center of town in the 15th-century **Vitelleschi Palace**. Even if you do not have time to savor all of the beautiful Etruscan vases and handsome carved stone sarcophagi, you must make at least a brief stop to view the astonishing winged horses dramatically displayed in a large room on an upper floor. You will be spellbound by these superb horses on an ornate relief that adorned the altar of the Queen's temple.

After your brush with Etruscan civilization, continue north for approximately 50 kilometers to Scalo/Orbetello where you turn east. The road crosses 6 kilometers of lagoons on a narrow spit of land (going through the town of Orbetello) before reaching the large, bulbous peninsula dominated by Monte Argentario. Turn left when you reach the peninsula (which looks like an island) and continue through the town of **Porto Ercole**, following signs to the exquisite resort of **Il Pellicano**, romantically perched on the cliffs overlooking the sea. If time and pocketbook allow, settle in to relax for a few days in this hideaway of the rich and famous before heading north. Enjoy the romantic setting, the swimming pool, tennis courts, and excellent food. Also explore the small peninsula, admire the many splendid yachts in the harbor at Porto Ercole, then continue on to the picturesque old fishing village of **Porto Santo Stefano**.

*NOTE:* If the luxurious Il Pellicano exceeds your budget, consider the **Hotel Torre di Cala Piccola**, located across the peninsula from Il Pellicano in Porto Santo Stefano. This is a less expensive hotel with a beautiful clifftop setting overlooking the sea. Or, if you would like to experience the natural, unspoiled beauty of Upper Latium, we highly recommend **Il Voltone**, located near the town of Farnese in an idyllic hamlet that has been converted into a small hotel. It is tucked far up in the hills above the coast next to the Selva del Lamone nature park. All of these hotels can be found on Map 10 and are described in the hotel section.

| DESTINATION II | CINQUE TERRE–LEVANTO |
|---|---|

*Leaning Tower of Pisa*

When it is time to continue, return to N1 and head north on the highway as it follows the coast. Get an early start if you want to stop in Pisa, Lucca, and Carrara along the way.

About 35 kilometers before you come to the large city of Livorno (which you want to avoid at all costs), the road divides. One split goes to Livorno and the other becomes the A12, which heads inland and bypasses the city. The next large town after Livorno is **Pisa**. Exit here and follow signs into the congested center of the old town. There is such a solid mass of tourists during the summer that you can hardly find a place to park close to the Piazza del Duomo, which is dominated by the Pisa's famous tower. The **Leaning Tower** is threatening to topple so it has been strengthened by massive cables that run to counterweights behind the square. Sitting photogenically beside the tower is the **Duomo**, built in marbles of alternating colors.

Even more interesting and not nearly so touristy as Pisa is the extremely picturesque city of **Lucca**, only a few kilometers to the north. Lucca too is an ancient city, even more perfectly preserved than its neighbor, Pisa. Completely surrounding the city is an enormous wall—a wall so wide that it even shelters pretty, small parks and a road that runs along the top. Lucca is truly a jewel. Take time to wander through her maze of narrow streets, admiring characterful mansions and colorful squares.

Leaving Lucca, return to the expressway A12 and head north to Genoa. Along the way you see what appears to be a glacier shimmering white in the mountains that rise to the right of the highway. This is not snow at all, but rather your introduction to the renowned white Italian marble. Unless it is too late in the day, detour to visit some of the marble quarries. Exit the highway at Carrara and take the winding drive up into the hills to the ancient village of **Colonnata**—famous through the ages for its marvelous white marble. As you wander this tiny town you're following the footsteps of Michelangelo, who used to come to here to choose huge blocks of marble from which to carve his masterpieces.

Take the small road from Carrara west to join the A12 and continue north for an entirely different kind of experience—exploring the five tiny isolated towns on the coast called **Cinque Terre**. This area is quickly becoming linked with civilization, so do not tarry if you love the thrill of discovering old fishing villages still untouched by time. En route you come to an exit to **La Spezia**, a large seaport and navy town. If you want to take a detour, go to La Spezia and from there take the short drive to the tip of the peninsula south of town to visit the old fishing village of **Portoverere** which clings to the steep rocks rising from the sea. This was one of Lord Byron's haunts when he lived across the bay at **San Terenzo**. Return to the A12, continue north, and take the exit for Levanto. We could not find suitable accommodations in any of the of the Cinque Terre villages, and therefore suggest **Levanto** as a hub for your explorations. Levanto, at one time a prosperous fishing port, lacks the luster of chic resorts, yet a faded, somewhat bedraggled charm remains. There are no luxury resorts here, just a smattering of simple places to stay. Our recommendation, **Hotel Stella Maris**, is a basic two-star hotel, which harks back to past grandeur. The small hotel is found up a narrow staircase leading to the second floor of a 17th-century palace, in its heyday a real showplace with manicured gardens stretching to the sea. Remnants of the past can be seen in frescoed ceilings, paneled walls, and antique furnishings. Although this is not a hotel for those who expect a decorator-perfect ambiance, the genuine hospitality grows on you.

Along the Cinque Terre there used to be five completely isolated fishing villages dotted along the coast between La Spezia to the south and Levanto to the north. First only a footpath connected these hamlets, then a train was installed, and now civilization is encroaching, with a road under construction which will open them up to greater commercialism. Three of these little villages, (**Riomaggiore**, **Monterosso**, and **Manarola**) are already accessible by road. Still completely cut off from car traffic are the fishing hamlets of **Vernazza** and **Corniglia**.

*Cinque Terre*

If you are staying in Levanto, you do not need your car. Instead, take a boat that connects the villages during the summer season. Alternatively, you can walk to the station and hop aboard one of the many trains in the direction of La Spezia. Most of these make stops at the Cinque Terre villages en route. Let your mood, the time, and the weather dictate your explorations. Another choice, instead of hopping on and off trains, is to hike between the towns along the spectacular trails that trace the rocky coast. Best yet, combine all these options. *NOTE*: Although it is not quite as close as Levanto, you can stay in **Tellaro** and use the delightful **Locanda Miranda** as your hub from which to explore the Cinque Terre. See the back of the book for more details.

If you have time to see only one of the scenic towns, Vernazza, which clings perilously to a rocky promontory that steps down to a tiny harbor, is the most picturesque. This colorful jewel has brightly painted fishermen's houses, quaint restaurants, a harbor with small boats bobbing in the clear water, and a maze of twisting narrow steps that lead up to the promontory overlooking the village.

## DESTINATION III                    PORTOFINO

After Cinque Terre, continue north beside the coast. Stop for lunch along the way in **Sestri Levante**, one of the most picturesque coastal villages en route. Continue along the small coastal road that goes through Chiàvari and on to San Margherita where you take the small road south for the short drive to the picture-book village of **Portofino**. This last section of the road, especially in summer, is jammed with traffic, but the prize at the end is worth the trials endured to reach it. Portofino is by no means undiscovered, but is well deserving of its accolades—it is one of the most picturesque tiny harbors in the world.

Before you reach Portofino, watch on your right for the sign for the **Hotel Splendido**. From the main road, a small lane winds up the wooded hillside to the magnificent villa-style hotel. Be prepared: the deluxe Splendido is a super-expensive hotel whose prices include breakfast and dinner. But what a glorious setting! The hotel is perched in the hills above Portofino with breathtaking views of the sea and the harbor. A swimming pool and tennis courts nestle below the hotel and enchanting little paths thread their way through the gardens, offering strategically placed benches for quiet moments to savor the stunning view. It is an easy walk into Portofino if you can bear to leave this haven. In 1998 the Splendido opened a "sister" hotel, the delightful **Splendido Mare**, for guests who want to be in the heart of town. *NOTE:* If you are on a tight budget, the **Hotel Eden** (a basic, 12-room hotel in the heart of town) is at the opposite end of the measure for ambiance and luxury, but has a good location and the warmth and caring of a family-owned small hotel.

Portofino is a national treasure—it truly is a jewel. Her tiny harbor is filled with glamorous yachts, small ferries, and colorful fishing boats. Enveloping the harbor are narrow fishermen's cottages, poetically painted in warm tones of sienna, ochre, and pink and all sporting green shutters. Bright flowerboxes accent the windows and the laundry flaps gaily in the breeze. Vivid reflections of these quaint little houses shimmer in the

*Portofino*

*Rome to Milan via the Italian Riviera*

emerald water. In the center of town is a small square, lined with restaurants, which faces the harbor. Forming a backdrop to the town are heavily forested hills which rise steeply to complete this idyllic scene.

*NOTE:* While staying in Portofino, if you appreciate gourmet dining, drive south to one of Italy's finest restaurants, the **Ca'Peo**, located in **Chiavari a Leivi.** You must make prior reservations because Franco and his wife, Melly, only take guests who call ahead since the food is specially prepared depending upon how many will be dining: tel: (0185) 31 90 90. The Ca'Peo, whose origins date back to a very old farmhouse, is located high in the hills overlooking the coast. Be forewarned: the meals are VERY expensive. If you want to spend the night, there are moderately priced suites available.

## DESTINATION IV          MILAN

*NOTE:* For those of you traveling to the French Riviera, we wish you farewell in Portofino. From Portofino continue to follow the coastal highway west to Genoa along the Italian Riviera into the principality of Monaco and then across the border to France.

For the rest of our group, after leaving Portofino, return to the A12 highway and continue west for about 30 kilometers to Genoa. As you circle the city, watch for the freeway A7 going north to Milan.

An interesting detour on the last leg of your journey is the **Pavia Carthusian Monastery** (*Certosa di Pavia*). Probably the simplest way to find it is to watch for the turnoff to Pavia (96 kilometers north of Genoa): take the road east to Pavia and from there go north about 10 kilometers to the monastery. Lavishly built in the 15th century, this splendid monastery is claimed by some to be one of the finest buildings in Italy. (Check carefully the days and hours open—the monastery is usually closed on Mondays and for several hours midday.) The outside of the building is lavishly designed with colorful marble and intricate designs. Inside, the small cloisters are especially charming with 122 arches framed by beautiful terra-cotta moldings. It also has a baroque fountain and several small gardens. Next to the monastery you find the **Palace of the Dukes of Milan** which is now a museum. After your tour of the monastery it is approximately 26 kilometers farther north to **Milan**.

The outskirts of Milan are not very inviting—frustrating traffic and modern commercial buildings. However, the heart of Milan has much to offer. Take time to see Leonardo da Vinci's famous mural, **The Last Supper**, which is once again on view in the church of **Santa Maria delle Grazie** after more than two decades of controversial restoration. (You must have an advance appointment for this—see page 33.) If you enjoy shopping (and Milan has some of the finest in Italy), pay a visit to the splendid **Galleria Vittorio Emanuele**, one of the prettiest shopping arcades in the world. Even if you are not a shopper, you should take time to browse. Located between Milan's other two sightseeing stars, the Duomo and La Scala, the Galleria Vittorio Emanuele is the forerunner of the modern shopping mall, but with much more pizzazz. In this Victorian-era fantasy there are two main, intersecting wings, both completely domed with intricately patterned glass. Along the pedestrian-only arcades you find many boutiques and colorful restaurants with outside tables.

After a stroll through the arcade, you emerge into an imposing square dominated by the truly spectacular **Duomo**, the third-largest cathedral in the world. Not only is the size impressive, but this sensational cathedral has a multi-colored marble façade enhanced by over 100 slender spires piercing the sky. This spectacular cathedral faces onto an enormous square which is lined with cafés, office buildings, and shops. Stop to have a snack at one of the outdoor restaurants—you could sit for hours just watching the people go by.

Also a "must-see" is Milan's opera house. Every opera buff knows about **La Scala**. Even if you have not been an opera enthusiast in the past, if you are going to be in Milan during the opera season (which usually runs from December to May), write ahead and try to get tickets. The theater is stunning and an experience not to be missed. When it is not opera season, there is usually some other performance or concert featured. If you haven't purchased seats in advance, you can try to buy them on the day of the performance (the ticket office is located down a flight of stairs to the left of the opera house).

Milan offers a large selection of places to stay. Until recently, most were modern hotels, seemingly way overpriced, with minimal old-world appeal. Happily, several hotels have recently emerged on the scene—some new, others opening after extensive renovations. If you want to splurge, the **Four Seasons Hotel Milano** is truly a superstar. Built within the walls of a 15th-century convent, the Four Seasons is just about as luxurious as you can get, offering every possible amenity. More in the tradition of old-world opulence is another gem, the deluxe **Grand Hotel et de Milan** which was closed for many years for a total face-lift and has now reopened. We also recommend several other hotels in Milan that are very nice and less expensive, such as the **Hotel de la Ville** and the **Antica Locanda dei Mercanti**. All of these are described in the hotel section.

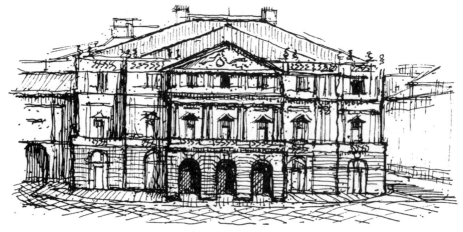

*La Scala, Milan*

# Highlights of
# Southern Italy

- ● Overnight stops
- * Suggested alternate hotels
- ○ Sightseeing
- ▨ Itinerary route
- ⋯ Suggested sidetrips

ROME

Anzio
Nettuno

Abbey of
Monte Cassino

Trani

Monopoli

Bari

Castel del Monte

Savelletri di
Fasano

Naples

Pompei

Salerno

Matera

Alberobello

to Corfu-Greece

Sorrento
Capri

Potenza

Taranto

Brindisi

Positano
Amalfi
Ravello

Paestum

Acquafredda

Marina de Pulsano

Santa Maria
di Castellabate

Maratea

Sibari

Tropea

Messina

Villa San Giovanni

Erice

PALERMO

Trapani

Cefalu

Taormina

Marsala

Gangvecchio

Catania

Selinunte

Enna

Agrigento

Piazza
Armerina

Syracuse

Ragusa

Rome

91

# Highlights of Southern Italy

*Amalfi Coast*

Having visited the justifiably famous trio of Rome, Florence, and Venice, many tourists think that they have seen Italy. Memories of childhood history lessons vaguely call forth such names as Pompeii, Herculaneum, and Paestum, yet, all too frequently, the urge to visit these jewels is lost in the misconception that southern Italy is an uninteresting destination. What a mistake: southern Italy has fascinating archaeological sites, gorgeous coastlines, medieval walled villages, beautiful sand beaches, marvelous hilltowns, and some of the most unusual sights in Italy. Many visitors who venture south from Rome are amazed to discover that the Emerald Grotto on the Amalfi Coast rivals the Blue Grotto of Capri and that the Greek ruins of Paestum outshine many found in Greece, and they are haunted by the mysterious town of Alberobello.

Therefore, for those of you who have already seen the fantastic highlights of northern Italy, we take pleasure in presenting to you the best of southern Italy. This itinerary makes a circle of the south in order to suit the travel needs of a wide selection of tourists. Follow the entire route or select the portion best for you since this itinerary is particularly suitable for the traveler who wants to take only a segment. For instance, the journey from Rome to Brindisi is a favorite one for the lucky tourists on their way to Greece, while the west coast is a popular drive for the tourist who wants to visit Sicily and then return to Rome by air or ferry. Most popular of all is the segment from Rome to the Amalfi Drive. This itinerary allows you to custom-tailor your journey and gives you tantalizing sightseeing along the way.

## ORIGINATING CITY                    ROME

**Rome** is a most convenient starting point to begin a tour of southern Italy, since its airport is the destination of planes from all over the world. In Rome you can immerse yourself in a wealth of history, art, architecture, museums, and monuments—and build a foundation for the sights that will be encountered on your journey southward. See pages 43–48 for suggestions of what to see and do in Rome.

There is a wide selection of accommodations in Rome in various price categories and locations. Choose the hotel that best suits your personality and budget from the hotel description section in the back of this guide. You will find that Rome has many excellent hotels and, even though the city is large, most of the hotels are still within walking distance of both shopping and sightseeing highlights. If you do not like to walk, ask the concierge at your desk to call you a taxi or direct you to the nearest subway station. Rome's main subway line stretches across the city—conveniently connecting most of the places of interest for the tourist.

When leaving the city by car, bear in mind that Rome always has a monumental traffic problem. Within the city look for strategically placed signs indicating that there is an expressway ahead. It might be quite a distance, but be patient as these signs lead you to the outskirts of Rome to the highway that makes a ring around the city with various spokes going off to different destinations. Follow the ring and take the exit for the A2, the expressway heading south toward Naples. Continue south for approximately 128 kilometers to the exit for **Cassino** where you leave the expressway. Actually, you can spot your destination from several kilometers away—the **Abbey of Monte Cassino** crowns the top of a large mountain to the left of the highway as you drive south. The road that winds up to the summit of the mountain to the Abbey is clearly marked about midway through Cassino. This abbey, founded by St. Benedict in 529 A.D., is extremely interesting both religiously and historically. For war historians it brings back many battle memories—this is where the Germans staunchly held out against the Allied forces for almost a year in World War II. When the mountain was finally conquered in May 1944, it opened the way for the Allies to finally move into Rome. As you read your history books, it seems strange that one fort could hold out for so long, but when you see the abbey you understand: it is an enormous building on the crest of a precipitous mountain. In the siege the abbey was almost destroyed, but it has been rebuilt according to the original plans.

*NOTE:* For those of you who for sentimental or historical reasons are especially interested in World War II, there is another destination you might well want to visit in this day's journey. **Anzio** is a town on the coast about 56 kilometers south of Rome and could easily be included as a stop before Cassino. It was at Anzio that the British and Americans forces landed in January 1944. The emotional reminder of this terrible battle is a few kilometers south at **Nettuno** where 8,000 white crosses and stars of David range—row after row across the green lawn. There is a circular drive around the beautifully manicured, parklike grounds where you also find a memorial chapel and small war museum. For those who lost family or friends during the invasion, there is an information office to the right as you drive in where you can stop to find out exactly where your loved ones are buried—you will need help because the park is huge.

From Cassino return to the expressway and continue south for about 60 kilometers until you see the sign for **Pompeii**. Unless you have absolutely NO interest in archaeology, you must see the city of your childhood history books. This is where time was frozen in 79 A.D. for the 25,000 people who were smothered by ashes from the eruption of **Mount Vesuvius**. If you are a dedicated student of archaeology, you must also visit the **National Archaeological Museum** in **Naples**, which houses many of the artifacts from Pompeii.

Time slips back 2,000 years and you feel the pulse of how people lived in ancient times as you wander the streets of Pompeii and visit the temples, lovely homes, wine shops, bakeries, and public baths. Many of the private homes have been reconstructed so you can marvel at the pretty inner courtyards, sumptuous dining rooms in Pompeii-red with intricate paintings on the walls, fountains, servants' quarters, bathrooms, and gardens. At the entrance to Pompeii there are souvenir stands where you can purchase a guidebook to the city, or, if you prefer, you can hire a private guide at the entrance. If you have time, visit the nearby ruins of **Herculaneum** which was also buried in the ashes of Vesuvius. See pages 48–49 for additional details about Pompeii.

Leaving Pompeii, head to the coast in the direction of Sorrento where the **Amalfi Drive** begins, tracing one of the most beautiful stretches of shoreline in the world. Be sure to make the journey in daylight because you want to savor every magnificent vista as well as safely negotiate this extremely twisty and precipitous road.

It is hard to recommend our favorite town along the Amalfi Drive since each has its own personality: **Sorrento** is an old fishing town perched on a rocky bluff overlooking the sea. It makes an especially convenient place to stay if you want to make a side trip to Capri by ferry or hydrofoil. **Ravello** is a tiny village tucked high in the hills above the coast with absolutely dazzling views down to the sea. **Positano** is an especially romantic coastal town with a picturesque medley of whitewashed houses terracing down an ever-so-steep embankment to a pebble beach dotted with brightly painted fishing boats. **Amalfi** is a small harbor town nestled in a narrow ravine.

*Positano*

There are many excellent places to stay along the Amalfi Drive—concentrated in just a few kilometers are some of the most splendid hotels in all of Italy. Study the various choices in Sorrento, Ravello, Amalfi, and Positano in the hotel descriptions section to see what most appeals to you.

From whatever hub you choose as your hotel base, venture out to do some exploring. The traffic during the tourist season is staggering, with buses, trucks, and cars all jockeying for position on the narrow twisting roads. Prepare for much shouting, waving of hands, honking, and general bedlam as long buses inch around the hairpin curves. The best advice is to relax and consider the colorful scene part of the sightseeing. Also, begin your excursions as early in the day as possible to try to avoid the major traffic.

If you are not overnighting in Ravello, you must plan to take the narrow winding road up to this romantic clifftop town. When you arrive, leave your car in one of the designated parking areas, pick up a map at the tourist office, then walk along the well-marked path to the **Villa Rufolo** and the **Villa Cimbrone**—both have beautiful gardens that are open to the public and enchanting views of the Bay of Salerno.

If you are not overnighting in Positano, by all means make this a day's excursion. The town is a photographer's dream—houses painted a dazzling white step down the impossibly steep hillside to a pebble beach lapped by brilliant blue water. To reach the small plaza dominated by a church topped by a colorful mosaic-tiled dome you have to climb one of the town's many staircases. Today Positano attracts artists and tourists from around the world, but in the 16th and 17th centuries it was an important sea port with tall-masted ships bringing in wares from around the world. When steamships came into vogue in the 19th century, Positano's prosperity declined and three-quarters of its population emigrated to the United States.

If you have not been able to include an interlude on **Capri** during your Italian holiday, it is easy to arrange an excursion to this enchanted island as a side trip from the Amalfi Coast. Steamers and hydrofoils depart regularly from Sorrento, Amalfi, and Positano. Ask at the tourist bureau or your hotel for the schedule. *NOTE:* If you have time, you could leave your car in Sorrento and spend several nights on Capri. See pages 50–52 for further information on what to see and do on Capri.

While exploring the Amalfi Coast, visit the **Emerald Grotto**, located between the towns of Amalfi and Positano. After parking, buy a ticket and descend by elevator down the steep cliff to a small rocky terrace. Upon entering the water-filled cave, you're rowed about the grotto in a small boat. Your guide explains how the effect of shimmering green water is created by a secret tunnel allowing sunlight to filter from deep below the surface. The cave is filled with colorful stalactites and stalagmites which further enhance the mysterious mood. There is also a nativity scene below the water which mysteriously appears and then drifts again from view.

## DESTINATION II          GULF OF POLICASTRO–MARATEA

When it is time to leave the Amalfi area, take the coastal road south as it twists and turns along the dramatic cliffs toward Salerno. At Salerno, join the expressway A3 for about 19 kilometers until the turnoff for **Paestum** which is located on a side road about a half-hour drive from the freeway. Magically, when you enter the gates of the ancient city, you enter a peaceful environment of a lovely country meadow dotted with some of the world's best preserved Greek temples. As you walk along the remains of streets criss-crossing the city, your senses are thrilled by the sound of birds singing and the scent of roses. Before leaving Paestum, stop for a snack at the **Marini Sea Garden**, a former villa set in a garden whose gates open onto the west side of the excavation.

From Paestum return to the A3 and continue south until you come to the Lagonegro Nord-Maratea exit. Do not be tempted by some of the short cuts you see on the map that lead to the coast, but stay on the main road 585. In about 25 kilometers the road comes to the sea where you turn north at Castrocucco, following signs to **Maratea**.

We have three hotel choices in this area, each lovely, each with its special merits. The **Santavenere Hotel** is a superb hotel in a glorious setting overlooking the sea; **La Locanda delle Donne Monache**, housed in an 18th-century convent, is snuggled in the

*Maratea, Gulf of Policastro*

hills above the quaint town of Maratea; and the **Villa Cheta Elite**, located a short drive north of Maratea in **Acquafredda**, is a moderately priced hotel whose gracious owners welcome guests as friends. If possible, spend several days in Maratea. Not well-known to foreigners, this lovely section of coast, known as the **Gulf of Policastro**, is a popular resort area for Italians. The loveliest section of the road is between Maratea and Sapri where the road traces the sea along a high corniche, providing lovely vistas of small coves and rocky promontories. This is not an area for intensive sightseeing, but provides a quiet interlude for several days of relaxation.

## DESTINATION III      ALBEROBELLO, MONOPOLI or SAVELLETRI

From the Gulf of Policastro, take road 585 back to the A3 and continue south for about 75 kilometers, turning east at Frascineto/Castrovillari toward the instep of Italy's boot. After about 25 kilometers you near the coast. Here you turn left on 106 to **Taranto**. Stop to see this ancient port which is connected by a bridge to the modern city. Even if you are not interested in ancient history, it is fun to see the Italian naval ships—giant gray monsters—sitting in the protected harbor.

From Taranto take 172 north and continue on for about 45 kilometers following signs to Alberobello. We suggest three hotels in this area, all conveniently located for sightseeing and relaxing. The first is in Alberobello, which is in the center of the Trulli district. The other two are located near the coast—one in Monopoli and the other close by in Savelletri. If you are staying in **Alberobello**, go into town and follow signs to the **Hotel dei Trulli**. If your chosen destination is **Monopoli** or **Savelletri**, do not go into Alberobello: instead, turn right and follow the ring road around town and continue on for 23 kilometers to Monopoli where you find the **Il Melograno**, a deluxe hotel built within a massive white 17th-century farmhouse. South of Monopoli is Savelletri where, just south of town, you will find **Masseria San Domenico**, a charming, beautifully managed hotel that exudes the character of its heritage, an old farm, built in the Moorish style. All three of the above places to stay are described in the hotel description section.

You are now in the province of **Apulia**, not a well-known destination, but all the more fun to visit because it is off the beaten path. With Monopoli, Alberobello, or Savelletri as your hub, venture out to explore the fascinating sights in the area. Some suggestions are listed below.

**Trulli District**: Trulli houses (whose origins date back to at least the 13th century) are some of the strangest structures in Italy—circular stone buildings, usually in small clusters, standing crisply white with conical slate roofs and whimsical, twisted chimneys. Outside ladders frequently lead to upper stories. Often several of these houses are joined together to form a larger complex. What a strange and

*Trulli Houses, Alberobello*

fascinating sight—these beehive-like little houses intertwined with cobbled streets form a jumble of a small village that looks as though it should be inhabited by elves instead of *real* people. The heart of the trulli region is Alberobello where there are so many trulli houses (more than 1,000 along the narrow streets) that the trulli district of town has been declared a national monument.

Trulli houses are not confined just to the town of Alberobello though this is where you find them composing an entire village. In fact, the trulli houses you see outside Alberobello are sometimes more interesting than those in the town itself. As you drive along the small roads, you spot gorgeous villas cleverly converted from trulli houses, which are now obviously the homes of wealthy Italians. Others are now farmhouses with

100             *Highlights of Southern Italy*

goats munching their lunch in the front yard. Occasionally you spot a charming old trulli home nestled cozily in the center of a vineyard. But most fun of all are the trulli homes of the free spirits: their homes, instead of displaying the typical white exteriors, have been painted a brilliant yellow, pink, or bright green with contrasting shutters.

**Grotte di Castellana**: As you are exploring the countryside near Alberobello, take the short drive north to see the Castellana Caves—the largest in Italy. In a two-hour tour you see many rooms of richly colored stalagmites and stalactites.

**Coastal Villages**: Be sure to include in your sightseeing some of the characterful towns along the coast. They look entirely different from the colorful fishing villages in the north of Italy. These are Moorish-looking, with stark-white houses lining narrow, alley-like streets. The Adriatic looks an even deeper blue as it laps against the white buildings, many of which rise from the sea with small windows perched over the water. Besides Monopoli, other coastal towns to see are **Polignano a Mare** and **Trani**.

**Castel del Monte**: On the same day that you explore the coastal villages, include a visit to the 13th-century Castel del Monte. Built by Emperor Frederick II of Swab, it is somewhat of a mystery, having none of the fortifications usually associated with a medieval castle. Nevertheless, it is dramatic—a huge stone structure crowning the top of a hill with 8 circular towers, which stretch 24 meters into the sky. There are stunning views in every direction.

When it is time to leave Apulia, you can breeze back to Rome by an expressway. Or, if your next destination is Greece, it is just a short drive to **Brindisi** where you can board the ferry for Corfu, Igoumenitsa, or Patras. Best of all, if you can extend your holiday in Italy, join the following itinerary, *Exploring the Wonders of Sicily*.

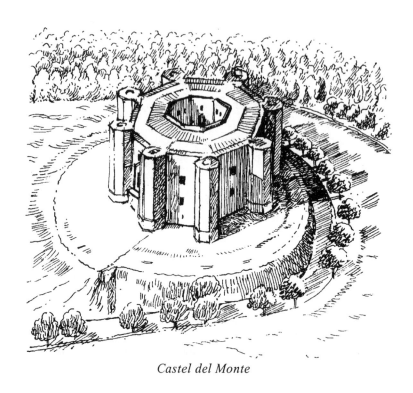

*Castel del Monte*

*Highlights of Southern Italy*

# *Exploring the*
## *Wonders of Sicily*

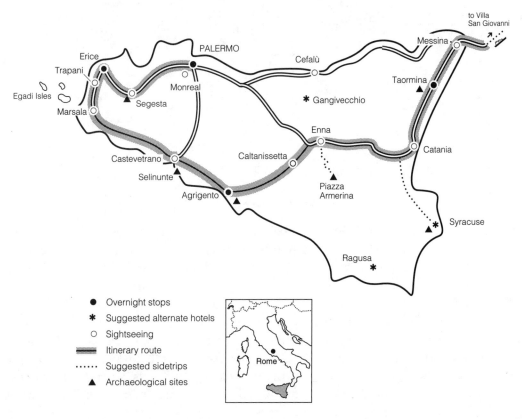

Egadi Isles

Trapani
Erice
Marsala
Segesta
Monreal
PALERMO
Castevetrano
Selinunte
Agrigento
Caltanissetta
Enna
Piazza
Armerina
Ragusa
Syracuse
Catania
Taormina
Gangivecchio
Cefalù
Messina
to Villa
San Giovanni

● Overnight stops
✳ Suggested alternate hotels
○ Sightseeing
▨ Itinerary route
⋯ Suggested sidetrips
▲ Archaeological sites

Rome

# Exploring the Wonders of Sicily

*Greek Theater, Taormina*

Sicily, the largest island in the Mediterranean, is a wondrous destination. This triangular hunk of land jutting out from the tip of Italy's toe became the crossroads of the ancient world. Nowhere in your travels can you discover a more diverse archaeological treasure-trove. Stone-Age tools and figures carved in the Grotta di Addaura at Monte Pellegrino indicate people were living in Sicily during the Palaeolithic Age. About 1270 B.C. the island was invaded by a Mediterranean tribe called Siculians, but they were not the only settlers: excavations show the arrival of tribes from Asia. Beginning in the 10th century B.C., pioneering Phoenicians took a fancy to this fertile land, followed later by their descendants, the Carthaginians. However, the true dawn of Sicily's reign of glory began with the colonization by the Greeks whose enormous influence permeates Sicily today.

However, the rich fabric of Sicily's heritage does not end with the Greek influence: later the Romans invaded, then the Normans, then the Spanish, and on and on. This resulting melting pot of cultures makes Sicily an absolute MUST for those who delight in the romance of archaeology. The true magic of Sicily is that most of the ruins are so natural in their setting. Frequently you discover you are alone—the only tourist walking through a field of wildflowers to gaze in awe at an exquisite temple.

As mentioned, the greatest age of glory for Sicily began when the Greeks founded their first colony here about 770 B.C. Apparently these early Greeks left their native country for economic and political reasons, but many were also undoubtedly motivated by pure curiosity—the desire to discover what awaited across the sea. Like the immigrants who came to America, the early settlers wanted a fresh start in a new land and an opportunity to establish a better life for themselves. And they did. Prospering enormously from the richness of the fertile soil, the early Greeks became extremely wealthy. As the *nouveaux riche* tend to do, they flaunted their success, building great cities, elaborate houses, theaters, spas, and stadiums—all bigger and better than those they left at home. Syracuse, the mightiest city in Sicily, eventually became more powerful than Athens. The temples they built surpassed in size and splendor those left in their native land. Not losing their passion for sports, every four years the new colonialists sent their finest athletes back to Greece where they dominated the Olympic games.

## ORIGINATING CITY　　　　TAORMINA

*Exploring the Wonders of Sicily* makes a natural extension from the previous driving tour, *Highlights of Southern Italy*. After ending that itinerary, drive to the tip of Italy's toe and take one of the ferries that cross the narrow channel twice an hour from **Villa San Giovanni** to **Messina**, Sicily. After buying your ticket, go to the indicated lane and wait with all the trucks, campers, and other cars for the signal to drive onto the boat. When on board, you may leave your car and go upstairs to the lounge area where you can buy snacks while traversing the short channel. In 35 minutes the large ferry draws up to the pier in Messina and you drive off to begin your adventures.

If you prefer to fly to Sicily, just reverse this itinerary. Start in Palermo and finish in Taormina. Alternatively, you can take a ferry from Naples to Palermo (a ten-hour journey).

**Taormina** makes an ideal starting point for your introduction to Sicily. Whereas good hotels are scarce in most of Sicily, there are many to choose from in Taormina. In the heart of town, we recommend the luxury-category, superb **Grand Hotel Timeo**. If you prefer to isolate yourself a bit from the bustle of tourists and yet be just a quick cable car ride away, the **Villa Sant'Andrea**, nestled just below the village on a beautiful little cove, is outstanding. If you are looking for a more moderately priced hotel, the **Hotel Belvedere** combines the charm of a family-run hotel with a stunning location overlooking the sea.

Picture-perfect Taormina, with the dramatic peak of **Mont Etna** as a backdrop, hugs the crest of a small peninsula that juts out to the sea. Steep cliffs drop to the unbelievably blue sea. Quaint streets wind through the colorful town where you can browse in the many smart boutiques, sip a cappuccino at a small café, or simply enjoy the incredible view. The scent of oranges is in the air and brilliantly colored bougainvilleas lace the medieval buildings.

However, it is not just the natural beauty of its spectacular setting that makes Taormina so popular. As in all of Sicily, your leisure pleasure is enhanced with fabulous sights to see. The prime archaeological target for your sightseeing is the **Greek Theater**. From the center of town an easy walk up Via Teatro Greco takes you to a magnificent theater dug into the sloping hillside above the town. Built by the Greeks in the 3rd century B.C., the open-air amphitheater has only a token few of its original columns remaining, making the effect even more romantic. As you gaze beyond the rows of seats to the stage below and out to the vivid blue sea beyond, you will think there is no prettier picture in all of Italy.

After visiting the Greek Theater, most of the remainder of your sightseeing can be done informally while strolling through town. First pick up a map and general information at the tourist office in the **Palazzo Corvaia,** a 15th-century palace located on the Piazza Vittorio Emanuele. From the Palazzo Corvaia, continue through town and stop at the 17th-century **St. Giuseppe Church** in Piazza Nove Aprile. As you walk on, be sure to step inside the 13th-century **cathedral** in the Piazza del Duomo to enjoy the paintings. Farther on you come to the 12th-century **Torre dell'Orologio**, the portal that leads into the oldest and most colorful part of Taormina, **Borgo Medieval**.

| DESTINATION I | AGRIGENTO |
|---|---|

When it is time to leave Taormina, follow the A18 south toward Catania. When you reach Catania, take the A19 west in the direction of Palermo, then when the highway splits (not long after passing Enna), instead of continuing north to Palermo, head southwest in the direction of Caltanissetta and Agrigento. After Caltanissetta, the expressway ends and you are on a two-lane road for the final leg of your journey to Agrigento.

Along the route from Palermo to Agrigento, we recommend two side excursions. It would make your day too long to include them both, but if you get an early start, you will have enough time to squeeze in one of them.

*Suggested Side Excursion*: If you are a Greek history buff, take this 128-kilometer detour to see one of the wealthiest, most powerful cities of the ancient Greek Empire (rivaling only Athens in importance). When you reach Catania, don't turn west toward Palermo, but continue south, following signs to **Syracuse**, founded in 734 B.C. by the Corinthians. In the **Archaeological Park** at the edge of town are two theaters—a 6th-century B.C. **Greek Theater** (one of the most magnificently preserved in the world) and the ruins of a 2nd-century A.D. **Roman Amphitheater** (one of the largest arenas the Romans ever built). From the Archaeological Park, skip the sprawling modern city and cross the Ponte Nuovo that spans Syracuse's harbor to **Ortygia,** the island where the Greeks first founded Syracuse. Visit the two main squares, the beautiful **Piazza del Duomo** where the cathedral (built upon the ancient temple of Minerva) is located and the **Piazza Archimede** enhanced by a baroque fountain. After sightseeing in Syracuse, return to Catania and take A19 west in the direction of Palermo.

*Suggested Side Excursion*: If you are a Roman history buff, take this 74-kilometer round-trip excursion to visit the Villa of Casale. En route from Taormina to Agrigento on the A19, turn south at Enna to **Piazza Armerina**. Continue southwest beyond Piazza Armerina for 5 kilometers to your sightseeing target, **Villa of Casale**, rivaling in splendor the home built by Tiberius on the island of Capri. The foundations of this sumptuous Roman villa were hidden under a blanket of mud for 700 years—not discovered by archaeologists until 1950. The fact that this ostentatious villa was built when the Roman Empire was on the verge of financial ruin is all the more fascinating. You cannot help wondering if the obviously vast expense of its construction was indicative of the flamboyant spending style that led to the collapse of the Roman Empire. Built in the 3rd century A.D., this mansion surely must have belonged to someone of enormous importance—perhaps Emperor Maximilian. The ruins are beautifully displayed in a covered museum with walkways guiding you from one opulent room to the next, each overlooking courtyards. But don't start until you have studied a mockup as you enter showing an artist's rendering of what the huge villa looked like in its prime—a look at this will increase your appreciation of the incredible grandeur of what you will be seeing. In all, the home covers an area almost three times the size of a football field. The outstanding feature is the 3,500 square meters of mosaics that decorated the floors of this sumptuous villa. Following the home's foundations are 40 mosaic floors of extraordinary quality. These beautifully preserved ancient Roman mosaics are considered the finest in the world. Slip back almost 1,700 years and imagine what life must have been like: the scenes show hunting expeditions, wild animals, mythical sea creatures, chariot races, cupids fishing, slaves working, girls cavorting. Once you have visited this Roman showplace, return north to Enna, then turn west following the route to Agrigento.

The hotels we suggest are not in the center of **Agrigento**, which is a congested, not very pretty city. Instead, follow the signs for the **Valle dei Templi**. This is the archaeological zone where both your sightseeing and our hotel recommendations are located. The name is misleading: the archeological site is actually on a plateau to the west of town—not in a valley at all. If you are lucky enough to get a reservation, go directly to the **Villa Athena**, and get settled. The Villa Athena has a somewhat commercial ambiance since,

because of its superb location, it is a favorite luncheon stop for small tour groups. But it is a very pretty villa, has a friendly staff, and a truly incomparable setting—in Agrigento, the Villa Athena is definitely THE place to stay for location. Ask for a room with a view of the archeological zone—these cost a bit more, but are worth it. To wake up in the morning and look across at the sun rising on the Temple of Concordia is certainly the way to begin your day of sightseeing. Just a short drive away from the ruins we also recommend the **Foresteria Baglio della Luna**, another lovely place to stay with prettily decorated rooms, a delightful terrace, and a view of the Valle dei Templi in the distance.

Plan to spend two nights in Agrigento so that you can spend one entire day leisurely seeing the ruins. From the gardens of the Villa Athena, walk down a footpath directly to the area where the temples are located. A wide pedestrian road connects the temples—start at one end and savor the haunting beauty of each. Most of these Doric temples are in ruins, with only enough columns remaining to give you an idea of what they used to be in their glory. The best preserved is the **Temple of Concordia**, which dates back to 440 B.C. See them all: the **Temple of Juno**, the **Temple of Hercules**, the **Temple of Dioscuri**, the **Temple of Jupiter**, and the **Temple**

of **Castor and Pollux**. The setting is beautiful with the sea in the distance and wildflowers in the surrounding fields. It is a thrill to stroll from one temple to the other, marveling at their grandeur and trying to envision what these incredible structures dedicated to Greek gods looked like 2,000 years ago.

To complement your sightseeing at the temples, walk to the **Archaeological Museum** (take the same path as to the temples, but go in the opposite direction). The museum has a mock-up of the Temple of Jupiter, plus many vases and artifacts from the site.

## DESTINATION II                    ERICE

From Agrigento, continue west on 115 toward Castelvetrano. About 10 kilometers before you arrive in Castelvetrano, turn left on the 115dir toward the coast, signposted to Selinunte. For such major ruins, there is little commercialism. You might well miss the main east entrance on the 115dir—as you drive toward the coast, look for a parking area to the right of the road (if you go under the railroad tracks, you have gone too far).

Park your car in the designated area, buy your ticket, and walk through the tunnel into the enormous field where the remains of the temples of Selinunte lie scattered amongst the wildflowers. In its prime, **Selinunte** was one of the finest cities in Sicily. It met disaster in 407 B.C. when the Carthaginians (it is thought under the command of Hannibal) razed the city, slaughtered 16,000 people, and took thousands into slavery. The giant temples, however, were probably destroyed by earthquake, not by the sword. Here, spread along a huge plateau overlooking the ocean, are the impressive remains of some of the most gigantic temples built by the Greeks. It is staggering to imagine how more than 2,500 years ago they had the skill and technology to lift and piece together these huge blocks of stone weighing over 100 tons each (slaves undoubtedly helped). Of the original seven temples, only one has been reconstructed, but the massive columns lying on the ground indicate the scope and grandeur of what used to be.

From Selinunte, return to the 115, taking the coastal route to Erice. En route, stop for lunch at one of the restaurants along the seafront promenade in **Mazara del Vallo**, an ancient city that was at one time a colony of Selinunte. Browse through the historic center of town to see the beautiful **Piazza della Repubblica** and the **cathedral**.

The next large town after Mazara del Vallo is **Marsala**, a large city well known throughout the world for its excellent wine. Ironically, it was not an Italian, but an Englishman, named John Woodhouse, who experimented by lacing the native wine with an extra bit of alcohol. Based on Woodhouse's formula, Marsala quickly became one of the staples of the British Navy and a special favorite of Lord Nelson. Along the road between Selinunte and Marsala are various wineries that are open to the public. One of the most popular is the **Florio Winery**—one of the three original companies to produce Marsala.

From Marsala, the road heads north to Trapani. Bypass Trapani and head northeast to **Erice**. Positioned over 750 meters above the coast (about 10 kilometers from Trapani), Erice is a delightful medieval

walled town, cooled by breezes from the sea. Park your car and walk through the **Porta Trapani** and up the cobbled street. A few blocks on your right is the **Moderno**, a friendly, well-run small hotel. The Moderno is simple, but very pleasant, and well located in the heart of town, close to restaurants and shopping. There are no deluxe hotels in Erice.

Erice is best discovered by exploring on foot. Narrow cobbled streets and steep stairways form a maze throughout the town, which is so small that you cannot get lost for long. Just wander, discovering tiny churches, picturesque squares, characterful stone houses, arcaded passageways, and shops selling the locally produced handmade carpets with colorful geometric designs. Walk to the **Castello Normanno**, built upon the ruins of the Temple of Venus. From the tower you have a splendid view looking over the town of Trapani and out to the sea.

*Erice, Sicily*

If you like to get off the beaten path, from Erice drive down to Trapani and take a hydrofoil to the **Egadi Isles**, all less than an hour away. Just a short distance off shore, **Favignana,** the largest of the three islands, was once a great center for tuna. The major cannery was owned by Ignazio Florio (the same Florio who founded the Florio Winery). **Levanzo**, the smallest of the islands, has a very small population due to its lack of fresh water. The island farthest from Trapani, **Maréttimo**, is basically a fishermen's island.

Erice also makes a convenient base for an excursion to **Segesta.** Wind down the hill from Erice and turn left on the A29 going east in the direction of Palermo. Thirty kilometers after getting on the freeway, take the Segesta exit and follow signs for the Segesta archaeological site, located close the highway. Although you have seen many ruins by this stage of your holiday in Sicily, don't miss this one—it is special.

First drive to the designated parking area and walk up the hillside to visit what most experts believe to be the world's finest example of a **Doric temple**. The temple with 36 columns looks much as it must have in 400 B.C. There is no roof—there never was because this isolated temple to some unknown god was never completed. One of the most superb aspects of this temple is its setting—there is nothing to jar the senses. The temple stands alone in a field of wildflowers with great natural beauty all around. Enjoy the romance of this gem at your leisure, then drive down the hill and park your car by the information center where there is a nice restaurant. Eat lunch here and then walk the marked path to see the **Greek Theater**. It is about a kilometer away, but a lovely walk through untouched fields. There are so few signs, you'll wonder if you are going the right way and be tempted to verify your destination with a fellow tourist you pass en route. Again, the location is what makes this theater so special. What an eye the Greeks had for beauty: the stage is set in such a way that the spectators look out across the mountains to the sea. The theater is mostly in ruins, but sit on one of the ancient benches, enjoy the beautiful surroundings, and imagine dramas that took place over 2,000 years ago.

## DESTINATION III                    PALERMO

From Erice return to the A29 and head east to Palermo. Palermo is a commercial, traffic-congested city , but there are some very interesting places to see both within the city and on its outskirts. Happily, Palermo has a couple of very good places to stay. The deluxe **Villa Igiea Grand Hotel**, located on the edge of the sea on the west edge of town, is expensive, but a welcome oasis of peace and quiet. It has a swimming pool on the bluffs above the sea and even has its own small ancient temple in the garden. If you want to be in the heart of Palermo, within walking distance of all the main sightseeing, the **Centrale Palace Hotel** is a superb choice. *NOTE:* If you want to skip overnighting in Palermo, the following sightseeing suggestions could also be accomplished from Erice.

The most dramatic sightseeing excursion (just 8 kilometers south of Palermo) is to visit **Monreale**, an awesome cathedral built by William II in 1174. It seems that William II was visited in a dream by an angel who told him of a secret treasure, and with his new-found wealth he built Monreale, one of the world's greatest medieval monuments. From the outside, the cathedral doesn't look special, but just wait: the interior is stunning. When you step inside you find 130 panels of shimmering mosaic, illustrating stories from both the Old and the New Testaments. The bronze doors of the cathedral are spectacular, designed by Bonanno Pisano in the 12th century. This is a cathedral not to be missed.

Another sight near Palermo is **Monte Pellegrino**, a 600-meter mountain rising on the west edge of the city. There are several caves in the mountain. The **Grotta di Addaura** is a three-chamber cave with carvings dating to the Palaeolithic Age. Another cave has been transformed into a chapel, the **Sanctuary of Santa Rosalia,** commemorating Santa Rosalia, the niece of King William II, who became a hermit—living and dying in this cave. You need to obtain permission from the National Archaeological Museum in Palermo if you want to visit these caves.

Another recommended side trip from Palermo is to visit the ancient fishing village of **Cefalù** built on a rocky peninsula about an hour's drive east from Palermo. Not only is this a very colorful fishing village, complete with brightly hued boats and twisting narrow streets, but there is also a splendid Norman **cathedral** built by King Roger II in the 12th century in fulfillment of a promise he made to God for sparing his life during a storm at sea.

When you are ready to leave Palermo, there are several choices. You can take one of the many flights from Palermo to Rome, board a ferry to Naples, or complete your circle of Sicily by driving to Messina for the short ferry ride back to the mainland.

# Hotel Descriptions

There is a fascinating area in southeastern Italy with a collection of strange round white buildings with gray-stone conical-shaped roofs. These ancient houses, which seem to be left over from some Moorish tribe that must have inhabited this part of Italy long ago, are called *trulli* and are usually seen in groups of two or three throughout the countryside. In the town of Alberobello you will discover a whole village of these whimsical little houses whose jumble of domed roofs, whitewashed walls, and crooked little chimneys creates a most unusual sight. Be sure to stroll through the pedestrian zone of Aberobello, which oozes charm. Fortunately there is a good hotel in the area that is located within walking distance of the center of the trulli village. Not only is its location excellent, but the hotel captures the mood of the area since it is constructed within some of the trulli houses. Small bungalows are scattered around a large parklike area connected by winding pathways under the pine trees. Each bungalow is a suite with a living room with fireplace, one or more bedrooms, and a private patio. The suites are spacious and have attractively tiled bathrooms. The dining rooms and the reception area each occupy their own trulli. Within the grounds are a pool and children's play yard. If you are on your way to Greece, you will find the Hotel dei Trulli a convenient choice: very close to Brindisi and Bari, the two major ferry ports.

*HOTEL DEI TRULLI*
*Manager: Riccardo Cottino*
*Via Cadore, 28*
*70011 Alberobello (BA), Italy*
*Tel: (080) 43 23 555, Fax: (080) 43 23 560*
*28 rooms, Double: Lire 360,000–420,000\**
*\*Rate includes breakfast & dinner*
*Open all year, Credit cards: all major*
*Restaurant open daily*
*68 km NW of Brindisi, 55 km SW of Bari*
*Region: Apulia, Michelin Map 431*

The choice place to stay in Amalfi is the deluxe Hotel Santa Caterina. It is not in the town center, but since Amalfi has the main highway separating it from the sea, the hotel has a far superior setting—just to the north of town on a cliff rising above the blue Mediterranean. Although larger than most hotels in our guide, the Santa Caterina has the intimacy and warmth of a small hotel. Since 1880 the property has belonged to the Gambardella family who have imbued in their excellent staff the art of making each guest feel special and with over 100 staff members for 70 rooms, you can understand how everyone is properly pampered. The hotel terraces down the hill from the highway to the sea where you find a large saltwater swimming pool. Guestrooms, all individual in décor, are charming, with whitewashed walls, antique accents in the furnishings, and colorful, local, handmade tiles on the floors and in the bathrooms. Many rooms have a balcony or terrace with a view to the sea. The main dining room is cheerful, with coved ceiling and sunlight streaming in through walls of glass. However, most guests choose to dine outside on the bougainvillea-bedecked terrace. On a terrace just above the swimming pool there is a second outdoor restaurant where lunch and special dinners are served. Almost all of the fruits and vegetables used in the restaurant are freshly gathered from the hotel's own gardens. If you want to splurge, there are several cottage suites tucked in amongst the lush lemon orchards.

*HOTEL SANTA CATERINA*      **New**
*Owners: Gambardella family*
*Manager: Armando Di Palma*
*S.S. Amalfitana, 9*
*84011 Amalfi (SA), Italy*
*Tel: (089) 87 10 12, Fax: (089) 87 13 51*
*E-mail: info@hotelsantacaterina.it*
*70 rooms, Double: Lire 560,000–1,500,000*
*Open all year, Credit cards: all major, Restaurant open daily*
*69 km S of Naples, 24 km N of Salerno*
*Region: Campania, Michelin Map 431*
*www.karenbrown.com/italyinns/santacaterina.html*

I Due Laghi, named for its position between the two Roman lakes of Bracciano and Martignano, was born 11 years ago with all the characteristics of an agritourism farm—and has remained the only one around Lake Bracciano. It has developed over time into more of a country hotel with all the service and upgraded amenities of a four-star establishment, yet conserves the informal, rustic flavor of a ranch. On 375 acres of cultivated fields and woods, horses and cattle graze and sports activities take center stage, from riding (even drag hunts organized) and biking to swimming in the pool. In addition, you can enjoy two nearby golf courses, tennis courts, and lake sailing. Its close proximity to Rome and surrounding Etruscan towns makes it a relaxing and peaceful haven for travelers. The equestrian theme prevails in the bar and lounge area and there is a large restaurant, La Posta de'Cavalieri, which has received a Veronelli rating. Matteo and his staff are very attentive to guests' needs and are thorough believers in the beauty that the area offers the more adventurous guest. Bedrooms, rather standard in decor, are all off one wing of the main house with suites that have separate garden entrances. *Directions*: From Rome leave the GRA ring road at exit 5—Cassia Bis—and follow it to the Bracciano-Anguillara exit left. Turn left again at the lake and follow signs to I Due Laghi 49 km from the airport.

*COUNTRY RELAIS I DUE LAGHI*  ***New***
*Owner: Matteo Marzano*
*Anguillara Sabazia (RM) 00061, Italy*
*Tel: (06) 99 60 70 59, Fax: (06) 99 60 70 68*
*E-mail: duelaghi@edl.it*
*32 rooms, Double: Lire 250,000–400,000*
*Open all year, Credit cards: all major*
*Restaurant open daily*
*39 km NW of Rome*
*Region: Lazio, Michelin Map 430*
*www.karenbrown.com/italyinns/iduelaghi.html*

If you've ever dreamed of waking up in an Italian villa and opening your windows to one of the world's most romantic views, the Albergo Villa Belvedere will surely capture your heart. This lovely 18th-century villa with its mustard-yellow façade, crisp-white trim, and dove-gray shutters has a superb setting. Only a private terrace separates it from Lake Como. Amazingly, this intimate inn is an incredible value—but do not expect a luxury hotel: the furnishings are simple. The guestrooms do have direct-dial phones, hairdryers, and satellite TVs, but no mini bars. What you get is much more: an incomparable setting, great warmth of welcome, and old-fashioned comfort enhanced by immaculate housekeeping. As an added bonus, the food is delicious. Giorgio Cappelletti oversees the kitchen, which produces not fancy gourmet dishes, but just simple home cooking in the best Italian tradition. There is a daily menu with several choices for each course, including of course the fresh catch of the day. Jane Cappelletti (born in Scotland) met and fell in love with Giorgio when visiting Italy. Her cheerful friendliness and eye for a tidy house are great assets. Jane and Giorgio are assisted by their charming, very efficient daughter, Michela. Boats depart from the dock just steps from the hotel. You can hop aboard to explore beautiful Lake Como with its clusters of romantic villages. Splurge and ask for a lakefront room (such as 7 or 15)—these are quieter and have spectacular vistas. *Directions*: Take the A9 north from Milan and exit at Como Nord. Take N340 north toward Menággio—after about 15 km you come to Argegno.

*ALBERGO VILLA BELVEDERE*
*Owners: Jane & Giorgio Cappelletti*
*Via Milano, 8*
*22010 Argegno, Lake Como (CO), Italy*
*Tel: (031) 82 11 16, Fax: (031) 82 15 71*
*18 rooms, Double: Lire 330,000–350,000\**
*\*Rate includes breakfast & dinner, Open mid-Mar to mid-Nov*
*Credit cards: none accepted*
*Restaurant open daily, 70 km N of Milan*
*Region Lombardy, Michelin Map 428*

As the road twists and turns ever further into the wooded hills above Assisi, one can't help wondering what treasure awaits at the trail's end, or if anyone could possibly have found this romantic hideaway before you. What a surprise then to finally turn off the graveled road and discover the parking lot filled with luxury cars. In this glorious hillside setting with its sweeping panorama of wooded hills, worldly cares quickly melt away. Although the hotel is built into a cluster of 10th-century stone houses, all the modern-day luxuries are present including a beautiful swimming pool on the right as you enter and, on a lower terrace, tennis courts. Behind the main building is a separate stone house where you find a most appealing lounge with deep-green sofas and chairs grouped around a giant fireplace. Doors from the lounge lead into an intimate little bar and beyond to a dining room with honey-colored stone walls, beamed ceiling, and terra-cotta floors with tables dressed in the finest of linens. Marvelous meals are served, prepared almost totally from ingredients from the hotel's own farm, which is part of the property. The individually decorated bedrooms sport a rustic, yet elegant, ambiance. The well-equipped bathrooms offer enormous towels, fragrant soaps, hairdryers, and bathrobes.
*Directions:* From Assisi follow signs toward Gualdo-Tadino and immediately as you leave the town walls of Assisi, watch for and take the road to the right signposted Armenzano. From Armenzano, the hotel is well marked.

*ROMANTIK HOTEL "LE SILVE DI ARMENZANO"*
*Manager: Daniela Taddia*
*06081 Localita: Armenzano, Assisi (PG), Italy*
*Tel: (075) 80 19 000, Fax: (075) 80 19 005*
*E-mail: hotellesilve@tin.it*
*15 rooms, Double: Lire 300,000*
*Open Mar to mid-Nov, Credit cards: all major*
*Restaurant open daily, 10 km E of Assisi*
*Region: Umbria, Michelin Map 430*
*www.karenbrown.com/italyinns/lesilvediarmenzano.html*

Asolo, a jewel of a village tucked into hills northwest of Venice, is one of Italy's best-kept secrets. While once again exploring this magical town, we were surprised to look up from the main square and see the Albergo al Sole nestled on the hill above us. Wondering how we could have missed this pretty mustard-yellow hotel, we walked the cobbled street up to the hotel and discovered it had just opened two weeks before. What a great addition to Asolo! The hotel, which had lain derelict for almost a quarter of a century, has been brought to new life after three years of extensive renovation by the De Checchi family. Fresh and new with excellent quality and pretty furnishings throughout, the Albergo al Sole is a terrific value. The guestrooms are spacious and decorated appealingly. The bathrooms too are exceptionally large and prettily tiled. All the rooms have satellite TV and mini bar. If you are on a budget, even the least expensive rooms are very lovely, although they do not have the view of the more expensive rooms that look out over the village. If you are looking for a truly special room, you need not splurge on a suite, but rather ask for a deluxe double. Our favorite, the Eleonora Duse, is a very pretty corner room decorated with antiques and with large windows overlooking Asolo. The entire hotel follows a basic color scheme that combines the cheerful colors of pretty blues and yellows. *NOTE:* A new fitness center has been added since our last visit.

*ALBERGO AL SOLE*
*Manager: Silvia De Checchi*
*31011 Asolo (TV), Italy*
*Tel: (0423) 52 81 11, Fax: (0423) 52 83 99*
*E-mail: sole@prometeo.com*
*23 rooms, Double: Lire 280,000–450,000*
*Open all year, Credit cards: AX, VS*
*No restaurant, breakfast only*
*65 km NW of Venice, 14 km E of Bassano*
*Region: Veneto, Michelin Map 429*
*www.karenbrown.com/italyinns/albergoalsole.html*

Asolo is a beautiful medieval town in the low-lying hills northwest of Venice, dominated by castle ruins on the hillside above and filled with charming streets, Gothic arcades, and frescoed façades. Here in this magical town one of our favorite hotels in Italy, the Villa Cipriani, is secreted in a garden just a short stroll from the center of the village. However, since the price tag at the Cipriani does not fit everyone's budget, for those who do not want to splurge on accommodations, a good alternative choice is the Hotel Duse. Its location is superb—right in the very heart of Asolo, surrounded by quaint streets lined with elegant shops. There is a tiny reception lobby leading up to freshly renovated guestrooms. Although small, each room is attractively decorated with a cozy provincial charm. The decor is similar throughout, with nicely framed prints over the beds, which have a pretty ribbon tied in a bow accenting the frame. The fabric matches the shades on the reading lamps. The cozy mood prevails in each room—only the color scheme varies. Although each room is very reasonably priced, they all offer air conditioning, television, direct-dial phone, mini bar, and a spotlessly clean bathroom. The hotel has changed hands since our last visit.

*HOTEL DUSE*
*Manager: Alessandro Avattiero*
*Via Browning, 190*
*31011 Asolo (TV), Italy*
*Tel: (0423) 55 241, Fax: (0423) 95 04 04*
*14 rooms, Double: Lire 180,000–850,000*
*Open all year, Credit cards: AX, VS*
*No restaurant, breakfast only*
*65 km NW of Venice, 14 km E of Bassano*
*Region: Veneto, Michelin Map 429*

The Villa Cipriani is just as I had envisioned in every dream of Italy: an old villa snuggled on a hill, her softly faded exterior emphasized by dark-green shutters, masses of roses creeping over trellises, columns adorned with vines, lazy views over rolling green hills, faded ocher-colored walls half-hidden by tall cypress trees dotting nearby hilltops, birds singing in the garden, the sentimental rhythmical peal of church bells, a pianist on the terrace playing old love songs, the fragrance of flowers drifting through the air like the finest perfume—perfection. My impression of a romantic paradise must not have been a unique experience for in the garden was a wedding party. A beautiful bride, a handsome groom, they had fallen in love at the Cipriani and had returned with family and friends from the United States for their marriage. The Villa Cipriani is located in Asolo, a charming, small, medieval walled hilltown less than two hours northwest of Venice which has an atmosphere so delightful that Robert Browning chose it as a residence. And the home he chose? The Cipriani. Luckily, his home is now a hotel and you, too, can live for a while in Asolo. Although the Villa Cipriani is a sophisticated, polished hotel, the warmth of reception is as gracious as in a small, family-run inn: all the guests are properly pampered.

*VILLA CIPRIANI*
*Manager: Giampaolo Burattin*
*Via Canova, 298*
*31011 Asolo (TV), Italy*
*Tel: (0423) 52 34 11, Fax: (0423) 95 20 95*
*E-mail: giampaolo_burattin@sheraton.com*
*31 rooms, Double: Lire 484,000–800,000\**
*\*Breakfast: Lire 58,500 per person*
*Open all year, Credit cards: all major*
*Restaurant open daily*
*65 km NW of Venice, 14 km E of Bassano*
*Region: Veneto, Michelin Map 429*
*www.karenbrown.com/italyinns/villacipriani.html*

The Hotel Subasio is located in Assisi with one wall forming part of the ancient square in front of the Basilica of St. Francis. The hotel is linked to the basilica by an arched colonnade. The setting is marvelous, with the rear of the hotel facing the beautiful Umbrian countryside. On the lower level there are several glorious terraces romantically shaded by vines. Many of the rooms also have splendid vistas over the valley. Request one of the deluxe rooms with a balcony—these are delightful. The Subasio's public rooms are pleasant, but rather stilted and formal; however, you will not be inside much anyway. The terraces are magic: to sit and watch the lovely fields mellow in the evening sun with that very special glow that is so characteristic of Umbria is certainly one of life's real pleasures. It is no wonder that many celebrities have chosen the Hotel Subasio for their residence when visiting Assisi: such famous names as Charlie Chaplin and James Stewart grace the guest book. Andrea Rossi personally oversees the management of the hotel and there is a friendliness in the air, from the gentle maid who turns down your bed at night to the charming waiter who helps select your local wine with dinner.

*HOTEL SUBASIO*
*Owner: Sergio Elisei*
*Manager: Andrea Rossi*
*Via Frate Elia, 2*
*06081 Assisi (PG), Italy*
*Tel: (075) 81 22 06, Fax: (075) 81 66 91*
*56 rooms, Double: Lire 310,000–400,000*
*10 suites: Lire 400,000*
*Open all year, Credit cards: all major*
*Restaurant open daily*
*177 km N of Rome, 26 km E of Perugia*
*Region: Umbria, Michelin Map 430*
*www.karenbrown.com/italyinns/subasio.html*

For a moderately priced place to stay in the heart of Assisi, the Hotel Umbra is an unbeatable choice. The hotel is located just a few steps down a narrow little alley that leads off the Piazza del Commune, one of the central plazas in town. The entrance is through wrought-iron gates that open to a tiny patio where you are treated to an idyllic oasis with tables set under a trellis covered by vines painting a lacy pattern of shadows. There is a lovely view from this intimate terrace. After passing through the patio, you enter into a lounge/reception area with doors opening into the dining room where very good meals are served. The public rooms have accents of antiques, but have a homey rather than grand ambiance. Steps lead to the simple bedrooms, which are individually decorated. Most have been recently refurbished and are very pleasant. Splurge and ask for a room (such as 34) with a panoramic vista of the Umbrian valley. However, do not be disappointed if one is not available—the rooms (such as 35) overlooking the jumble of tiled roofs are also very nice. If you like small, family-run hotels that are not decorator-perfect in every detail, but offer great heart and hospitality, the Hotel Umbra is an excellent choice. The delightful Alberto Laudenzi family oversees every detail of this small inn and makes guests feel at home. The staff too is extremely gracious and accommodating. Best of all, the location is absolutely perfect.

*HOTEL UMBRA*
*Owners: Alberto Laudenzi family*
*Via degli Archi, 6–Piazza de Comune*
*06081 Assisi (PG), Italy*
*Tel: (075) 81 22 40, Fax: (075) 81 36 53*
*E-mail: humbra@mail.caribusiness.it*
*26 rooms, Double: Lire 170,000–210,000*
*Closed mid-Jan to mid-Mar, Credit cards: all major*
*Restaurant closed Sundays, Central location off main square*
*177 km N of Rome, 26 km E of Perugia*
*Region: Umbria, Michelin Map 430*
*www.karenbrown.com/italyinns/hotelumbra.html*

Il Palazzo, a three-star hotel in the heart of Assisi, offers surprisingly attractive accommodations for a modest price. Built in the 1500s as a palace for the prosperous Bindangoli-Bartocci family, its foundations date back even further. Amazingly, the hotel is still owned by Bartocci descendants. Indications of the palace's rich heritage can still be seen in the many important oil paintings and 18th-century tempera mythical scenes. As you enter off the street there is a simple reception area. Beyond is a large, beamed-ceilinged living room with comfortable sitting areas. The hotel has no restaurant, but this is not a problem in Assisi. Breakfast is served in a cozy lower-level room with a low, vaulted ceiling and thick stone walls. To reach the bedrooms, you walk out into a central courtyard and then up an exterior steel staircase. I assure you the climb is worthwhile because once you throw open the shutters of your bedroom, you are treated to a stunning panorama of the Umbrian countryside. Definitely splurge—request one of the superior bedrooms, all very spacious and attractively furnished with appealing antiques. One of my favorites, 204, has twin beds with pretty, painted iron headboards. Room 203, a corner room, is also a real winner with a canopy bed—it would be my first choice except that the bathroom is not very large. As with all the hotels in Assisi, take just a small overnight suitcase. Closest parking: Piazza San Francesco.

*IL PALAZZO*
*Manager: Arianna Bartocci Fontana*
*Via San Francesco, 8*
*06081 Assisi (PG), Italy*
*Tel: (075) 81 68 41 2, Fax: (075) 81 23 70*
*E-mail: hotel.ilpalazzo@edisons.it*
*12 rooms, Double: Lire 140,000–200,000*
*Closed mid-Jan to mid-Mar, Credit cards: all major*
*No restaurant, breakfast only*
*Between Piazza del San Francesco & Piazza del Comune*
*177 km N of Rome, 26 km E of Perugia*
*Region: Umbria, Michelin Map 430*
*www.karenbrown.com/italyinns/ilpalazzo.html*

A reader highly recommended La Fortezza, saying that it was a wonderful bargain and that he enjoyed the best meal of his entire trip there. We too were immediately captivated by this simple, charming place to stay in the center of Assisi. The restaurant seems to be the star attraction, with Guglielmo Chiocchetti in the kitchen cooking while his wife, Tina, takes care of the many dinner guests. Their two wonderful sons, Luca and Lorenzo, are also totally involved in this family operation, helping out wherever needed, assisted by Luca's pretty wife who was serving the day we stopped by. Without a doubt, it is the gentle, caring Chiocchetti family with their exceptional warmth that makes La Fortezza so special. Their restaurant's superior food features many Umbrian dishes, served in a cozy dining room with vaulted stone ceiling and wooden chairs painted a cheerful red. The guestrooms, which are an outstanding value, are located on two floors above the restaurant. Although not large, each is spotlessly clean and very tastefully decorated in an appropriate, simple, country style. The choice bedroom even has its own little terrace. The hotel is hidden up a lane of stone steps at the northeast corner of the Piazza del Comune. Luca suggested we remind readers there are lots of steps getting to their hotel, but then this is true throughout Assisi, which seems pasted to the side of the hillside. Just remember, bring only a small suitcase. Closest parking: Piazza Matteotti.

*LA FORTEZZA*
*Owners: Chiocchetti family*
*Piazza del Comune*
*06081 Assisi (PG), Italy*
*Tel: (075) 81 24 18, Fax: (075) 81 98 035*
*E-mail: lafortezza@lafortezzahotel.com*
*7 rooms, Double: Lire 105,000–120,000*
*Open all year, Credit cards: all major*
*Restaurant closed Thursdays*
*Above NE corner of Piazza del Comune*
*177 km N of Rome, 26 km E of Perugia*
*Region: Umbria, Michelin Map 430*
*www.karenbrown.com/italyinns/lafortezza.html*

The Grand Hotel Villa Serbelloni is certainly appropriately named—it is definitely "grand." Indeed, the public rooms will take your breath away with their intricately frescoed ceilings, gold mirrors, ornate columns, Oriental carpets, gilded chairs, massive chandeliers, and a sweeping marble staircase. The bedrooms too are lovely and the quality throughout is superb: fine percale sheets, soft down pillows, and large towels. The service too excels with a friendly staff eager to please. The parklike grounds—enhanced by colorful beds of well-tended flowers—stretches to the very edge of the lake where a large swimming pool holds center stage. There are two more indoor pools (one for adults and one for children) opening to the garden. In addition, there are a fitness/beauty center, squash court, and two tennis courts. For sightseeing and shopping, the quaint port of Bellagio is adjacent to the hotel. If you want to explore some of the other charming lakeside villages, the ferry is just steps away—or the concierge can arrange a private boat to pick you up at the hotel's pier. For opulent surroundings and palatial splendor, the Grand Hotel Villa Serbelloni can't be beat. *Directions*: In the center of Bellagio.

*GRAND HOTEL VILLA SERBELLONI*
*Owners: Gianfranco Bucher family*
*Manager: Giuseppe Spinelli*
*22021 Bellagio-Lake Como (CO), Italy*
*Tel: (031) 95 02 16, Fax: (031) 95 15 29*
*E-mail: inforequest@villaserbelloni.it*
*83 rooms, Double: Lire 631,000–1,325,000*
*13 apartments with cooking facilities\**
*\*Rates on request, 1-week minimum*
*Open Apr to Oct 31, Credit cards: all major*
*Restaurant open daily*
*80 km N of Milan, 31 km NE of Como*
*Region: Lombardy, Michelin Map 428*
*www.karenbrown.com/italyinns/grandhotelvillaserbelloni.html*

The Hotel Florence offers moderately priced accommodations in the charming ancient port of Bellagio. The location is prime—facing the lake in the heart of the old part of town. Across the road from the hotel, next to the lake, is a romantic, wisteria-covered terrace where meals are served when the weather is balmy. If you are lucky enough to snare a front room with a balcony, you can step out through your French doors and be treated to a splendid view of Lake Como. The lounge, which is just off the reception area, is the oldest part of the building, dating back to the 18th century. Here you find a beamed ceiling and a large fireplace. There is also a bar where jazz sessions are held every Sunday during the summer. A staircase leads to the upper floor where the guest dining room is located—it has no view of the lake, but does have a fireplace to warm the room on chilly days. There is also a gourmet restaurant open to the public. All of the individually decorated guestrooms have antique furnishings, satellite TVs, safety boxes, and hairdryers. Splurge and ask for the corner room with French doors opening onto a large terrace with lounge chairs invitingly set for viewing the lake. The hotel is owned by the Ketzlar family, who are real pros—the inn has been in their family for over 150 years. It is now managed by Freidl Ketzlar, her son, Ronald, and her daughter, Roberta. The family tradition lives on. When I last visited, it was fun to see three of Freidl Ketzlar's grandsons working at the hotel.

*HOTEL FLORENCE*
*Owners: Ketzlar family*
*Piazza Mazzimi, 42*
*22021 Bellagio-Lake Como (CO), Italy*
*Tel: (031) 95 03 42, Fax: (031) 95 17 22*
*E-mail: hotflore@tin.it*
*32 rooms, Double: Lire 280,000–340,000*
*Open Apr to Oct, Credit cards: all major*
*Restaurant open daily, Lakefront location, 80 km N of Milan*
*31 km NE of Como, Region: Lombardy, Michelin Map 428*
*www.karenbrown.com/italyinns/hotelflorence.html*

I fell instantly in love with La Pergola, a charming hotel nestled in a quaint hamlet just a short walk over the hill from Bellagio. Although it officially rates only one star, in my estimation this romantic hotel deserves far more. Originally a 15th-century convent, it came into Marilena Mazzoni's family in 1732 and has been passed down from generation to generation ever since. The pretty, creamy-yellow building with dark-green shutters snuggles right by the lake and features an enchanting terrace-restaurant at the edge of the water where guests dine under an ivy-draped trellis. The charm of the hotel continues within where a fresh, uncluttered, old-world ambiance is displayed throughout. The dining room is most attractive, with fresh white walls accented by gleaming copper pots, simple wooden chairs and tables, and a vaulted ceiling. The spacious guestrooms differ in size but each is decorated with excellent taste, features some antique furnishings, and has a modern, tiled bathroom. I was instantly captivated by La Pergola, but Signora Mazzoni was reluctant to have her property featured in our guide for fear that it would attract the wrong kind of guests—those looking for more amenities than her simple hotel provides. I assured her our readers are different, valuing charm and comfort rather than luxurious amenities. Please convince her that I am telling the truth! *Directions*: Take the road from Como to Bellagio. Just before entering Bellagio, turn right toward Lecco, then left toward Pescallo. The hotel is in the tiny town plaza.

*LA PERGOLA*
*Owner: Marilena Mazzoni*
*Piazza del Porto, 4, Pescallo*
*22021 Bellagio–Lake Como (CO), Italy*
*Tel: (031) 95 02 63, Fax: (031) 95 02 53*
*11 rooms, Double: Lire 160,000–180,000*
*Open all year, Credit cards: none accepted*
*Restaurant closed Tuesdays*
*80 km N of Milan, 31 km NE of Como*
*Region: Lombardy, Michelin Map 428*

L'Orto degli Angeli is a rare jewel. Located in the historic center of Bevagna (a small, picture-perfect walled village of Roman origin), this intimate inn exudes the genuine warmth of a private home, yet offers the comfort and sophistication of a fine hotel. The handsome stone house has been in the family of your gracious host, Francesco Antonini, since 1788. He and his sweet wife, Tiziana, welcome guests with such a gentle kindness that you will be immediately captivated by their charm. On the first floor is a pretty breakfast room for guests and an outstanding restaurant (built upon the ruins of a Roman temple), which is as cozy as can be with deep-yellow walls, beamed ceiling, soft lighting, and cheerful blue chairs. An impressive staircase leads up to the guest lounge, which has a stunning frescoed ceiling and comfortable sofa and chairs grouped around an immense stone fireplace. All of the individually decorated guestrooms have pretty, tiled bathrooms, some antique furnishings, and color-coordinating fabrics on the bedspreads and curtains. Many of the rooms overlook a central garden, built upon an old Roman theater. Bevagna is rich in historical importance—don't miss the stunning little 19th-century opera house, the well-preserved mosaics in the Roman baths, and the many picturesque churches. *Directions:* From Perugia take 75 to Assisi-Foligno. Exit to the 316 to Bevagna and look for L'Orto degli Angeli signs.

*L'ORTO DEGLI ANGELI*
*Owners: Tiziana & Francesco Antonini*
*Via Dante Alighieri, 1*
*06031 Bevagna (PG), Italy*
*Tel: (0742) 36 01 30, Fax: (0742) 36 17 56*
*E-mail: orto.angeli@ortoangeli.it*
*9 rooms, Double: Lire 250,000–400,000*
*Closed Jan, Credit cards: all major*
*Restaurant closed Tuesdays*
*25 km S of Assisi*
*Region: Umbria, Michelin Map 430*
*www.karenbrown.com/italyinns/lortodegliangeli.html*

Although surrounded by a sprawling, uninteresting concrete metropolis, the center of Bologna shelters a fascinating maze of ancient twisting streets, arcaded passageways, marvelous shopping under porticoed walkways, and some of the best food in all of Italy. The Corona d'Oro, ideally located in the heart of the medieval quarter, is a small, well-managed hotel whose elegantly designed construction conserves architectural elements of various periods. In the inner courtyard (covered over with a skylight that rolls back to allow the room to return to its original open-air status) you can admire a portico that dates back to the 14th century. The hall and stairwell, exquisitely done in the Liberty style of the early 1900s, lead up to the bedrooms, which are individually decorated, mostly with modern furnishings, but with a touch of the traditional in the sedate color schemes and prints nicely displayed on the walls. Some of the rooms have recessed block-panel ceilings with paintings of coats of arms and landscapes dating back to the 15th and 16th centuries. The hotel does not charge a premium for the few rooms that have small balconies or terraces. *Directions*: Located on a small side street just a few blocks from the large, central plaza. The hotel is very difficult to drive to because of one-way streets. The best bet is to arrive by train and take a cab. If driving, ask the hotel for detailed directions. Good luck.

*HOTEL CORONA D'ORO 1890*
*Manager: Mauro Orsi*
*Via Oberdan, 12*
*40126 Bologna, Italy*
*Tel: (051) 23 64 56, Fax: (051) 26 26 79*
*E-mail: hotcoro@tin.it*
*35 rooms, Double: Lire 380,000–525,000*
*Closed Aug, Credit cards: all major*
*No restaurant, breakfast only*
*In the heart of Bologna*
*Region: Emilia-Romagna, Michelin Map 429/430*
*www.karenbrown.com/italyinns/coronadoro.html*

The Villa Clementina is a gem of a small hotel, romantically secreted behind high walls. It is not until the green gates swing slowly open that the stunning gardens and charming inn come magically into view. This gorgeous property was once the home of a famous artist, Lorenzo Vespignani, and your enchanting young host, Dimitri Bonnetti, is also a well-known painter and studied under Vespignani. Today Dimitri uses the same light-filled studio that was once his mentor's. However, one of his greatest masterpieces isn't on canvas—it is the Villa Clementina. The property is truly a work of art: each room has hand-painted frescoed walls, lamps and beds made by Dimitri, furniture placed in perfect positions, handsome fabrics, and quality in every detail. My favorite guestroom, Romana, is a particularly spacious room with a fireplace and replicas of ancient Roman frescoes enhancing the walls. The inn is built within several houses nestled on terraces that step down a gentle hill. The grounds are like a beautiful park, with many exotic trees and perfectly manicured gardens filled with the fragrance of jasmine and the sweet song of birds. On one of the terraces there is a charming restaurant, on another a large swimming pool, and on the lowest level, a clay tennis court. The Villa Clementina's location is superb: it is within an easy drive of the Rome airport, making it a perfect choice for your first few days in Italy. Then, when you feel up to the bustle of Rome, a train from Bracciano will whiz you into the heart of the city in just about half an hour.

*HOTEL VILLA CLEMENTINA     **New***
*Owner: Dimitri Bonetti*
*Via Traversa Quarto del Lago, 12*
*00062 Bracciano (RM), Italy*
*Tel & fax: (06) 99 86 268*
*E-mail: villaclementina@tiscalinet.it*
*7 rooms, Double: Lire 250,000–400,000*
*Open: Apr to Nov (rest of the year by request)*
*Credit cards: all major, Restaurant by request*
*30 km NW of Rome, Region: Lazio, Michelin Map 430*
*www.karenbrown.com/italyinns/villaclementina.html*

In 1550, King John of Portugal decided to give a "little" gift to the Emperor Ferdinand of Austria, so he purchased an elephant in India, shipped it to Genoa, then planned to walk it to Austria. This giant beast grew weary about the time it reached Bressanone and was stabled for two weeks at the Am Hohen Feld Inn. Young and old came from far and wide to see this impromptu circus. The proprietor of the Am Hohen Feld was obviously a master at marketing: to maintain the fame of his establishment, he promptly renamed his hotel—you guessed it—the Elephant. A picture of our friend the elephant was painted on the front of the building to commemorate the sensational event. But even without an elephant story this hotel is a winner with its old-fashioned charm. The sitting room, hallways, and dining rooms (three cozy rooms) incorporate antiques, museum-quality paintings, and magnificent paneling. The Elephant is also well-known for its good food—fresh vegetables and fruits come from the adjacent walled garden where you also find the swimming pool and an old home that has been converted into very nice bedrooms. I particularly liked our room 12 for its spaciousness, room 11 for its corner location, and room 29 for its comfortable decor and balcony. *Directions:* Leave the autostrada at Bressanone and follow the main road through town. The hotel is well signposted in the quiet pedestrian zone.

*HOTEL ELEPHANT*
*Director: Heinrich Radmüller*
*Manager: Elisabeth Heiss*
*Via Rio Bianco, 4*
*39042 Bressanone (Brixen) (BZ), Italy*
*Tel: (0472) 83 27 50, Fax: (0472) 83 65 79*
*E-mail: elephant.brixen@acs.it*
*44 rooms, Double: Lire 372,000–492,000*
*Open Mar to Nov & Christmas, Credit cards: all major*
*Restaurant closed Mondays*
*40 km NE of Bolzano, near Brenner Pass*
*Region: Trentino-Alto Adige, Michelin Map 429*
*www.karenbrown.com/italyinns/elephant.html*

If you are captivated by nature at its finest, then you must detour to the tiny Relais Torre Pratesi. Stop for a few days to refresh your soul, become acquainted with the gentle kindness of Letty and Nerio Raccagni, dine memorably on food from the farm, and sleep in lovely, peaceful surroundings. The Relais Torre Pratesi, a picturesque, salmon-colored farmhouse with a typical tiled roof, brown shutters, and a sturdy, 16th-century stone watchtower, sits serenely in the center of a meadow high on a hilltop. The sweeping views in every direction are breathtaking—gently rolling hills with terraced fields of grapes, pine forests, groves of olive trees, and square patches of manicured fields stretch to the distant mountains. Amazingly, considering that you are far off the beaten track, the accommodations are fantastic. The lovingly decorated bedrooms are very large (most are suites) and offer every comfort. The most romantic room is tucked at the top of the tower where small windows on all four walls frame views in every direction like miniature oil paintings. Meals, featuring produce fresh from the farm, are served in a charmingly rustic dining room. The owners, Letty and Nerio Raccagni, speak no English, but their radiantly warm welcome overcomes all language barriers. *Directions:* From A14 take the Faenza exit, following Firenze and Brisighella signs around Faenza. Go through Brisighella to Fognano. At the end of the village, turn right toward Zattaglia, then follow signs to Relais Torre Pratesi.

*RELAIS TORRE PRATESI*
*Owners: Letty & Nerio Raccagni*
*Via Cavina, 11*
*48013 Brisighella (RA), Italy*
*Tel: (0546) 845 45, Fax: (0546) 845 58*
*E-mail: torrep@tin.it*
*7 rooms, Double: Lire 250,000–300,000*
*Open all year, Credit cards: all major*
*Restaurant open daily*
*75 km SE of Bologna*
*Region: Emilia-Romagna, Michelin Map 430*
*www.karenbrown.com/italyinns/torrepratesi.html*

The Cenobio dei Dogi was formerly the summer home of the Genoese doges, so it is no wonder that it has such an idyllic location nestled on a small hill that forms one end of Camogli's miniature half-moon bay. From the hotel terrace there is an enchanting view of the tiny cove lined with marvelous narrow old fishermen's cottages painted in all shades of ochres and siennas. The hotel has a very nice swimming pool, as well as a private (though pebbly) beach. Many of the bedrooms have balconies boasting romantic views of this storybook scene. There is a tennis court for tennis buffs, although I cannot imagine anyone wanting to play tennis with all the beautiful walking trails, which make enticing spider-web designs on the peninsula. The Cenobio dei Dogi is a larger, less-personalized hotel than most that appear in this guide, but although its decor seems a bit dated, the hotel possesses a solid, comfortable, no-nonsense kind of charm. It is not chic in the jet-set style of hotels frequently found on the Riviera. However, if you relate to lovely flower gardens, exceptional views, and slightly faded old-world comfort, you will like this hotel. To reach the hotel, exit the A12 at Recco and follow signs to Camogli. The hotel is located at the east end of town. *NOTE:* Since our last visit the hotel has been renovated.

*HOTEL CENOBIO DEI DOGI*
*Manager: Mauro Siri*
*Via Nicolo Cuneo, 34*
*16032 Camogli (GE), Italy*
*Tel: (0185) 72 41, Fax: (0185) 77 27 96*
*107 rooms, Double: Lire 260,000–510,000*
*Suite: Lire 610,000–700,000*
*Open all year, Credit cards: all major*
*Restaurant open daily*
*Near Portofino–Italian Riviera*
*20 km SE of Genoa, Region: Liguria, Michelin Map 428*
*www.karenbrown.com/italyinns/cenobiodeidogi.html*

Just when we thought we had seen almost every castle in Italy, another pops up offering hospitality in a private, historic home, enabling the fortunate traveler to personally experience an entirely new dimension of Italian culture and history. The Castello di Magona in Maremma, a lesser-known part of Tuscany opposite Elba, is truly a dream—sumptuous accommodation within the walls of a gray-stone castle dating to the days of Leopoldo II, Grand Duke of Tuscany. Situated atop a hill below the charming village of Campiglia Marittima, the restored home with its turreted tower peeking above the surrounding trees offers five luxurious suites, three double rooms, and the Grand Duke's spacious bedroom. The luminous bedrooms are decorated with exquisite antiques, and every modern amenity such as air conditioning and satellite television linked to the Web is cleverly incorporated. Rooms look out onto a lovely garden with access to a shaded swimming pool whose surrounding trees hide the view of a rather drab modern town below. Guests can gaze at 16th-century paintings while relaxing in one of several formal, painted sitting rooms before an enormous fireplace and enjoy a buffet breakfast in the stately dining room. Although containing museum-quality furnishings, the impeccable castle with its earth-tone colors exudes warmth and comfort. *Directions*: Coming from Rome, leave the Aurelia route 1 at Venturina/Campiglia and follow signs through Venturina to Campiglia. The castle is marked at 2 km from Venturina, before Campiglia.

*CASTELLO DI MAGONA*     **New**
*Owner: Cesare Merciai*
*Via Venturina, 27*
*57021 Campiglia Marittima (LI), Italy*
*Tel: (0565) 85 12 35, Fax: (0565) 85 51 27*
*9 rooms, Double: Lire 400,000–630,000*
*Restaurant for hotel guests only*
*Open Mar to Nov, Credit cards: all major*
*252 km NW of Rome, 68 km S of Livorno*
*Region: Tuscany, Michelin Map 430*

Relais Il Canalicchio is snuggled within a medieval village on a hilltop overlooking a breathtaking vista of vineyards, olive groves, tiny villages, and forested hills that melt into the horizon. Because the hotel occupies almost the entire romantic village, it has secret little terraces and enchanting nooks to explore. You feel you have stepped back in time as you walk the cobbled lanes with the solitude broken only by the singing of the birds. The castle dates back to the 13th century and in its excellent restoration, great care was taken to preserve its original architectural features such as terra-cotta floor tiles, beamed ceilings, thick stone walls, massive fireplaces, and arched brick doorways. The ancient Roman fortified walls of the village are incorporated into one side of the hotel and allow for a romantic lush garden that stretches to the edge of the wall and, on a lower terrace, a splendid swimming pool and a panoramic restaurant. Giant terra-cotta pots filled with brilliant red geraniums add color to the immaculately tended grounds. Inside, everything is decorator-perfect with a homelike, comfortable ambiance created by the use of fine antiques and lovely fabrics. The spacious bedrooms have the feel of an English country manor, with pretty floral fabrics, coordinating wallpapers, and accents of antiques. All have air conditioning, mini bar, satellite TV, and, best yet—fabulous views. *Directions*: From Perugia go south on E45 in the direction of "Roma/Terni," exit at Ripabianca-Foligno, and follow signs to the hotel.

*RELAIS IL CANALICCHIO*
*Manager: Orfeo Vassallo*
*Via della Piazza, 4*
*06050 Canalicchio di Collazzone (PG), Italy*
*Tel: (075) 87 07 325, Fax: (075) 87 07 296*
*34 rooms, Double: Lire 250,000–400,000*
*Open all year, Credit cards: all major*
*Restaurant open daily*
*39 km SW of Assisi, 20 km N of Todi*
*Region: Umbria, Michelin Map 430*
*www.karenbrown.com/italyinns/relaiscanalicchio.html*

Maria Carla Gallinotto presides over her family hotel in this little lakeside resort just south of the Swiss border. With her four children (Felice, Samuele, Annalisa, and Alfredo) working alongside her, you can be certain that you will meet caring family members during your stay. The family is always improving the hotel–one of the wonderful things about returning here on a regular basis is that you can personally check out the most recent changes. Ferries that visit all the delightful resorts and islands of Lake Maggiore leave from the dock in front of the hotel. However, do not confine your explorations to the lake, for the valleys and mountains to the west offer spectacular scenery. On the other hand, the hotel is so delightful that you may wish to limit your excursions to the pool and strolls along the lakeside pedestrian promenade. Lake-facing bedrooms are found on four floors—all are charming. Additional guestrooms look out to the swimming pool, as do ten self-catering apartments that can accommodate from two to four persons. Dinner is served in the lovely lakefront restaurant. *Directions:* Cannero Riviera is located 20 km south of Locarno (Switzerland), 12 km north of Verbania (Italy) on Lake Maggiore, and 75 km from Malpensa International Airport. Arriving at the lake, drive north along the pedestrian promenade to the hotel. If space is not available next to the hotel, you will be directed to the hotel's parking lot in the village.

*CANNERO LAKESIDE HOTEL*
*Owners: Gallinotto family*
*28821 Cannero Riviera*
*Lake Maggiore, Verbania (VB), Italy*
*Tel: (0323) 78 80 46, Fax: (0323) 78 80 48*
*E-mail: info@hotelcannero.com*
*55 rooms, Double: Lire 240,000–280,000\**
*1-bedroom apartment (2–4 persons): Lire 190,000\*\**
*\*Rate includes breakfast & dinner, \*\*Breakfast only*
*Open Mar 10 to Nov 3, Credit cards: all major*
*Restaurant open daily, 12 km N of Verbania, 20 km S of Locarno*
*Region: Piedmont, Michelin Map 428*
*www.karenbrown.com/italyinns/cannerolakeside.html*

The Morganos are superb hoteliers, maintaining a family tradition that traces back for three generations in Capri, and when I first visited the Casa Morgano, Nicolino Morgano's pretty, young daughter was helping behind the desk, a welcome hint that the hotel business will continue into yet another generation. The brothers currently own the Grand Hotel Quisisana, La Scalinatella, and the Casa Morgano, all fine hotels that feature proudly in our guide. From the Via Tragara, one of Capri's prettiest walkways, a flagstone path, fragrant with honeysuckle, leads you to the entrance of the Casa Morgano. The essence of Capri is captured in the spacious, airy reception hall with its whitewashed walls, bright-yellow sofas, gorgeous blue-and-white-tiled floor, Oriental carpets, and walls of windows. Doors lead out to a terrace where an incredible view is enhance by towering pines. The guestrooms are nestled on various levels of the hotel as it terraces down the hillside. Each is beautifully furnished in color-coordinating drapes and bedspreads. Best of all, each guestroom looks out to the sea and has a balcony or terrace so that you can enjoy the vista to its fullest. There is also a large swimming pool where guests can relax and enjoy the sun. Although there is no formal restaurant as such, next to the pool is a bar where refreshing drinks and light lunches are served. Although deluxe, this hotel exudes the character of a small, intimate, family-run establishment.

*CASA MORGANO     **New***
*Owner: Nicolino Morgano*
*Via Tragara, 6*
*80073 Capri (NA), Italy*
*Tel: (081) 83 70 158, Fax: (081) 83 70 681*
*28 rooms, Double: Lire 480,000–700,000\**
*\*Rate includes breakfast*
*Open mid-Mar to Nov, Credit cards: none accepted*
*Poolside bar for light lunch*
*Island of Capri, ferry from Sorrento or Naples*
*Region: Campania, Michelin Map 431*

The Grand Quisisana, a stately, elegant hotel, has a superb setting, right in the heart of Capri. You can't miss this handsome building, which is painted a creamy yellow with white trim and has jaunty flags decorating the entrance. It conjures the image of a hideaway for the rich and famous. The women, adorned in jewels and the latest swimming ensembles, lounge in the sun and gossip about current scandals while their husbands (or boyfriends?) sit pool-side drinking Scotch and playing the game of grown boys—discussing their latest business ventures. But it is all great fun and quite in the mood of Capri which has been a playground for the wealthy since the time of the early Romans. The Grand Quisisana is an imposing hotel with a gorgeous oval pool overlooking the blue Mediterranean. The air of formal elegance appears as soon as you enter the lobby decorated with marble floors, sumptuous furnishings, Oriental carpets, ornate statues, crystal chandeliers, and beautiful paintings. All the bedrooms are well appointed and the deluxe rooms even have separate his-and-hers half-baths. Room rates include breakfast and lunch or dinner and you can choose from almost anything on the menu. The opulent, Grand Hotel Quisisana most definitely provides a setting and atmosphere to reflect the image of, and cater to, their jet-set clientele.

*GRAND HOTEL QUISISANA*
*Owners: Morgano family*
*Manager: Gianfranco Morgano*
*Via Camerelle, 2*
*80073 Capri (NA), Italy*
*Tel: (081) 83 70 788, Fax: (081) 83 76 080*
*150 rooms, Double: Lire 440,000–700,000*
*Suite: Lire 700,000–1,250,000*
*Open mid-Mar to Nov, Credit cards: all major*
*Restaurant open daily*
*Island of Capri, ferry from Sorrento or Naples*
*Region: Campania, Michelin Map 431*
*www.karenbrown.com/italyinns/quisisana.html*

The Hotel Luna savors one of the most beautiful, tranquil locations on the island of Capri. It is just a short walk from the village yet, in atmosphere, it seems a world away from the bustle and noise. The overall mood at the hotel is set by its delightful approach, a covered trellis pathway which in summer is completely shaded by brilliant bougainvillea and grape vines and bordered by flowers: a wonderful introduction to the Hotel Luna and to a restful interlude by the sea. To the left of the path as you approach the hotel, you see the Luna's large swimming pool surrounded by flowers and a view to the sea. The hotel is perched on the cliffs overlooking a spectacular coastline of green hills dropping straight into the sea, from which emerge giant rock formations. On two sides of the hotel there is a terrace with comfortable chairs where guests may enjoy this spectacular view. Just below the terrace is an open-air bar set on a balcony that hangs out over the cliffs with an unsurpassed panorama of the sea. The reception area and the lounges are attractively decorated using a pleasing, fresh color scheme of white, blue, and yellow. The bar is especially appealing with slip-covered chairs that pick up the rich colors in the tiled floors. There are a few antiques around to add charm. The guestrooms are also attractive. If you want to splurge, ask for one of the guestrooms facing the sea—although these cost more, the vista is memorable.

*HOTEL LUNA*
*Manager: Luisa Vuotto*
*Viale Giacomo Matteotti, 3*
*80073 Capri (NA), Italy*
*Tel: (081) 83 70 433, Fax: (081) 83 77 459*
*50 rooms, Double: Lire 380,000–600,000*
*Open Apr to Oct, Credit cards: all major*
*Restaurant open daily*
*Island of Capri, ferry from Sorrento or Naples*
*Region: Campania, Michelin Map 431*
*www.karenbrown.com/italyinns/capriluna.html*

Hugging a hillside with a ship's prow position overlooking the sea, the Hotel Punta Tragara is definitely one of Capri's landmarks. Whereas most of the island's villas and hotels have white façades that sparkle in the sunlight, the Hotel Punta Tragara is painted a deep sandy beige, accented by wrought-iron grills, dark-green shutters, and, of course, the profusion of flowers and greenery that make Capri so special. The hotel is reached by a pleasant 15-minute walk from the center of town—a path that dead-ends at the point where the hillside drops steeply down to the sea. Here the picturesque Faraglioni Islands thrust their jagged peaks just below the hotel, affording fabulous views. Perhaps this spectacular setting is what made Eisenhower and Churchill choose the Punta Tragara for accommodation when they visited Capri. There is a certain formality to this small hotel—the staff seems professionally accommodating, but there is not the warmth often found in a small, family-run establishment. Sea chests, paintings of old sailing vessels, aged-bronze divers' helmets, ships' bells, and antique maps create a pleasing, nautical theme. It is not the decor, but rather the setting that makes Hotel Punta Tragara special. Request a deluxe room with a view. However, even if your room is not one of the deluxe category, you can settle by one of the two swimming pools and soak up the sun.

*HOTEL PUNTA TRAGARA*
*Manager: Ceglia Goffredo*
*Via Tragara, 57*
*80073 Capri (NA), Italy*
*Tel: (081) 83 70 844, Fax: (081) 83 77 790*
*50 rooms, Double: Lire 650,000–800,000*
*Open Easter to Oct, Credit cards: all major*
*Restaurant open daily*
*Island of Capri, ferry from Sorrento or Naples*
*Region: Campania, Michelin Map 431*

La Scalinatella, although with far fewer rooms than its beautiful "big sister," the Grand Hotel Quisisana, radiates the same opulent luxury. A courtyard in front, dotted with small tables and chairs, leads to an imposing glass doorway majestically flanked by two stone lions. There is a slightly Moorish feel to the sparkling white building embellished by a crenellated roof that lends a whimsical, castle-like character. Inside, colorful tiled floors, handsomely framed portraits, and ornate furnishings create the mood of a formal, grand, private home. Snuggled next to the hotel is one of its most outstanding features: an absolutely stunning terrace where, shaded by trees and enhanced by gardens, you find a splendid swimming pool. This terrace is obviously the heart of the hotel where guests relax on comfortable lounge chairs strategically placed to enjoy the sun and capture the breathtaking view. You have no need to leave this oasis, for next to the pool is a bar serving drinks and delicious light lunches. La Scalinatella terraces down the hillside, and the guestrooms are staggered on various levels that offer beautiful vistas. All of the attractive bedrooms are tastefully furnished and offer every deluxe amenity. If you are looking for a luxurious, ornate ambiance and yet prefer the intimacy of a small hotel, La Scalinatella might be just your cup of tea. It is owned by Enrico Morgano, one of the three Morgano brothers whose small deluxe hotels are all stars in Capri.

*LA SCALINATELLA*     **New**
*Owner: Enrico Morgano*
*Via Tragara, 10*
*80073 Capri (NA), Italy*
*Tel: (081) 83 70 633, Fax: (081) 83 78 291*
*30 rooms, Double: Lire 600,000–880,000*
*Open mid-Mar to Nov, Credit cards: none accepted*
*Poolside bar for light lunch*
*Island of Capri, ferry from Sorrento or Naples*
*Region: Campania, Michelin Map 431*

The Villa Brunella is a tiny jewel located on the picturesque via Tragara, only a ten-minute walk to the center of town. This romantic hotel, overlooking the Marina Piccola, squeezes the greatest advantage from its narrow, deep lot. It is built on terraces starting at the street level where its superb restaurant with a view balcony is located, and stepping down the steep hillside to the blue swimming pool. The hotel is run more like a private home than a commercial hotel. The charming owner, Vincenzo Ruggiero (whose father was a fisherman) was born on Capri. He built the villa and named it after his lovely wife Brunella. This is truly a family operation: Vincenzo and Brunella are now ably assisted by their three handsome sons (Massimo Salvatore, Luigi) and charming daughter (Antonella). The whole family seems to take genuine pleasure in entertaining guests and making them feel welcome. The 20 bedrooms, each with private bath, telephone, mini bar, and air conditioning, are tastefully put together with pretty pink or powder-blue floral bedspreads and matching curtains. The cool ceramic-tiled floors, creamy-white walls, and potted plants add to the charm. Splurge and ask for one of the deluxe-category rooms—these offer dramatic views of the sea and islands from their own private terraces. Simply heavenly. *NOTE*: The setting is spectacular but because the rooms are on a steep hillside, be aware there are many steps.

*VILLA BRUNELLA*
*Owners: Brunella & Vincenzo Ruggiero*
*Via Tragara, 24*
*80073 Capri (NA), Italy*
*Tel: (081) 83 70 122, Fax: (081) 83 70 430*
*E-mail: villabrunella@capri.it*
*20 rooms, Double: Lire 380,000–550,000*
*Open Mar 19 to Nov 6, Credit cards: all major*
*Restaurant open daily*
*Island of Capri, ferry from Sorrento or Naples*
*Region: Campania, Michelin Map 431*
*www.karenbrown.com/italyinns/villabrunella.html*

If you are approaching Florence from the west, perhaps on your way from Milan, we highly recommend stopping just before you reach Florence at the Paggeria Medicea. The hotel's address is Artimino, but the town is so small that I doubt you will find it on any map. Mark Carmignano on your map instead and when you arrive there, you will find signs to Artimino, only a few minutes' drive farther on. The hotel is cleverly incorporated into what were once the pages' quarters for the adjoining 16th-century Medicea Villa La Ferdinanda. The long, narrow structure has been cleverly restored, preserving the many original chimneys that adorn the heavy, red-tiled roof. An open corridor whose heavily beamed ceiling is supported by a stately row of columns forms a walkway in front of the rooms. All of the guestrooms are simple, but very inviting, with tiled floors, pretty prints on the white walls, hand-loomed-looking white drapes hanging from wooden rods above the windows, and attractive antiques or copies of antiques as accents in each room. There is a snack bar in the same wing as the hotel, but the main restaurant, Biagio Pignatta (which serves simple but delicious Italian cooking), is located in a nearby building which at one time housed the butler for the villa. If you are a guest at the hotel, you can enjoy the villa's swimming pool, two tennis courts, and a running track. In addition there is an interesting small Etruscan museum situated in the vaults of the Medicea Villa La Ferdinanda.

*PAGGERIA MEDICEA*
*Manager: Alessandro Gualtieri*
*Viale Papa Giovanni XXIII*
*50040 Carmignano-Artimino (FI), Italy*
*Tel: (055) 87 18 081, Fax: (055) 87 18 080*
*37 rooms, Double: Lire 260,000–350,000*
*Open all year, Credit cards: AX, VS*
*Restaurant closed Wednesdays & Thursdays for lunch*
*20 km SW of Florence, 15 km S of Prato*
*Region: Tuscany, Michelin Map 430*
*www.karenbrown.com/italyinns/paggeriamedicea.html*

The Solarola, a sunny yellow villa, as its name implies, in the flat countryside around Bologna is, in a word, "perfect." Gracious hosts Antonella and Valentino (a renowned architect) took over the vast family property, transforming one of its two turn-of-the-century villas into a private home and the other into a guesthouse with five double rooms, a restaurant, living room, billiard room, outdoor gazebo, and beautiful swimming pool. Ten more rooms with air conditioning and all amenities were opened after that in the former barn directly in front with downstairs living room and library. Antonella decorated the guest villas to be romantic and refined, yet warm and inviting. Each room is named after a flower and everything—wallpaper, botanical prints, fluffy comforters, motifs on lampshades and bed frames, bouquets, and even room fragrance—conforms to the floral theme. Victoriana abounds in details such as antiques filled with china, lace curtains and doilies, dried-flower bouquets, old family photos, and Tiffany lamps. The real treat at Solarola is the inventive cuisine created by chef Bruno Barbieri who has earned two Michelin stars. *Directions*: Exit from autostrada A14 at Castel S. Pietro and turn right towards Medicina for 5 km. Turn right at Via S. Paolo, follow the road to the end then turn right on Via S. Croce to Solarola.

*LOCANDA SOLAROLA*
*Owners: Antonella Scardovi & Valentino Parmiani*
*Via San Croce, 5*
*Castel Guelfo (BO) 40023, Italy*
*Tel: (0542) 67 01 02 or 67 00 89, Fax: (0542) 67 02 22*
*13 rooms, 1 suite, Double: Lire 360,000–420,000*
*E-mail: solarola@imola.queen.it*
*Open all year, Credit cards: all major*
*Restaurant closed Mondays & Tuesdays for lunch*
*28 km E of Bologna*
*Region: Emilia-Romagna, Michelin Map 429/430*
*www.karenbrown.com/italyinns/locandasolarola.html*

If your dream is to discover a small luxury hotel in Tuscany that is truly "off the beaten path," look no further—the romantic Locanda Le Piazze is about as remote as you will find. Tucked in the heart of Tuscany's richest wine-growing region, the hotel crowns a gentle hill. In every direction there is nothing but a breathtaking patchwork of vineyards sweeping like the open sea across undulating hills, dotted with enchanting old farmhouses. After three years in which the buildings were totally renovated and a beautiful pool added, the hotel opened to guests in the summer of 1995. It is no wonder the design and decor are in absolutely faultless taste: the owner, Maureen Bonini, has for over 40 years been a design consultant in Florence. All of the hotel's rooms exude sophisticated country elegance. Huge bouquets of fresh flowers highlight white walls, terra-cotta floors, and beamed ceilings. Each of the guestrooms has its own personality, but all exude a similar comfortable, home like ambiance. The fabrics used throughout are all from Maureen's good friend, Ralph Lauren. The stunning swimming pool, tucked in amongst the vineyards, is reached by a path that threads through fragrant beds of lavender. *Directions*: From Castellina take the road toward Poggibonsi. Just as you leave Castellina, turn left at the first road, marked to Gagliole, Castellare, and Castagnoli and follow signs to the hotel—about a 15-minute drive over a narrow graveled road (ask them to fax directions).

*LOCANDA LE PIAZZE*
*Owner: Maureen Bonini*
*Localita: Le Piazze*
*53011 Castellina in Chianti (SI), Italy*
*Tel: (0577) 74 31 90, Fax: (0577) 74 31 91*
*E-mail: lepiazze@chiantinet.it*
*20 rooms, Double: Lire 320,000–420,000*
*Open Apr to Nov, Credit cards: all major*
*Restaurant closed Wednesdays for dinner*
*Midway between Castellina & Poggibonsi*
*Region: Tuscany, Michelin Map 430*
*www.karenbrown.com/italyinns/locandalepiazze.html*

The Tenuta di Ricavo is unique—not a hotel at all in the usual connotation, but rather a tiny, very old, Tuscan hamlet with peasants' cottages that have been transformed into delightful guestrooms. The stables are now the dining room and the barn is now the office. Unlike many of the over-renovated hotels in Tuscany where most of what you see is actually new construction, Ricavo is *all* real. The guestrooms have been lovingly restored to enhance their original rustic charm and are attractively furnished with country antiques. You enter the large property following a lane through a vast pine forest that leads to the cluster of weathered stone cottages, romantically embellished by climbing roses. Flowers are everywhere and in one of the gardens are two swimming pools, one on an upper terrace, and the other on a lower terrace. Before it became a hotel, the village was the summer-holiday retreat of a Swiss family who, after World War II, transformed their home into a unique, village-style hotel. However, the Tenuta di Ricavo is not for everyone. It is quiet. It is remote. But it is a haven for the traveler for whom a good book, a walk through the forest, a swim in the pool, a drink at sunset, and a delicious dinner are fulfillment. Excellent English is spoken—especially by the gracious manager, Christina Lobrano, whose charming husband, Alessandro, is the talented chef. *Directions*: From Castellina, take the road to San Donato. A long way out of town, the hotel is on your right.

*ROMANTIK HOTEL TENUTA DI RICAVO*
*Owners/Managers: Christina & Alessandro Lobrano*
*53011 Castellina in Chianti (SI), Italy*
*Tel: (0577) 74 02 21, Fax: (0577) 74 10 14*
*E-mail: ricavo@ricavo.com*
*23 rooms, Double: Lire 290,000–600,000*
*3–5-night minimum, 7-night minimum high season*
*Open mid-Mar to mid-Nov, Credit cards: MC, VS*
*Restaurant closed Tuesdays, reservations required*
*21 km N of Siena on road 22, Region: Tuscany, Michelin Map 430*
*www.karenbrown.com/italyinns/romantikhoteltenutadiricavo.html*

Castelrotto is the loveliest of medieval towns in the western Dolomites. Surrounded by high mountain meadows dotted with chalets and backed by towering mountains, it's a sight to behold. Snuggled in the heart of town, the 14th-century Cavallino d'Oro has a deep-mustard-color façade highlighted by dark-green shutters and flowerboxes overflowing with cheerful geraniums. There is a traditional, old-world atmosphere throughout this small inn. The guestrooms are individual in decor, and delightfully furnished in a typical Tyrolean style—three rooms with light-pine, four-poster beds are especially pretty. From the beginning of its history the Cavallino has always offered accommodations, originally being a coaching station providing food and rooms for weary travelers and facilities to care for the horses. This hospitality is certainly ongoing— Susanne and Stefan (both of whom speak excellent English) have now taken over as the third generation of the Urthaler family to run the hotel. Not only do they exude boundless enthusiasm and gracious warmth of welcome, they are also constantly improving their small hotel by incorporating more antiques into the decor and continuously renovating and upgrading. The restaurant has an excellent reputation, with the chef specializing in regional dishes. The hotel's sauna beckons you to relax after skiing or walking. *Directions*: Exit at Bolzano Nord from the Verona-Brennero autostrada and follow signs for Siusi and Castelrotto. The hotel faces the market square in the cobbled center of town.

*HOTEL CAVALLINO D'ORO*
*Owners: Susanne & Stefan Urthaler*
*39040 Castelrotto (Kastelruth) (BZ), Italy*
*Tel: (0471) 70 63 37, Fax: (0471) 70 71 72*
*E-mail: cavallino@cavallino.it*
*24 rooms, Double: Lire 110,000–220,000*
*Open all year, Credit cards: all major*
*Restaurant closed Tuesdays*
*140 km S of Innsbruck, 24 km NE of Bolzano*
*Region: Trentino-Alto Adige, Michelin Map 429*
*www.karenbrown.com/italyinns/hotelcavallinodoro.html*

The family-run Relais San Pietro is an absolute dream. It offers the finest quality throughout, gorgeous views, excellent location, spectacular swimming pool, and outstanding cuisine, all at remarkably reasonable prices. This gem of a little hotel has the added benefit of superb hospitality: Luigi Protti, your host, radiates a gentle, old-fashioned, welcoming kindness. Upon retirement he and his wife, Antonietta, decided to move back to the peaceful Tuscan countryside, along with their son, Franco, and his wife, Franca, and open a hotel. They bought a long-neglected farmhouse only a few kilometers from the town where Signora Protti had been born and after two years of restoration, opened it at the end of 1998 as a small, intimate hotel. The interior of the hotel has a refreshing light, fresh, uncluttered appeal. All of the original architectural features such as beamed ceilings and beautiful brick archways have been meticulously preserved. Bedrooms feature beautiful wrought-iron headboards, white bedspreads, excellent lighting, doors painted with regional designs, and superb bathrooms. The romantic dining rooms occupy what were formerly the stables. Signora Protti and her daughter-in-law preside over the kitchen and the food is fabulous. *Directions*: From Cortona, go north on 71 toward Arezzo. At Castiglion Fiorentino, turn right toward Città di Castello. After about 6 km, turn left at a sign to Polvano. Go up the hill. Relais San Pietro is on the left side of the road.

*RELAIS SAN PIETRO*
*Owner: Luigi Protti*
*Localita: Polvano*
*52043 Castiglion Fiorentino (AR), Italy*
*Tel: (0575) 65 01 00, Fax: (0575) 65 02 55*
*E-mail: polvano@technet.it*
*7 rooms, Double: Lire 300,000–400,000*
*Closed Nov 5 to Mar 15, Credit cards: all major*
*Restaurant open daily for hotel guests*
*14 km N of Cortona, Region: Tuscany, Michelin Map 430*
*www.karenbrown.com/italyinns/relaissanpietro.html*

A book on the most charming hotels in Italy would not be complete without including one of the world's premier hotels, the Villa d'Este. Originally the hotel was a private villa built in 1568 by Cardinal Tolomeo Gallio. He obviously had elegant (and expensive) taste, for the Villa d'Este is truly a fantasy come true. From the moment you step into the vast lobby with its sweeping staircase, huge Venetian-glass chandeliers, marble columns, statues, and soaring ceiling, you will feel you are entering a dream. The bedrooms are all elegantly furnished—no two are alike, but all are beautiful with color-coordinated carpets, wall-coverings, and bedspreads. Some of the bedrooms have prime locations with enchanting views out over the lake. Although the interior is outstanding, it is the outside where the fun really begins. The hotel opens onto a large terrace where guests relax with refreshing drinks. Just a short distance beyond the terrace is the lake where there is a dock for boats and a very large swimming pool that extends out over the water, plus an indoor pool and a very popular state-of-the-art spa. Tucked away in the park there are eight tennis courts, and in the nearby area, seven golf courses. However, the most stunning feature of the Villa d'Este is the park: it surrounds the hotel with lovely pathways winding between the trees, a jogging course, glorious flower gardens, statues, and even a formal garden with dramatic mosaic colonnade. *Directions*: Well-signposted in the center of Cernobbio.

*VILLA D'ESTE*
*Manager: Claudio Ceccherelli*
*22010 Cernobbio, Lake Como (CO), Italy*
*Tel: (031) 34 81, Fax: (031) 34 88 44*
*E-mail: info@villadeste.it*
*158 rooms, Double: from Lire 1,000,000, Suite: from Lire 2,750,000*
*Open Mar to Nov, Credit cards: all major*
*Restaurant open daily*
*53 km N of Milan, 5 km N of Como (town)*
*Region: Lombardy, Michelin Map 428*
*www.karenbrown.com/italyinns/villadeste.html*

La Frateria di Padre Eligio, a very special, enchanting hotel, makes an outstanding base for exploring the beauties of Tuscany and Umbria. The guestrooms of this 13th-century convent (founded by St. Francis) are the original guest quarters where the friars lodged passing pilgrims. They are simply, yet tastefully, furnished with antiques. There is nothing to interrupt the enchantment—bathrooms and telephones are the only concessions to the modern era. The silence is sweetened by the song of birds and the air by the fragrance of flowers. A centuries-old forest surrounds the hotel with beckoning paths where you can stroll in perfect stillness. The restoration of this masterpiece of history is superb, but the miracle is how it was accomplished. La Frateria di Padre, in addition to housing a deluxe hotel, is home to a commune of once-troubled young people who toiled for 12 years to restore the Convento San Francesco to its former beauty. Today these remarkable young men and women awaken at dawn to begin long days of labor. They meticulously groom the gardens, tend the vegetable garden, run the hotel, bake the fresh breads, prepare the meals (exclusively using produce from the farm), and serve in the restaurant. *Directions*: Exit the A1 at Chiusi Chianciano and follow signs to Cetona. Go through town towards Sarteano. Just after leaving Cetona, turn left at a sign "Mondo X," "La Frateria di P. Eligio." Go about 700 meters to the hotel.

*LA FRATERIA DI PADRE ELIGIO*
*Manager: Maria Grazia Daolio*
*Convento San Francesco*
*53040 Cetona (SI), Italy*
*Tel: (0578) 23 80 15 or 23 82. 61, Fax: (0578) 23 92 20*
*E-mail: frateria@ftbcc.it*
*6 rooms, Double: Lire 380,000–500,000*
*Closed Nov, Credit cards: all major*
*Restaurant open daily*
*89 km SE of Siena, 62 km NW of Orvieto*
*Region: Tuscany, Michelin Map 430*
*www.karenbrown.com/italyinns/lafrateriadipadreeligio.html*

The Villa Anna Maria is located in Champoluc, a small town at the end of the beautiful Ayas Valley, which stretches north into the Alps almost to the Swiss border. The glaciers of the Monte Rosa (one of the 4,000-meter peaks of the Alps) provide a glorious backdrop as you drive up the valley. Champoluc is a well-known ski center in winter as well as a favorite mountain summer resort. The Villa Anna Maria is not a luxury hotel, but rather a simple, charming mountain chalet with great warmth of welcome from Miki Origone and his gracious son, Jean Noël. Together they run the villa with meticulous care for every comfort of their guests. Inside there is a delightful dining room that exudes a romantic coziness with its wooden Alpine-style country chairs, wooden tables, and gay red-checked curtains—just the place to return to for a good lunch or dinner after walking in the mountains (organized walks can be arranged). Upstairs, the bedrooms are spotlessly clean and very comfortable, with wooden paneling on the walls and a rustic ambiance. The atmosphere is homey—wonderful for those seeking a friendly, family-oriented country inn in a mountain village. *Directions:* Exit the A5 at Verres and follow the valley as it winds up to Champoluc. Drive through Champoluc and you see a small sign for the Villa Anna Maria on the right side of the road just before you leave town. Turn right on this little lane, which winds up the hill, and the Anna Maria is on your right.

*VILLA ANNA MARIA*
*Owners: Miki & Jean Noël Origone*
*Via Croues, 5*
*11020 Champoluc, Monte Rosa (AO), Italy*
*Tel: (0125) 30 71 28, Fax: (0125) 30 79 84*
*E-mail: hotelannamaria@tiscalinet.it*
*20 rooms, Double: Lire 150,000–185,000*
*Open all year, Credit cards: MC, VS*
*Restaurant open daily*
*175 km NW of Milan, 100 km N of Turin*
*Region: Valle d'Aosta, Michelin Map 428*
*www.karenbrown.com/italyinns/villaannamaria.html*

The Ca'Peo, a well-known restaurant serving some of the finest food in Italy, is located high in the coastal hills south of Genoa. You might think you will never arrive as the road winds ever upward from the coast through groves of olive and chestnut trees. But the way is well signposted, and just about the time you might be ready to despair, you will find a wonderful old farmhouse, owned by the charming Franco Solari, who is host and in charge of the wines, and his talented wife, Melly, who is the chef. Their enchanting daughter, Nicoletta, who will immediately win your heart, helps out wherever needed. The intimate dining room, which has only nine tables, is enclosed on three sides by large arched windows to take advantage of a sweeping view to the sea. Be aware that the meals are expensive, but if you appreciate fine food and wines, superb. Dining is definitely the main feature; however, in a modern annex there are five rooms (most are suites) available for guests who want to spend the night. The decor here is simple, but after lingering over a wonderful meal accompanied by delicious wines, how nice to walk just a few steps to your bed. The Ca'Peo is only about half-an-hour's drive from the popular resort of Portofino, so you might want to stay here instead or at least treat yourself to a memorable meal—but call ahead as reservations are necessary. *Directions*: Exit the A12 at Chiavari. Follow signs to Leivi, then pick up and follow signs to Ca'Peo.

*CA'PEO*
*Owners: Melly & Franco Solari*
*Via dei Caduti, 80*
*16040 Chiavari a Leivi (GE), Italy*
*Tel: (0185) 31 96 96, Fax: (0185) 31 96 71*
*E-mail: nicosol@libero.it*
*5 rooms, Double: Lire 200,000*
*Closed Nov, Credit cards: all major*
*Restaurant closed Mondays*
*6 km N of Chiavari toward Leivi*
*44 km SE of Genoa, 22 km NE of Portofino*
*Region: Liguria, Michelin Map 428*
*www.karenbrown.com/italyinns/capeo.html*

The 16th-century Locanda del Sant'Uffizio, originally a Benedictine monastery, then a farm, has been converted over the years by Signor Giuseppe Firato (Beppe), a native of this tiny village, into a delightful resort offering 35 guestrooms and an exquisite restaurant serving the finest of Piedmontese cuisine. All furnishings are antique and every detail of the decor has been rigorously overseen personally by Signor Beppe and his wife, Carla, with the result being a very tasteful, elegant, yet relaxed hotel with its own swimming pool and tennis courts cozily nestled amongst vineyards. Our favorite bedrooms are the cloister rooms looking towards the swimming pool with either terrace or balcony. The Firato family (Beppe, Carla, and sons Fabio and Massimo) is responsible for the ambiance of warmth and hospitality that radiates throughout the hotel. The food is outstanding, but be aware that the meals, the wines, and the before-dinner aperitifs (which some readers thought were complimentary) are expensive, as would be expected in a one-Michelin-star restaurant. *Directions*: Exit the A21 at Asti Est, turn right, then next right on the 457 towards Casale Monferrato. After passing through Calliano go 1 km and turn right for Cioccaro and follow signs to the Locanda.

*LOCANDA DEL SANT'UFFIZIO*
*RISTORANTE DA BEPPE*
*Owner: Giuseppe Firato*
*Near Moncalvo*
*14030 Cioccaro di Penango (AT), Italy*
*Tel: (0141) 91 62 92, Fax: (0141) 91 60 68*
*35 rooms, Double: Lire 340,000\**
*\*Rate includes breakfast & dinner*
*Closed Jan & Aug 10–20, Credit cards: all major*
*Restaurant open daily*
*5 km SE of Moncalvo, 60 km E of Turin*
*21 km N of Asti toward Moncalvo*
*Region: Piedmont, Michelin Map 428*

The Palazzo del Capo is a handsome, pastel-yellow hotel accented by white trim, with an imposing location on a bluff overlooking the sea. You will find this hotel on the west coast, a bit off the beaten path, as you head south toward Italy's "tip of the toe." It is no wonder the setting is so special since this property (whose origins date back to the 11th century) was originally a palace belonging to the dukes of De Aloe. Now a polished, slick, sophisticated hotel has been created within the renovated shell of this once-grand old palace. As you approach, you see in front of the property a large swimming pool surrounded by a beautifully tended lush lawn. As you enter, the reception is on your left, while to the right is a charming small, private chapel. Continuing on, you come to an inviting inner courtyard, enclosed on three sides, one of which is an ancient tower that houses several romantic suites. This pleasant courtyard is dotted with tall palm trees and faces onto a handsome, three-tiered, arcaded grand entry where the majestic marble staircase is open to the air. The public rooms are all pleasantly furnished and exude a traditional, formal ambiance. The bedrooms too are very attractive and many have a view of the sea. A spacious terrace wraps around the back of the hotel and overlooks an impressively wide, pebbly beach and crystal-clear water. For guests who would rather swim in the sea than in the hotel pool, there is a staircase descending from the terrace to the beach.

*PALAZZO DEL CAPO*     **New**
*Manager: Antonio Goffredi*
*Via C. Colombo, 5*
*87020 Cittadella del Capo-Bonifati (CS), Italy*
*Tel & fax: (0982) 95 674 or (0982) 95 675*
*16 rooms, Double: Lire 470,000–520,000\**
*\*Rate includes breakfast & dinner*
*Open all year, Credit cards: all major*
*Restaurant open daily*
*150 km N of Reggio-Calabria, 75 km N of Cosenza*
*Region: Calabria, Michelin Map 431*

From what readers had written about the Hotel Zunica, I had expected it to be a pleasant place to stay with excellent home cooking. This was right on target—great food and far-better-than-average guestrooms. What came as a marvelous surprise was the tiny town of Civitella del Tronto—it is awesome! Civitella del Tronto is a 12th-century fortress that stretches across the entire ridge of a hill. It is now open as a museum where you can wander the entire length of the ridge, imagining the battles of days gone by and savoring the beautiful, 360-degree view. The walled village nestles just below the castle, its medieval stone buildings clinging to the side of the hill. The Hotel Zunica is easy to find. Just after you drive through the walled gate, you will see the attractive cream-colored building with brown shutters facing the main square. The hotel seems to be where all the action in town takes place—a wedding and a first communion were being celebrated while we were there. Our bedroom was an excellent value. Furnished in a modern style with built-in headboards and a desk, it had a good-sized bathroom with great shower and even a hairdryer. Wonderful home-cooked meals are available in a large, old-fashioned dining room. A simple breakfast is served in a small room by the bar. *Directions*: From the A14 take the Val Vibrata exit and then follow signs to Civitella del Tronto.

*HOTEL ZUNICA*
*Owners: Zunica family*
*Piazza F. Pepe, 14*
*64010 Civitella del Tronto (TE), Italy*
*Tel: (0861) 913 19, Fax: (0861) 918 150*
*21 rooms, Double: Lire 170,000\**
*\*Rate includes breakfast*
*Closed Nov 23 to Dec 2*
*Credit cards: all major*
*Restaurant closed Wednesdays*
*18 km S of Ascoli Piceno, 200 km NE of Rome*
*Region: Abruzzo, Michelin Map 430*

The Hotel Petit Dahu is positively enchanting. This 18th-century stone farmhouse with heavy slate roof oozes charm just as it stands, but what makes the hotel so absolutely adorable is that it is nestled in a garden of colorful flowers and decorated with a profusion of pots of brilliant red geraniums. Truly, I have never seen a sweeter-looking hotel at any price—and this one is incredibly inexpensive. The location is also stunning. If you love the mountains, you will be overwhelmed by the location of the Petit Dahu: it sits in a national park at the tip of the finger of the Cogne Valley where the road ends, blocked by the Gran Paradiso. From here only trails beckon you onward into the mountains. Nothing is deluxe or fancy. The bedrooms are small, but as tidy as can be and reflect the same ambiance of delightful rustic simplicity as the rest of the house. The light-pine walls are enhanced throughout by the previous owner's creativity—bouquets of dried flowers are everywhere, prettily displayed in baskets with a ruffle of lace that she made by hand. Also on the walls are figures fashioned of dough, dressed in the regional costumes of the area. Your hosts, Cecilia and Luciano Fraschetto, recently purchased the hotel and we have not had the opportunity to meet them yet. Cecilia is also the chef and most of the produce comes from her own garden. *Directions*: Exit the A5 at Sarre and follow the road up and through Cogne to Valmontey—the hotel is on your left.

*HOTEL PETIT DAHU*
*Owners: Cecilia and Luciano Fraschetto*
*Valmontey 27, 11012 Cogne (AO), Italy*
*Tel & fax: (0165) 74 146*
*8 rooms, Double: Lire 160,000–240,000\**
*\*Rate includes breakfast & dinner*
*Open Dec to Oct, Credit cards: MC, VS*
*Restaurant closed Mondays to Wednesdays*
*3 km S of Cogne, 30 km S of Aosta*
*Region: Valle d'Aosta, Michelin Map 428*

Leaving behind the road from Perugia with its developing industries, a country gravel road takes you up to the splendid 17th-century Villa di Montesolare overlooking in all directions its hilly estate of olive groves and vineyards. A wide, gray-stone staircase leads up to an elegant salon with marble fireplace and crystal chandelier off which are eight lovely guestrooms and two suites on two floors. They are individually appointed with authentic period antiques, which harmonize perfectly with the original features of the villa left intact. Five newer suites and five bedrooms are located within two 350-year-old farmhouses just down the road, offering magnificent views and utter tranquillity. A separate breakfast room is inside one of these two houses. Back at the main house, guests enjoy a drink at the bar before dinner served in one of the two intimate, frescoed dining rooms where varied Tuscan cuisine is presented along with a selection of 120 Umbrian wines. Summer concerts are held in a chapel in the formal Italian garden. Other activities include swimming in one of the two hillside pools, tennis, or horseback riding. Gracious and warm hosts Filippo and Rosemarie do an absolutely superb job of making guests feel totally pampered at their romantic retreat. *Directions*: From Perugia take S.S. 220 toward Citta di Pieve. After Fontignano (3 km), turn right at Colle Sao Paolo to the villa (4 km).

*ROMANTIK HOTEL VILLA DI MONTESOLARE*
*Owners: Rosemarie & Filippo Strunk Iannarone*
*Localita: Colle San Paolo*
*06064 Panicale (PG), Italy*
*Tel: (075) 83 23 76, Fax: (075) 83 55 462*
*E-mail: info@villamontesolare.it*
*20 rooms, Double: Lire 310,000–360,000*
*Closed mid-Dec to mid-Jan, Credit cards: all major*
*Restaurant open daily for hotel guests*
*25 km SW of Perugia*
*Region: Umbria, Michelin Map 430*
*www.karenbrown.com/italyinns/villadimontesolare.html*

Baita Fraina sits in a meadow looking out to the craggy, saw-toothed peaks of the Dolomites with the chic resort of Cortina d' Ampezzo hidden in the valley below. It's an idyllic spot to enjoy excellent food and top-of-the-line, value-for-money accommodation at a fraction of the cost of a hotel room in Cortina. Adolpho Menardi sees that guests are well taken care of while brother Alessandro makes sure that they are well fed. Guests dine outside on the terrace in summer or in one of the traditional, cozy, paneled dining rooms during inclement weather. The Fraina is primarily a well-established and esteemed restaurant cited in top restaurant guides and specializing in pastas with fresh mushrooms as well as the exquisite local *fartaies* dessert with wild-berry sauce. Bedrooms are not fancy but neat and tidy, traditionally paneled in pine with fitted pine furniture and each has a spotless bathroom. Beyond the hotel, meadows stretch in every direction, children romp on the sturdy play structures, and hiking paths beckon to walkers. A sauna, Jacuzzi, and sun terrace are extra features. You can bask in all this bucolic scenery, yet in a few minutes be in the heart of Cortina. *Directions:* Arriving from Belluno, pass the town limit sign and watch for a little yellow signpost on your right, indicating a right-hand turn for Baita Fraina. Follow the road for 1.2 km to the hotel.

*BAITA FRAINA*
*Owners: Menardi family*
*Localita: Fraina*
*32043 Cortina d'Ampezzo (BL), Italy*
*Tel: (0436) 36 34, Fax: (0436) 86 37 61*
*6 rooms, Double: Lire 150,000–220,000*
*Closed May, Jun, Oct & Nov, Credit cards: MC, VS*
*Restaurant closed Mondays in low season*
*133 km E of Bolzano, 71 km N of Belluno*
*Region: Veneto, Michelin Map 429*

As Cortina has grown from a mountain outpost to a chic resort, so the Hôtel de la Poste has grown from a simple mail coach stop to a resort hotel, the last big expansion being made to accommodate visitors to the 1956 Olympics. The Manaigo family has been at the helm for the last century and the current generation—Marisa, her nephew Gottardo, and her daughter Michela—continues to keep the hotel in tip-top condition while offering guests the warmest of welcomes. Add to family involvement a long-term staff and you have a winning combination. Bedrooms vary from a sumptuous suite in the oldest, thick-walled building to a snug single room with small shower room in the new wing. You can choose from mountain views to town views and decor that varies from traditional to modern. Breakfast is taken in the snug breakfast room or outside on the patio in sunny weather. Dinner is enjoyed in the grand dining room with its soaring ceiling and ornate plasterwork. In winter skiing is *de rigueur,* while in summer walking in the mountains, shopping in the sophisticated stores, and simply just enjoying stunning views of the Dolomites are the order of the day. *Directions:* When you arrive in Cortina keep on the one-way system round town until you come to the Hôtel de la Poste garage. Park here to unload. You can leave your car here (25,000 lire per day) or at a free car park in town.

*HOTEL DE LA POSTE*
*Owners: Manaigo family*
*32043 Cortina d'Ampezzo (BL), Italy*
*Tel: (0436) 42 71, Fax: (0436) 86 84 35*
*E-mail: posta@hotels.cortina.it*
*80 rooms, Double: Lire 310,000–740,000\**
*\*Rate includes breakfast & dinner*
*Closed Apr to mid-Jun & Oct to Dec 23*
*Credit cards: all major*
*Restaurant open daily*
*133 km E of Bolzano, 71 km N of Belluno*
*Region: Veneto, Michelin Map 429*
*www.karenbrown.com/italyinns/hoteldelaposte.html*

The Hotel Menardi, over 200 years old, was originally a farmhouse, but as Cortina's popularity as a fabulous ski center has spread, so has the town, and now the farm is located on the outskirts of town. The Menardi farm just naturally evolved into a hotel. At first it gave shelter to the men carting loads over the Cimabanche Pass who needed a place to sleep. Today the inn is a simple but wonderful small hotel whose special ingredient is the old-fashioned warmth and hospitality of the gracious Menardi family— Franca Menardi assisted by her three sons Antonio, Alberto, and Andrea. The hotel maintains a country flavor with old prints on the walls, old clocks, giant dowry chests, Oriental carpets, and beautiful hanging cupboards all set off by the warmth and gaiety of flowers everywhere. The dining room is most appealing and serves an excellent dinner— be sure to request the half-pension rate. The individually decorated bedrooms are all attractive, several have balconies and all have double-glazing to guard against road noise. Several delightful rooms are located across the garden, with three lovely rooms sacrificing a mountain view for a private terrace. *Directions:* Arriving in Cortina, follow the one-way system around town and signposts for Dobbiaco. You find the hotel on your right on the outskirts of town.

*HOTEL MENARDI*
*Owners: Menardi family*
*112 Via Majon*
*32043 Cortina d'Ampezzo (BL), Italy*
*Tel: (0436) 24 00, Fax: (0436) 86 21 83*
*E-mail: hmenardi@sunrise.it*
*51 rooms, Double: Lire 200,000–360,000*
*Open Jun 20 to Sep 20 & Christmas to Apr 10*
*Credit cards: all major, Restaurant open daily*
*133 km E of Bolzano, 71 km N of Belluno*
*Region: Veneto, Michelin Map 429*
*www.karenbrown.com/italyinns/menardi.html*

If you are looking for a place to stay in the heart of the charming walled hilltown of Cortona, the Hotel San Michele is a real winner. Originally a magnificent palazzo, it still maintains its fine architectural details. The mood is set as you enter: look up and you will see a marvelous vaulted stone ceiling. As you walk the halls, notice the arched doorways, frescoed walls, massive stone fireplaces, and intricate beamed ceilings. The guestrooms are tucked along a maze of hallways connected by a series of stone staircases—finding your room is like a treasure hunt. All of the guestrooms are different, but similar in ambiance with tiled floors, off-white walls, prettily framed antique prints, wrought-iron headboards, and antique armoires or dressers. The suites cost only a little bit more than the standard doubles. The honeymoon suite is really special, having a small sitting room with windows on three sides capturing a memorable view of the Val d'Chiana. However, you must be young and nimble to stay in this suite because a wooden ladderlike stairway leads very steeply up to the sleeping alcove and the bathroom is tiny, with an open shower. For the older romantics, suite 241 is spacious and has a beautifully designed beamed ceiling that slopes almost to the floor. *Directions*: Follow signs to the center of Cortona. On the lower edge of town, park close to the main gate, *Porta San Agostino* (near the Agip station), go through the gate, and follow Via Guelfa to the hotel.

*HOTEL SAN MICHELE*
*Owner/Manager: Paolo Alunno*
*Via Guelfa, 15*
*52044 Cortona (AR), Italy*
*Tel: (0575) 60 43 48, Fax: (0575) 63 01 47*
*E-mail: sanmichele@ats.it*
*40 rooms, Double: Lire 250,000–280,000*
*Open Mar to Jan, Credit cards: all major*
*No restaurant, breakfast only*
*Region: Tuscany, Michelin Map 430*
*www.karenbrown.com/italyinns/sanmichele.html*

If you want to find the perfect little hotel to use as a base from which to explore the wonders of Tuscany and Umbria, look no farther than Il Falconiere—a jewel snuggled in the countryside just a few kilometers outside the walled city of Cortona. From this convenient location you can venture out each day to such beauties as Siena, Florence, Assisi, San Gimignano, Orvieto, and Pienza, all of which all easily accessible by car. The joy is that you can return each evening to relax by the gorgeous swimming pool, enjoy some of the best food in Italy, then sleep peacefully in the hushed tranquillity of the countryside. And what a value! You can stay here for much less than you would pay for a deluxe room in Florence or Rome. Il Falconiere is owned by Silvia and Riccardo Baracchi, a charming, talented young couple who have achieved amazing results (even being invited to join the Relais & Châteaux affiliation) from their labor of love and long years of hard work. Riccardo, who inherited the property from his grandmother, was born in the small pretty villa that now houses several of the guestrooms. His wife, Silvia, was born nearby and is the incredibly talented chef whose superb meals lure Italians from far and near to dine here. The guestrooms are individually decorated with great flair. Many antiques are used throughout, creating a comfortable, quietly sophisticated elegance. Il Falconiere is truly a very special place offering superb quality, charm, and genuine hospitality. *Directions*: Just north of Cortona, signposted off the road to Arezzo.

*IL FALCONIERE RELAIS E RISTORANTE*
*Owners: Silvia & Riccardo Baracchi*
*Localita: San Martino, 43*
*52044 Cortona (AR), Italy*
*Tel: (0575) 61 26 79, Fax: (0575) 61 29 27*
*E-mail: ilfalcon@ilfalconiere.com*
*12 rooms, Double: Lire 430,000–520,000, Suite: Lire 670,000*
*Open all year, Credit cards: all major*
*Restaurant open daily, Relais & Châteaux, 3 km N of Cortona*
*Region: Tuscany, Michelin Map 430*
*www.karenbrown.com/italyinns/ilfalconiererelaiseristorante.html*

For a simple small restaurant-hotel, Locanda del Molino offers an unexpected air of style and charm. You quickly understand this when you hear that the delightful owner/chef, Graziella Balducci, is the energetic mother of Silvia Baracchi who (along with her husband, Riccardo) operates Il Falconiere, one of Tuscany's most romantic little inns. Don't be put off by the fact that the Locanda del Molino fronts onto the main road with a service station nearby. Once you step inside the centuries-old stone building, you discover an exceptionally pretty restaurant specializing in typical Tuscan-style food—all homemade, including the wonderful pastas. One wall of stone and the others painted butter-yellow set off to perfection tables covered in layers of checkered tablecloths in cheerful hues of yellow, red, green, and blue. Fresh flowers abound, including a dramatic arrangement in the middle of the room artistically set in giant ceramic olive-oil vats. As you might expect from the name, the building was a mill, so you won't be surprised to find the old millstream still flowing behind the hotel. In warm weather meals are served outside on a balcony overlooking the stream. A small swimming pool has been added for guests' enjoyment. The bedrooms are air-conditioned and tastefully furnished with antiques and offer a good value. Ask for one of the rooms with a new bathroom. *Directions*: 8 km east of Cortona on the road to Montanare.

*LOCANDA DEL MOLINO*
*Owner: Graziella Balducci*
*Localita: Montanare*
*52040 Cortona (AR), Italy*
*Tel: (0575) 61 41 92, Fax: (0575) 61 40 54*
*E-mail: l.locandadelmolino@tin.it*
*8 rooms, Double: Lire 180,000–220,000*
*Closed Jan & Feb, Credit cards: all major*
*Restaurant open for dinner*
*9 km E of Cortona*
*Region: Tuscany, Michelin Map 430*
*www.karenbrown.com/italyinns/locandadelmolino.html*

Corvara is a lovely Alpine village sitting high in the Dolomites and ringed by towering peaks. Fortunately, it's one of those places that combines an exquisite setting with a superb hotel run by the most welcoming of families, the Costas. You will doubtless meet Ernesto, Anny, sons Michil, Maxi, and Mathias, and daughter-in-law Petra during your stay. From the exterior the hotel looks like a typical Alpine hotel but once inside you realize that this is very different—all five lovely dining rooms are rooms from very old local houses that have been re-built here. The conservatory breakfast room offers the largest breakfast selection I have ever seen, from fresh-squeezed juices to eggs cooked any way you want them. The indoor swimming pool with its whirlpool features is a swimming adventure, though if you prefer swimming outdoors, there is also a large garden pool. Bedrooms are absolutely delightful, ranging from standard rooms with balconies offering stunning mountain views to two exquisite junior suites decked out in white pine accented by blue-and-white fabric. In winter this is a skiers' paradise and in summer a walkers'. It's a wonderful base for exploring the Dolomites and if you do not want to explore alone, you can join in the hotel's activities of picnics and walks. *Directions:* Corvara is 50 km west of Cortina d' Ampezzo. Arriving in the town, you find the hotel on the hill next to the church.

*ROMANTIK HOTEL LA PERLA*
*Owners: Costa family*
*39033 Corvara (BZ), Italy*
*Tel: (0471) 83 61 32, Fax: (0471) 83 65 68*
*E-mail: perla@altabadia.it*
*52 rooms, Double: Lire 340,000–720,000*
*Open Jul to Oct & Dec to Easter*
*Credit cards: all major, Restaurant closed Mondays*
*65 km E of Bolzano, 47 km W of Cortina*
*Region: Trentino-Alto Adige, Michelin Map 429*
*www.karenbrown.com/italyinns/romantikhotellaperla.html*

Elba is a beautiful small island, easily accessible in one hour by car ferry from Piombino. After exploring Tuscany, or while en route along the coast heading north from Rome, you will find that Elba makes a delightful stopover where you can happily spend several days relaxing and exploring the island's many pretty inlets and picturesque fishing villages. The Hotel Villa Ottone is idyllically nestled in a tranquil park and has its own private beach (there is also a swimming pool). The original part of the hotel is a romantic villa (which belonged to Signor Di Mario's grandfather) facing directly onto the sea. If you want to splurge, ask for a deluxe room in the villa. Some of the guestrooms are located in an attractive building that also houses the reception area and the dining room, while more guestrooms are found in a separate wing nestled amongst the trees. The furnishings throughout are tasteful and everything is immaculately maintained. Be sure to visit the bar, which has a stunning ceiling of intricate plasterwork and lovely frescoes. In high season you need to take the modified American plan (MAP), which includes breakfast and either lunch or dinner. However, this is no problem as the food is very good and beautifully served. Villa Ottone is a hotel with great personality, overseen with meticulous attention to detail by the gracious Signor Di Mario.

*HOTEL VILLA OTTONE*
*Owners: Di Mario family*
*Localita: Ottone*
*57037 Portoferraio (LI), Isola di Elba, Italy*
*Tel: (0565) 93 30 42, Fax: (0565) 93 32 57*
*75 rooms, Double: Lire 280,000–680,000\**
*\*Rate includes breakfast & lunch or dinner*
*Open May to Oct, 3-night minimum*
*Credit cards: all major, Restaurant open daily*
*11 km SE of Portoferraio*
*Region: Tuscany, Michelin Map 430*
*www.karenbrown.com/italyinns/villaottone.html*

For many generations the 15th-century hamlet of Il Voltone (along with the surrounding 1,000 acres) has belonged to the Parenti family. When the last farmers and their families moved out of Il Voltone in 1960, the tiny community fell into ruin but, happily for the traveler, the charming Parenti sisters, Daniela and Donatella, have meticulously restored the small cluster of abandoned buildings into a delightful small hotel. You enter through an open archway into a courtyard framed by connecting houses and a tiny church—all painted in pastel hues of pinks and creams. The guestrooms are spacious and prettily decorated with color-coordinating fabrics and nice pieces of furniture. The restaurant serves delicious meals accompanied by wine produced on the property. But what makes this hotel truly special is its setting: Il Voltone crowns a gentle hill and in every direction there is a sweeping view of forests, vineyards, lush pastures, and hilltop towns. Guests can enjoy this view from teak deck chairs placed under the chestnut trees or by the swimming pool. Another plus—Il Voltone is in the center of rich archeological sites, great Etruscan ruins, and fascinating hilltop towns. Daniela and Donatella have prepared a series of day tours to help you explore the countryside. *NOTE:* It is an adventure to find Il Voltone—have a detailed map and ask for directions when making reservations.

*IL VOLTONE*
*Owners: Daniela & Donatella Parenti*
*Localita: Voltone*
*01010 Farnese (VT), Italy*
*Tel & fax: (0761) 42 25 40*
*E-mail: info@voltone.it*
*30 rooms, Double: Lire 200,000–240,000*
*Open Apr 7 to Nov 7, Credit cards: MC, VS*
*Restaurant open daily*
*12 km N of Farnese, 45 km N of Tarquinia*
*Region: Lazio, Michelin Map 430*
*www.karenbrown.com/italyinns/ilvoltone.html*

Sitting high above the valley, the delightful village of Völs nestles beneath the Schlern Mountain—hence you see local signposts for Völs am Schlern. At the heart of the village the Romantik Hotel Turm dates back to the 13th century when it functioned as a castle. Today it is certainly not a castle of drafty corridors and sparse rooms but a delightful hotel that displays its castle origins in its barrel-vaulted rooms and thick stone walls. Instead of a gloomy dungeon you have an indoor swimming pool (as well as an outdoor one set on a grassy garden terrace). Karl Pramstrahler's art collection lines every available inch of wall space and includes everything from old oil paintings to contemporary art. His son Stefan, who is responsible for the delicious food, assists Karl in the running of the hotel. Bedrooms come in all shapes and sizes, from lovely rooms set beneath the eaves to a turret suite with a four-poster bed and a little house (Wagenhaus) with traditional pine paneling, a sitting room and child's bedroom downstairs, and a master bedroom upstairs. *Directions*: Exit at Bolzano Nord from the Verona-Brennero autostrada. Follow signs for Siusi and Fiè (also called Völs) and at the main intersection in the village turn left, following the road round to the hotel, which is next to the church.

*ROMANTIK HOTEL TURM*
*Owners: Karl & Stefan Pramstrahler*
*Kirchplatz, 9*
*39050 Fiè allo Sciliar/Völs am Schlern*
*Sudtirol (BZ), Italy*
*Tel: (0471) 72 50 14, Fax: (0471) 72 54 74*
*24 rooms, Double: Lire 320,000–384,000*
*Closed early Nov to Dec 19, Credit cards: MC, VS*
*Restaurant closed Thursdays*
*16 km E of Bolzano, 7 km S of Siusi (Seis)*
*Region: Trentino-Alto Adige, Michelin Map 429*

The Punta Est is a delightful villa perched on a hilltop overlooking the sea. When the home was converted to a hotel, an annex was added to provide more bedrooms, but it still radiates the friendly ambiance of a private home. This warmth of reception and attention to detail are the result of the management of the gracious Podestà family who own and personally manage the inn. They seem dedicated to making your stay as enjoyable as possible—even their German Shepherd wags his tail in welcome. This small hotel is constantly being maintained with loving care. Every time we visit the property has been upgraded—the latest addition being two beautiful new suites. There are little terraces with lovely views snuggled at various levels among the trees and on one of these terraces is a swimming pool. There is also access to the public beach (where the hotel has its own area with lounge chairs), which can easily be reached by walking down the path to the main highway and following the tunnel beneath the highway to the beach. The rooms in the main villa are smaller and more old fashioned than those in the newer annex, which are more reminiscent of an American motel. There is a small dining room for breakfast, which is especially inviting with its blue-and-white English bone-china service. The hotel is located east of Finale Ligure, just before the tunnel.

*HOTEL PUNTA EST*
*Owners: Podestà family, Manager: Attilio Podestà*
*Via Aurelia N.1*
*17024 Finale Ligure (SV), Italy*
*Tel & fax: (019) 60 06 11*
*40 rooms, Double: Lire 340,000–440,000*
*Suite: Lire 440,000–840,000*
*Open May to Oct, Credit cards: all major*
*Restaurant open daily*
*72 km SW of Genoa*
*Region: Liguria, Michelin Map 428*
*www.karenbrown.com/italyinns/puntaest.html*

The Grand Hotel Villa Cora is a mansion, originally built during the 19th century by the Baron Oppenheim as a gift for his beautiful young bride. Among the many romantic tales of the Villa Cora is the one about Oppenheim's wife who, so the story goes, became enamored of one of her many admirers. The jealous baron was so enraged that he threatened to burn the entire mansion, but, luckily for you and me, he was stopped in time from this mad endeavor by his friends, and today this magnificent villa is a stunning hotel. Although only about a 5-minute taxi ride from the center of Florence (or a 20-minute walk), the Grand Hotel Villa Cora is eons away in atmosphere—you feel more like a guest on a country estate rather than in a city hotel. The interior of the hotel is rather ornate and sumptuous. The villa is set in intricate gardens and even has a pool. You can almost hear the sounds of laughter and music drifting through the gardens, and indeed the mansion has always been famous for its dramatic parties: at one time the villa was the residence of Napoleon's wife, Empress Eugenia, whose gay entertaining was the talk of Florence. Now this grand, palace-like home can be yours for days of dreams and romance. Another excellent bonus is free limousine service to/from the heart of Florence.

*GRAND HOTEL VILLA CORA*
*Manager: Luigi Zaccardi*
*Viale Machiavelli, 18/20*
*50125 Florence, Italy*
*Tel: (055) 22 98 451, Fax: (055) 22 90 86*
*E-mail: info@villacora.com*
*48 rooms, Double: Lire 520,000–830,000*
*Suite: Lire 900,000–1,600,000*
*Open all year, Credit cards: all major*
*Restaurant open daily*
*20-minute walk from the heart of Florence*
*Region: Tuscany, Michelin Map 430*
*www.karenbrown.com/italyinns/hotelvillacora.html*

When we first saw the Hotel Continental in the 1980s, we thought its location and views were outstanding, but the hotel—whose decor was extremely modern—did not reflect the style of our guides. However, when we revisited in 1998 we were pleased to see that the hotel had been renovated. There are still reminders of the hotel's previous modern image, but overall, the ambiance is now much more conservative. Fabrics in pretty pastel hues, traditional-style furniture, and even some antiques have replaced the brilliant colors and modern furniture. The Continental can't compare in luxurious, old-world elegance with its sister hotel, the Lungarno, which sits across the river, but it certainly has a great deal to offer. As for location, it just can't be beat—the hotel sits on a corner, facing one of Florence's most famous landmarks, the Ponte Vecchio. The most outstanding feature of this small hotel is its stunning roof garden, the Terrazza de'Consorti, an incredibly romantic garden terrace with a 180-degree view of the city, the river, and the Ponte Vecchio. This outstanding place provides a perfect spot to have a drink in the evening and watch the glow of sunset descend upon the Arno. In addition, special events (such as dinner with live jazz or classical music, wine-tasting, and seasonable programs) are held on the terrace, always of course according to the weather. For those who want to splurge, this same view (but with a 360-degree panorama) is available from the Continental's magical 12th-century tower penthouse.

*HOTEL CONTINENTAL*
*Manager: Martin Elsner*
*Lungarno Acciaiuoli, 2*
*50123 Florence, Italy*
*Tel: (055) 27 262, Fax: (055) 28 31 39*
*48 rooms, Double: Lire 510,000–590,000*
*Penthouse: from Lire 1,000,000*
*Open all year, Credit cards: all major*
*No restaurant, breakfast only, In the heart of Florence*
*Region: Tuscany, Michelin Map 430*

In our estimation, the Hotel Helvetia and Bristol is one of the finest luxury hotels in the center of Florence. Nothing has been spared to make this showplace a true beauty—the decor is outstanding. The lounges, exquisitely decorated with an elegant, yet extremely comfortable, homelike ambiance, exude quality without flamboyance. Each of the guestrooms is also superbly decorated, and, as in a private home, no two are alike. Abundant use of exquisite padded-fabric wall coverings, with color-coordinated draperies, upholstered chairs, and bedspreads along with lovely antiques make each one special. I fell in love with each of the rooms, but my very favorites were the mini-suites: room 257 in gorgeous shades of muted green and room 363 in lovely golds, creams, and dusty pinks, with a sumptuous marble bathroom with Jacuzzi tub, heated towel racks, plus the added bonus of a tiny terrace. The dining room, cozy yet elegant with dark walls and soft lighting, features Tuscan cuisine. For light refreshments, a cool drink, or just relaxing, the Giardino d'Inverno (Winter Garden) is a marvelous retreat—light and airy with a domed, old-fashioned skylight, potted plants, and nostalgic wicker furniture. The Helvetia and Bristol is expensive, but no more so than the other luxury hotels in Florence, and for those who appreciate quality and refinement, it is unsurpassed.

*HOTEL HELVETIA AND BRISTOL*
*Manager: Pietro Panelli*
*Via dei Pescioni, 2*
*50123 Florence, Italy*
*Tel: (055) 28 78 14, Fax: (055) 28 83 53*
*E-mail: information_hbf@charminghotels.it*
*67 rooms, Double: Lire 649,000–869,000*
*Suite: Lire 979,000–2,090,000, breakfast not included*
*Open all year, Credit cards: all major*
*Restaurant open daily*
*In the heart of Florence*
*Region: Tuscany, Michelin Map 430*
*www.karenbrown.com/italyinns/hotelhelvetiaandbristol.html*

Moderately priced accommodations are rare in Florence, so we were happy to discover the Hotel Il Guelfo Bianco, which combines reasonable rates with a choice location in the heart of Florence, just steps to all the prime tourist spots. Most importantly, this small hotel has an owner, Alessandro Bargiacchi, whose presence is seen and felt. He speaks only a little English, but his smile and genuine warmth of welcome make guests feel right at home. Everyone who assists him is exceptionally friendly and all converse in several languages, including the gracious manager, Carlo Cenni, and two charming ladies, Antonella and Gaia. When it first opened, the Il Guelfo Bianco had only 29 rooms, but it has added an annex, the adjacent Hotel Cristallo, bringing the total to 39. The unpretentious but inviting lobby sets the tone of the hotel. The intimate reception area ends in a cozy bar, and from there a hall leads to the breakfast room (although, when the weather is pleasant, breakfast is served outside in the pretty central courtyard). The bedrooms vary in size and position, as one would expect in an historical 14th-century building. All are nicely decorated and some even have beautiful paintings on the ceilings. One of my favorite rooms, number 11, has an especially pretty outlook over a back garden. The Hotel Il Guelfo Bianco is not a deluxe hotel, nor does it pretend to be, but it makes an excellent choice for a friendly, pleasant place to stay in the heart of Florence.

*HOTEL IL GUELFO BIANCO*
*Owner: Alessandro Bargiacchi*
*Manager: Carlo Cenni*
*Via Cavour, 29*
*50129 Florence, Italy*
*Tel: (055) 28 83 30, Fax: (055) 29 52 03*
*E-mail: info@ilguelfobianco.it*
*39 rooms, Double: Lire 300,000–385,000*
*Open all year, Credit cards: all major*
*No restaurant, breakfast only*
*In the heart of Florence, Region: Tuscany, Michelin Map 430*
*www.karenbrown.com/italyinns/hotelilguelfobianco.html*

The Hotel Lungarno, one of our favorite hotels, is superbly located directly on the River Arno, a few minutes' walk from the Ponte Vecchio. Although it is basically of new construction, the architect cleverly incorporated into the hotel an ancient stone tower, which houses several romantic suites. The hotel changed hands in 1997 and the new owners have renovated the entire hotel and made it even more perfect. The new decor is superb, with fine-quality furnishings accented by an appealing color scheme of pretty blues and creamy whites. In addition to the redecoration of all the rooms, a restaurant was opened in 1999. Also added were six splendid two-bedroom, two-bath apartments, which are an exceptional value if you are traveling with friends or family. Throughout the hotel a gracious ambiance of understated elegance prevails—enhanced by admirable management and a warm reception. Bountiful bouquets of fresh flowers and an outstanding collection of original art add the final touch of perfection. When making a reservation, request a bedroom overlooking the Arno—one might not be available, but you can always try. If you plan far in advance, you might even be lucky enough to snare a room with a large terrace overlooking the river—these are very special and well worth the extra cost. What a treat to sit on your own terrace in the evening and watch the Arno fade into gold in the setting sun.

*HOTEL LUNGARNO*
*Manager: Mr. Aleseio Ianna*
*Borgo San Jacopo, 14*
*50125 Florence, Italy*
*Tel: (055) 27 26 1, Fax: (055) 26 84 37*
*69 rooms, Double: from Lire 650,000*
*Suite: from Lire 900,000*
*Open all year, Credit cards: all major*
*Restaurant closed Sundays*
*On the Arno near Ponte Vecchio*
*Region: Tuscany, Michelin Map 430*

The Regency is a superb, intimate hotel built into several beautiful homes that face a small, parklike square. Although only a ten-minute walk from the heart of Florence, the hotel seems a world away in atmosphere—instead of the noise of motorcycles and the bustle of tourist-filled streets, you encounter utter tranquillity. From the moment you step through the front door, the mood is one of an exquisite home. Happily lacking is any feeling of commercialism. You are greeted warmly, not at an impersonal reception counter, but at an intimate desk. The charming parlors also exude the refined elegance of a private home with exquisite fabrics, many antiques, the finest quality furnishings, and bouquets of fresh flowers. The wood-paneled dining room, which overlooks the lovely rear garden, is exquisite, plus the food is outstanding and the service impeccable. The spacious, luxurious bedrooms also meet the highest standards with opulent fabrics, lavish antique mirrors, excellent lighting, and beautiful marble bathrooms. Although the Hotel Regency is small, it offers all the luxuries that are frequently available only in larger hotels, including a concierge to assist you with any of your personal needs.

*HOTEL REGENCY*
*Owner: Amedeo Ottaviani*
*Manager: Monica Landi*
*Piazza Massimo d'Azeglio, 3*
*50121 Florence, Italy*
*Tel: (055) 24 52 47, Fax: (055) 23 46 735*
*E-mail: info@regency-hotel.com*
*34 rooms, Double: Lire 540,000–695,000*
*Suite: Lire 800,000–1,100,000*
*Open all year, Credit cards: all major*
*Restaurant open daily*
*10-minute walk to the city center*
*Region: Tuscany, Michelin Map 430*
*www/karenbrown.com/italyinns/hotelregency.html*

Mario's came highly recommended to us by several readers, and after seeing the hotel for ourselves, we agree that it is a delightful small hotel, moderately priced for Florence. It is conveniently located two blocks from the train station, and within easy walking distance of the city's major sightseeing. From the street, the appeal of the hotel is not readily evident as it is housed in a rather nondescript building. But after ascending the stairs to the second floor and stepping into the cozy, beamed-ceilinged lobby, you know you've arrived at a well-tended small hotel with an old Florentine ambiance. Facing the reception desk is a sitting area with sofas arranged under a wall of pictures, Oriental carpets enhancing the dark tile floors, and artfully arranged pictures and plants setting off the cream-colored walls. All of the guestrooms have a country-fresh feeling with antique armoires, wrought-iron headboards, rustic wooden desks and chairs, and pretty bedspreads. The rooms are not large, but are very pleasing and immaculately tidy. A copious breakfast is served buffet-style in a charming room whose walls are hung with many pictures. Guests choose from a wonderful selection of breads, cheese, salami, ham, yogurt, boiled eggs, coffee, tea, and chocolate. The nicest aspect of this hotel is the fact that it is small enough to be very personalized. Mario sees that every guest feels special, and will even (upon prior arrangement) give driving tours around Tuscany.

*MARIO'S*
*Owner: Mario Noce*
*Via Faenza, 89*
*50123 Florence, Italy*
*Tel: (055) 21 68 01, Fax: (055) 21 20 39*
*E-mail: hotel.marios@hotelmarios.com*
*16 rooms, Double: Lire 170,000–310,000*
*Open all year, Credit cards: all major*
*No restaurant, breakfast only*
*2 blocks from the Florence train station*
*Region: Tuscany, Michelin Map 430*
*www.karenbrown.com/italyinns/marios.html*

The Torre di Bellosguardo is a romantic villa nestled on the shelf of a hill with an unsurpassed view of Florence. Below the hotel, the tiled rooftops, steeples, towers, and domes of the city seem like a fairyland at your fingertips. It is not surprising that the setting of the Torre di Bellosguardo is so breathtaking: it was chosen by a nobleman, Guido Cavalcanti (a friend of Dante's), as the most beautiful site in Florence. The villa is owned today by Amerigo Franchetti who inherited the fabulous property from his grandmother, a baroness. Amerigo takes great pride in his stunning home and, with a passion for perfection, is restoring the villa to its original glory. The guestrooms are decorated in antiques and vary in size as they would in a private home. The most splendid features of the hotel are its incredible setting and meticulously groomed garden, which highlights a swimming pool nestled on a terrace overlooking Florence. What happiness to relax after a day of sightseeing and watch the superb buildings below you melt in the twilight, to reappear as a panorama of twinkling lights. In summer lunch is served by the swimming pool—otherwise breakfast is the only meal available. For dinner, you must wind down a narrow twisting road to go to a restaurant. If you want to walk into Florence, ask about the "secret" path—a short cut down the hill to the city.

*TORRE DI BELLOSGUARDO*
*Owner: Amerigo Franchetti*
*Via Roti Michelozzi, 2*
*50124 Florence, Italy*
*Tel: (055) 22 98 145, Fax: (055) 22 90 08*
*E-mail: torredibellosguardo@dada.it*
*16 rooms, Double: Lire 490,000—690,000\**
*\*Breakfast not included*
*Open all year, Credit cards: all major*
*No restaurant, breakfast only*
*Lunch served by the pool during summer*
*5-minute drive to city center*
*Region: Tuscany, Michelin Map 430*
*www.karenbrown.com/italyinns/torredibellosguardo.html*

The Villa Montartino, which opened as a deluxe small hotel in 1999, is located on the outskirts of Florence with the advantage of being easy to find and providing convenient parking. In the future a shuttle service to and from the city is planned, and in the meantime taxis are readily available. In the 11th century Montartino was built as a watchtower to insure safe transit for goods coming into Florence. As you enter the gates and wind up to the enchanting small villa crowning the hilltop, you can quickly see why this site was chosen for protection since the Ema Valley stretches below as far as the eye can see. You feel like a guest in a secluded country estate, yet Florence is only 3 kilometers away. The house, which for years had been totally neglected, has been lovingly restored with great care taken to retain its original architectural features. As you step into the house terra-cotta floors, whitewashed walls, beamed ceilings, handsome wooden furniture, and many beautiful antiques create the ambiance of a noble home. The guestrooms are all spacious and the decor luxurious without being pretentious. All of the rooms are air-conditioned, have satellite TV, safe, mini bar, direct-dial phone, and even a computer line. An added bonus is a large, heated swimming pool. *Directions*: From the A1, take the Florence Certosa exit. At the second stop light turn right on Via Gherardo Silvani, at the far end of the square. Continue on Via Gherado Silvani for 1.3 km. When the road splits, keep to the right. The hotel is on the left, behind a gated entrance.

*VILLA MONTARTINO*
*Director: Patrizia Caciolli*
*Via Gherardo Silvani, 151*
*50125 Florence, Italy*
*Tel: (055) 22 35 20, Fax: (055) 22 34 95*
*E-mail: info@montartino.com*
*7 rooms, Double: Lire 460,000–520,000*
*Open all year, Credit cards: all major*
*Restaurant by reservation*
*3 km S of Ponte Vecchio*
*Region: Tuscany, Michelin Map 430*
*www.karenbrown.com/italyinns/villamontartino.html*

If you want to see Florence, yet be blissfully removed from its swarm of tourists and congestion of traffic, the Villa La Massa makes a fabulous choice for a place to stay. Here you can enjoy the best of all worlds—the tranquil beauty of the countryside combined with the convenience of a courtesy bus to take you to and from the heart of the city (just 15 minutes away). This gorgeous Renaissance villa originally belonged to the rich and powerful Giraldi family—inscribed tombstones, underground tunnels, and a chapel still remain from this period of the villa's history. What makes Villa La Massa so stunning is not only the appeal of the hotel, but also its setting. This idyllic property sits on a gentle bluff that hugs the edge of the River Arno as it loops its way east from Florence. During the day guests relax by a lovely swimming pool in the central garden courtyard. The restaurant is very special, with tables set on a terrace right above the Arno, making dinner truly romantic as guests dine under the stars while overlooking the river. In 1998 Villa La Massa was bought by the owners of the Villa d'Este (one of Italy's premier hotels) and totally renovated, with the hotel emerging as a shining new gem in the Florence scene. The grounds are now meticulously groomed, the gardens are splendid, and the interior lovely—reflecting the same standard of excellence as the Villa d'Este. *Directions*: Exit the autostrada A1 at Firenze Sud and follow signs to Bagno A Ripoli and Candeli. At Candeli, watch for a sign on the left marked to the hotel.

*HOTEL VILLA LA MASSA*
*Manager: Giampaolo Ottazzi*
*50012 Candeli (FI), Italy*
*Tel: (055) 62 611, Fax: (055) 63 31 02*
*37 rooms, Double: Lire 720,000–1,455,000*
*Open Mar to Nov, Credit cards: all major*
*Restaurant open daily*
*On the Arno river, 7 km E of Florence*
*Region: Tuscany*
*Michelin Map 430*

Fiesole, a small town tucked in the green wooded hills above Florence, has long been a favorite of ours. Staying here gives you the best of both worlds—you can enjoy the peacefulness of the countryside while being just a short ride away from Florence's wealth of attractions. If you are looking for ultimate luxury, nothing can compete with the Villa San Michele, but the Hotel Villa Fiesole offers a delightful alternative for those on a more conservative budget. You can easily spot the Villa Fiesole, set just above the road as it loops up the wooded hillside. Originally a private mansion, the Villa Fiesole was converted into a delightful small hotel in 1995, being equipped with all the finest modern amenities but keeping the overall ambiance of an exquisite home. In this part of the hotel, the rooms vary somewhat in size because of the nature of the building. A new wing has been added and the construction, although obviously recent, was done in excellent taste so that it blends in beautifully with the original villa. Here the rooms are almost identical in size and furnishings. Each is especially spacious and decorated in a most appealing way, using tones of rich blue and whites, giving an overall ambiance of refined good taste. The hotel does not have a formal restaurant but, in addition to breakfast, a light lunch, dinner, and simple buffet supper are available for guests. Next to the hotel is a small swimming pool, prettily nestled beneath a medieval tower.

*HOTEL VILLA FIESOLE*
*Director: Simone Taddei*
*Via Beato Angelico, 35*
*50014 Fiesole (FI), Italy*
*Tel: (055) 59 72 52, Fax: (055) 59 91 33*
*E-mail: info@villafiesole.it*
*28 rooms, Double: Lire 340,000–490,000*
*Open all year, Credit cards: all major*
*Restaurant for guests only*
*8 km NE of Florence*
*Region: Tuscany, Michelin Map 430*
*www.karenbrown.com/italyinns/hotelvillafiesole.html*

The Bencista is a real find for the traveler looking for a congenial, unpretentious, family-run hotel near Florence that has charm and yet is reasonably priced. The villa, romantically nestled in the foothills with a bird's-eye view of Florence, is owned and managed by the Simoni family who are always about, personally seeing to every need of their guests. Simone Simoni speaks excellent English, and on the day of my arrival he was patiently engrossed in conversation with one of the guests, giving him tips for sightseeing. Downstairs there is a jumble of sitting rooms, bars, and parlors, each decorated with dark Victorian furniture. Upstairs are the bedrooms, which vary in size, location, and furnishings. Some are far superior to others, but they are all divided into only two price categories: with or without private bathroom. Many people return year after year to their own favorite room. During the season, reservations are usually given only to guests who plan to spend several days at the hotel—this is an easy requirement because the hotel is beautifully located for sightseeing in both Florence and Tuscany. (If you do not have a car, you can take the bus that runs regularly into Florence from the top of the road.) Two meals (breakfast and a choice of lunch or dinner of family-style Italian cooking) are included in the price. One of the outstanding features of the pensione is its splendid terrace where guests can enjoy a sweeping panorama of Florence.

*PENSIONE BENCISTA*
*Owner: Simone Simoni*
*50014 Fiesole (FI), Italy*
*Tel & fax: (055) 59 163*
*44 rooms, Double: Lire 320,000\**
*Double without private bath: Lire 280,000\**
*\*Rate includes breakfast & lunch or dinner*
*Open all year, Credit cards: none accepted*
*Restaurant open daily for guests only*
*8 km NE of Florence*
*Region: Tuscany, Michelin Map 430*

It would be difficult to find another hotel with as many attributes as the Villa San Michele—in fact, almost impossible. How could you surpass a wooded hillside setting overlooking Florence, a stunning view, gorgeous antiques, impeccable management, gourmet dining, and, as if this were not enough, a building designed by Michelangelo. The Villa San Michele was originally a monastery dating back to the 15th century occupied by Franciscan friars until Napoleon turned it into his headquarters. The adaptation of its rooms and public areas to today's standards has been made without affecting the ambiance of serenity and history. Most of the rooms are in the historical building and although some are not large, having been monks' cells in the past, they are decorated with taste and somber elegance. Eleven suites are located in the Italian garden and two in the *Limonaia*, once the greenhouse for storing lemon plants during the winter. All have stunning views of Florence and the Arno Valley. The lounges, dining rooms, terraces, and gardens are also exquisite. Meals can be enjoyed either in a beautiful dining room or on a lovely veranda that stretches along the entire length of the building. A beautiful swimming pool has been built on a secluded terrace above the hotel. The pool is perfectly situated to capture the view and surrounded by fragrant gardens.

*VILLA SAN MICHELE*
*Manager: Maurizio Saccani*
*Via Doccia, 4*
*50014 Fiesole (FI), Italy*
*Tel: (055) 56 78 200 or 59 99 23, Fax: (055) 56 78 250*
*38 rooms, Double: Lire 1,575,000–1,880,000\**
*\*Rate includes breakfast & lunch or dinner*
*Open Mar to Dec, Credit cards: all major*
*Restaurant open daily*
*7 km NE of Florence*
*Region: Tuscany, Michelin Map 430*

Nestled in a small village in the foothills of the Alps, you'll find one of our favorite hotels, the very special Romantik Hotel Villa Abbazia, situated across from a picturesque 12th-century abbey. When you enter into the 17th-century palazzo—which is graced by fine antiques, Oriental carpets, fine fabrics, and bouquets of fresh flowers—the Zanon family welcomes you as if you were a friend in their own home. All of the palazzo's bedrooms and suites are stunning. Each guestroom has been splendidly decorated and exudes the ambiance of an English country manor. Meticulous care and tender love has gone into every tiny detail, including the fresh flowers and individual breakfast china, which reflects the color scheme of each room. In addition to the bedrooms in the Palazzo, there are eight beautiful suites in the magnificently restored 19th-century, Liberty-style villa across the garden. The Abbazia is surrounded by excellent places to dine, including its own restaurant, La Corte, where one can find delicious foods typical of the region in a pleasant and intimate environment. The Villa Abbazia is located in a region rich in medieval villages and Palladian villas, most appealing for lovers of art and architecture. The historic towns of Asolo and Vittorio Veneto are nearby.

*ROMANTIK HOTEL VILLA ABBAZIA*
*Owners: Zanon family*
*Via Martiri della Liberta*
*31051 Follina (TV), Italy*
*Tel: (0438) 97 12 77, Fax: (0438) 97 00 01*
*E-mail: info@hotelabbazia.it*
*17 rooms, Double: Lire 300,000–330,000*
*8 suites: Lire 440,000–600,000*
*Open all year, Credit cards: all major*
*Restaurant closed Sundays*
*90 km S of Cortina, 60 km NW of Venice*
*Region: Veneto, Michelin Map 429*
*www.karenbrown.com/italyinns/villaabbazia.html*

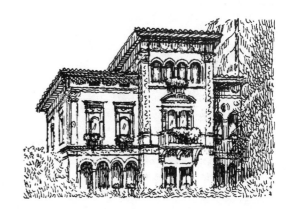

When dreaming of Tuscany, one usually envisions sweeping fields of vineyards and gentle hills dotted with olive trees. L'Ultimo Mulino has a totally different type of setting, in a heavily wooded nook by a small stream. This small hotel was originally a medieval olive mill and the antique millstone in the lounge stands testament to the hotel's colorful past, as do many architectural features, including 13 dramatic brick arches, which form a vaulted ceiling in the lounge. The primary color scheme throughout is white and blue—seen in the sofas and also in the dining room in the cushions and the table linens and china. The guestrooms all have a rustic ambiance, appropriate to the old mill, with wrought-iron headboards used throughout. The price of the rooms depends upon the size and the amenities. The least expensive rooms are fairly small but those in the upper category are large, and several have their own private terrace. The bathrooms are especially nice, and many have the added luxury of Jacuzzi tubs. All the rooms have air conditioning, direct-dial phones, mini bars, good lighting by the beds, and satellite televisions. One of the most pleasant features of the hotel is a 20-meter swimming pool built into a terrace above the hotel. There are also bicycles available for guests' use. *Directions*: From Radda in Chianti, take the road for Gaiole and Siena. About 5 km from Radda, turn left at the sign to L'Ultimo Mulino. The hotel is about midway between Radda and Gaiole.

*L'ULTIMO MULINO*
*Manager: Andrea Mencarelli*
*Localita: La Ripresa di Vistarenni*
*53013 Gaiole in Chianti (SI), Italy*
*Tel: (0577) 73 85 20, Fax: (0577) 73 86 59*
*13 rooms, Double: Lire 350,000–400,000*
*Closed mid-Jan to mid-Feb, Credit cards: all major*
*Restaurant open daily for hotel guests*
*50 km S of Florence, 30 km N of Siena*
*Region: Tuscany, Michelin Map 430*

I was enchanted with the Villa Fiordaliso (a fetching pink and white villa superbly located on the shore of Lake Garda) when I spent the night in one of its antique-filled bedrooms overlooking the lake many years ago. At that time, I wrote a glowing description of this beautiful little hotel, only to learn the villa was closing to the public. Nevertheless, when researching for a later edition, I went by the Villa Fiordaliso for old times' sake and, to my delight, found it open again as a small hotel. Although the emphasis now is definitely on dining (the meals are expensive, but excellent), there are seven bedrooms—each unique in decor, yet each with every modern comfort. The rooms facing the lake have a lovely view and are quieter since they are away from the noise of the street. Throughout the interior there is a blend of antique and stylish modern furniture, nicely set off by ornate parquetry floors, cool marble pillars, and magnificent gilded and painted ceilings. For history buffs, the villa offers a bit of romance—the Villa Fiordaliso was a gift from Mussolini to his mistress, Claretta Petacci. In fact, Claretta's bedroom is one of the rooms available and is a real winner, with an enormous marble bathroom. The Villa Fiordaliso is owned and managed by the Tossetti family whose warmth of welcome mellows the sophisticated ambiance of this small hotel.

*VILLA FIORDALISO*
*Owner: Giuseppe Tossetti*
*Via Zanardelli, 132*
*Lake Garda, 25083 Gardone Riviera (BS), Italy*
*Tel: (0365) 20 15 8, Fax: (0365) 29 00 11*
*7 rooms, Double: Lire 400,000–700,000*
*Suite: Lire 1,000,000*
*Open Mar to Dec, Credit cards: all major*
*Restaurant closed Mondays & Tuesdays for lunch*
*66 km W of Verona*
*Region: Lombardy, Michelin Map 428/429*

La Foresteria Serègo Alighieri is on a working farm producing wine and olive oil. Only a discreet brass sign on the gate hints at any commercialism, yet it is indeed a fabulous place to stay. Each reasonably priced guestroom is a one- or two-bedroom apartment with a well-equipped kitchen, charming living room, and a large bathroom tiled in local marble. The decor throughout reflects tasteful, elegant simplicity—whitewashed walls set off country antiques, and comfortable sofas are upholstered in Venetian pure-cotton fabrics in green and cream stripes. Soft green is repeated in the pretty cotton drapes and bedspreads. It is not surprising that La Foresteria has been developed with such love and meticulous care to maintain the estate's authentic charm—the present owner, the gracious Count di Serègo Alighieri, is the 20th generation to own the property! Family records indicate the first ancestor to own the land was the poet Dante's son, who purchased the estate in 1353. This vast farm was almost doomed at the end of World War II when the retreating armies had orders to destroy it. As a forestalling tactic, the present count's father invited the commanding officers to a magnificent party. Perhaps it was the abundance of the excellent wines served, but happily the officers forgot their orders. To celebrate this miracle of the saving of the town, every April the local town people make a pilgrimage to the estate to celebrate mass—followed, of course, by a little wine.

*LA FORESTERIA SERÈGO ALIGHIERI*
*Owner: Count Pieralvise di Serègo Alighieri*
*Via Stazione, 2*
*37020 Gargagnago di Valpolicella (VR), Italy*
*Tel: (045) 77 03 622, Fax: (045) 77 03 523*
*E-mail: serego@easynet.it*
*8 apartments, Double: Lire 190,000–340,000*
*Closed Jan, Credit cards: all major*
*No restaurant*
*18 km NW of Verona*
*Region: Veneto, Michelin Map 428/429*
*www.karenbrown.com/italyinns/laforesteriaseregoalighieri.html*

The entrance to Baia d'Oro is off the narrow cobbled street that runs through the quaint lakeside town of Gargnano-Villa (be prepared—parking is difficult). Inside, there are a small lounge, bar, and a dining room. To truly appreciate the attributes that make this small inn special, you must step outside to the terrace stretching out over the water. In the daytime this sun-drenched oasis is a favorite with the luncheon crowd, then in the evening as the sun sets, fresh flowers and candles are placed on small tables dressed with fresh linens. Although open only in high season, the restaurant lives up to all expectations: the pasta is homemade in the kitchen, the fish is fresh from the lake. As you dine, there is a constant parade of beautiful yachts pulling up to the dock, unloading their cargo of chicly dressed, obviously well-to-do Italians who have come to dine. After dinner, you go up a narrow staircase to the basic bedrooms, which are ideal for the young of heart who are not expecting decorator-perfect furnishings (room 14, which has two windows overlooking the lake, is one my favorites). Bedrooms and bathrooms are being renovated. The Baia d'Oro is owned by the Terzi family (Gianbattista Terzi is a well-known artist). Their son, Gabriele, has taken over the management and personally orchestrates dinner each evening. Be forewarned: several readers have mentioned that what they thought was a free "welcome drink" was actually not complimentary.

*BAIA D'ORO*
*Owners: Terzi family*
*Manager: Gabriele Terzi*
*Via Gamberera, 13, 25084 Gargnano-Villa*
*Lake Garda (BS), Italy*
*Tel: (0365) 71 17 1, Fax: (0365) 72 56 8*
*13 rooms, Double: Lire 220,000*
*Open mid-Mar to mid-Nov, Credit cards: none accepted*
*Restaurant open daily in high season*
*140 km E of Milan, 78 km W of Verona*
*Region: Lombardy, Michelin Map 428/429*
*www.karenbrown.com/italyinns/baiadoro.html*

The Frascati hillside wine area just south of Rome is an alternative to staying in the city. Before opening its doors in 1997, the 16th-century Villa Grazioli undertook ten years of tedious restoration work—it was imperative to conserve the architecture, grounds, and the many important frescoed ceilings by G.P. Pannini. After the restoration it was transformed into a splendid hotel under the strict regulations of the Ministry of Historical Buildings. The spacious reception area and four inviting frescoed sitting rooms on the first floor remind us that this was once a private residence. Ten spacious double rooms and two suites are offered right in the villa off the impressive *galleria*—a head-spinning vaulted hall completely frescoed from floor to ceiling, overlooking the front garden. The remaining more standard rooms are located across the garden in what was originally the lemon-tree greenhouse, all decorated conservatively with antiques and rich fabrics and offering all the modern amenities. An underground tunnel connects the two buildings. The four formal, high-ceilinged dining rooms have an enormous terrace taking in the surrounding park, Italian gardens, and a panoramic view over Rome. Besides being close to both airports, the hotel has a shuttle service to Frascati, Rome, or the local train station. *Directions*: From the GRA (the circle road around Rome) exit onto the N21/22. Go south to Grottaferrata. At the far end of town, a sign to the left marks the way to the hotel.

*PARK HOTEL VILLA GRAZIOLI*
*Director: Rolf Rampf*
*Via Umberto Pavoni, 19*
*00046 Grottaferrata (RM), Italy*
*Tel: (06) 94 54 00, Fax: (06) 94 13 506*
*E-mail: info@villagrazioli.com*
*58 rooms, Double: 430,000–480,000*
*Open all year, Credit cards: all major*
*Restaurant open daily*
*20 km south of Rome*
*Region: Lazio, Michelin Map 430*
*www.karenbrown.com/italyinns/hotelvillagrazioli.html*

Gubbio is one of Umbria's many jewels: a small, wonderfully intact medieval town that presses against the wooded hillside. A not-to-be-missed sight in Gubbio is the Piazza Grande, considered to be one of the boldest examples of medieval town planning, and facing onto this awesome masterpiece is the Relais Ducale. Gazing from the square, you would hardly know that a hotel is secreted within the building, but you will notice a large, open, stone passageway. Enter here and climb up the stairs through a tunnel-like corridor where you will emerge into a little lane. Continue on until you come to a hotel sign by the gate on a stone wall. Ring the bell for entrance and suddenly the hotel reveals itself with a charming inner garden courtyard off which you find the discreet reception office. The hotel, once the guest quarters for the Ducale Palace, has been sleekly renovated, but impressive features of its past are seen throughout with massive thick walls, high vaulted ceilings, and stone archways. On the fourth level of the hotel there is a romantic garden, walled on three sides, but with one side enclosed by a carved stone balustrade, where you can gaze out to a beautiful panoramic view. Fine antique furniture is used for accent, handsome oil paints adorn the walls, and Oriental carpets brighten the floors. The pretty guestrooms have a sedate, refined decor, showing an effort to preserve the aristocratic aura of the hotel's heritage.

*RELAIS DUCALE*
*Owner: Rodolfo Mencarelli*
*Via Ducale, 2*
*06024 Gubbio (PG), Italy*
*Tel: (075) 92 20 157, Fax: (075) 92 20 159*
*E-mail: mencarelli@mencarelligroup.com*
*32 rooms, Double: Lire 340,000–400,000*
*Open all year, Credit cards: all major*
*Restaurant open daily*
*54 km NW of Assisi, 92 km E of Arezzo*
*Region: Umbria, Michelin Map 430*
*www.karenbrown.com/italyinns/relaisducale.html*

La Posta Vecchia, a spectacular villa nestled on the edge of the ocean just north of Rome's airport, was the home of the late John Paul Getty. There are 17 bedrooms (mostly suites) tucked into a stunning mansion secluded by manicured gardens artfully designed to emphasize the ruins of the Pompeii-like villa. The magic starts from the moment you ring the bell at the gated entrance—the gate swings open, you drive through a vast park, and suddenly, the storybook villa comes into view. Within the mansion, priceless antique furniture, statues, and fine fabrics richly adorn the rooms, creating an opulent, tasteful splendor in the lounges and the guestrooms. The dining room is exquisite, but even more romantic is to dine on balmy evenings on the terrace perched above the ocean. When Getty was installing the magnificent pool in the northern wing, he discovered the foundations of a Roman villa—thought perhaps to be the weekend retreat of Julius Caesar. Getty, who was profoundly interested in archaeology, spared no expense to preserve this antiquity. These Roman ruins are now encompassed by the lower level of the home and guests can view the splendid mosaic floors, walls, and pottery—displayed as if in a living museum. La Posta Vecchia is expensive, but a once-in-a-lifetime experience. It is truly like being a guest in a private home. *Directions*: Exit the A12 at Ladispoli and follow signs to town. La Posta Vecchia is in Palo Laziale, 2.2 km south of Ladispoli.

*LA POSTA VECCHIA*
*Manager: Franco Ottaviani*
*00055 Palo Laziale, Ladispoli, (RM), Italy*
*Tel: (06) 99 49 501, Fax: (06) 99 49 507*
*17 rooms, Double: Lire 775,000–2,400,000*
*E-mail: info@postavecchia.com*
*Open mid-Mar to early Nov, Credit cards: all major*
*Lunch or dinner: Lire 140,000 per person*
*Restaurant open daily, Relais & Châteaux*
*25 km N of Rome Airport*
*Region: Lazio, Michelin Map 430*
*www.karenbrown.com/italyinns/lapostavecchia.html*

Cinque Terre is the name given to five villages (Monterosso, Riomaggiore, Vernazza, Manarola, and Corniglia) that are built into the mountainous coast of Liguria. Several of these picturesque villages are accessible only by foot or train. There are several choices of places from which you can explore these tiny fishing hamlets, one of these being the modest, rather dated resort of Levanto. The Hotel Stella Maris is a simple, two-star hotel, but it exudes warmth and caring, and is recommended to the traveler who is looking for a reasonably priced place to stay and who values hospitality rather than decorator-perfect accommodation. Not that the hotel is lacking in character: it is located on the second floor of a 17th-century palazzo and remnants of its past grandeur remain. Many of the bedrooms feature high, elaborately frescoed ceilings and handsome antique beds. I think my favorite is number 4, an especially inviting room with a romantic wooden, French-style headboard. The dining room also has a frescoed ceiling and a fancy mural depicting a maharajah and his elephant train. Breakfast and dinner are included in the room rate. Although only a little English is spoken, Renza and Sandro exude a merry warmth that is sure to touch your heart.

*HOTEL STELLA MARIS*
*Owners: Renza & Alexandro Italiani*
*Via Marconi, 4*
*19015 Levanto (SP), Italy*
*Tel: (0187) 80 82 58, Fax: (0187) 80 73 51*
*E-mail: renza@hotelstellamaris.it*
*14 rooms, Double: Lire 340,000–360,000\**
*\*Rate includes breakfast & dinner*
*Closed Nov, Credit cards: all major*
*Restaurant open daily*
*83 km SE of Genoa, 36 km NW of La Spezia*
*Region: Liguria, Michelin Map 428*
*www.karenbrown.com/italyinns/stellamaris.html*

Limone sul Garda is a small town tucked into a pocket of a hillside at the edge of Lake Garda. This very old town of pastel-colored houses adorned with bougainvillea and twisting cobbled streets attracts so many visitors that in high season it is wall-to-wall tourists. Nevertheless, the town is very quaint, and especially appealing off season when you can avoid some of the crowds. The Hotel Le Palme (in a building dating back to the 17th century) is in the heart of town, directly on the lake. Whereas many of our suggestions in the Lake Garda area are intimate, family-operated inns, Le Palme is a hotel with a more commercial ambiance. You enter into the lobby and go down a few steps to a small bar and an especially attractive dining room with handsome wooden, antique-style, high-back chairs and beautifully set tables. From the dining room, French doors open onto an appealing outside dining area on a balcony overlooking the lake. Along the side of the hotel is another, more casual, place to eat in a garden terrace overlooking the lake where white wrought-iron tables and chairs are set under the centuries-old palm trees among many plants and colorful flowers. The rooms, all with satellite TV and air conditioning, are pleasant and a few have some antique pieces of furniture. Prime rooms overlook the lake. The Risatti brothers who own Le Palme own several hotels in town and guests can use the pool at another of their hotels, La Pergola.

*HOTEL LE PALME*
*Owners: Risatti family*
*Via Porto, 36*
*25010 Limone sul Garda (BS), Italy*
*Tel: (0365) 95 46 81, Fax: (0365) 95 41 20*
*E-mail: lepalme@limone.com*
*28 rooms, Double: Lire 140,000–250,000*
*Open Easter to Oct, Credit cards: MC, VS*
*Restaurant open daily*
*160 km NE of Milan, 97 km NW of Verona*
*Region: Lombardy, Michelin Map 428/429*
*www.karenbrown.com/italyinns/hotellepalme.html*

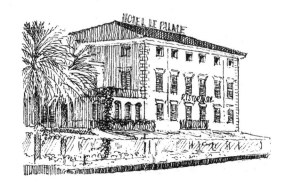

Lucca is an outstanding walled town—truly one of Italy's jewels—but it does not offer any deluxe hotels. However, just a ten-minute drive away sits the sumptuous Locanda L'Elisa, a pretty, deep-lavender villa with white trim peeking out from a frame of trees. The hotel has the appearance of a private home and, happily, this intimate, homelike quality remains even after you step inside where you are warmly greeted. As you look around, it is obvious that this was previously the residence of a wealthy family. Fine antiques, splendid paintings, and luxurious fabrics combine to create a mood of refined elegance. All of the guestrooms are individually decorated, but exude a similar old-world ambiance created with dark woods and opulent materials. The walls are richly covered in damask fabrics that color-coordinate with the draperies and bedspreads. However, the mood changes dramatically in the appealing dining room, found in a glass-enclosed conservatory. During the day, sunlight streams in through the windows and guests can enjoy both excellent cuisine and a view of the trees, green lawn, and colorful, well-tended beds of flowers. In this same garden you find a refreshing swimming pool. The Locanda L'Elisa is very small and very special—a real luxury hideaway with a gracious warmth of welcome. *Directions:* Take the A11 to Lucca then take N12r (not 12) toward Pisa. Soon after leaving Lucca, watch for a sign on the left for Locanda L'Elisa.

*LOCANDA L'ELISA*
*Owner: Ruggero Giorgi*
*Via Nuova per Pisa, N12r, Massa Pisana*
*55050 Lucca, Italy*
*Tel: (0583) 37 97 37, Fax: (0583) 37 90 19*
*8 rooms, Double: Lire 450,000–790,000*
*Breakfast: Lire 32,000 per person*
*Open Mar to Nov, Credit cards: all major*
*Restaurant closed Sundays, Relais & Châteaux*
*4.5 km S of Lucca on N12r, 65 km W of Florence*
*Region: Tuscany, Michelin Map 430*

The Luz family bought and restored this lovely turn-of-the-century villa across from the lake 30 years ago. It retains its "Liberty"-style decor (1920s) throughout the several sitting and dining rooms with high, frescoed ceilings, stained-glass and lead windows, and ornate chandeliers. The reception area has an old-fashioned wooden bar with leather stools, velvet sofas and armchairs, Oriental carpets, and an enormous stone fireplace. Bedrooms upstairs vary in size (single, double, or suite) and are in keeping with the general decor of the accommodation. Many amenities are offered such as air conditioning and hydrojet baths in suites. A garden surrounds the villa where in the summer months tables and umbrellas are set up for dinner or buffet breakfast. Gracious Signora Renate runs the show, assisting her guests with various itineraries around the lake area. Guests have access as well to the family's other lakefront hotel, with alternative restaurant, park, and swimming. This place exudes old-world charm. *Directions*: Luino is halfway up the eastern side of the lake and the hotel is easily found right in town.

*CAMIN HOTEL LUINO*     **New**
*Owners: Luz family*
*Viale Dante 35*
*21016 Luino (VA), Italy*
*Tel: (0332) 53 01 18, Fax: (0332) 53 72 26*
*E-mail: caminlui@tin.it*
*12 rooms, Double: Lire 240,000–270,000*
*Open all year, Credit cards: all major*
*Restaurant open daily*
*100 km NW of Milan, 20 km S of Locarno*
*Region: Lombardy, Michelin Map 428*
*www.karenbrown.com/italyinns/hotelluino.html*

The Albergo del Sole, located about an hour's drive south of Milan, came highly recommended to us as one of Italy's finest restaurants with rooms so we arrived eagerly for our first visit. Happily, this little inn surpassed our expectations, offering an elegantly rustic setting and delicious meals. This 600-year-old farmhouse is a food connoisseur's dream come true. From the moment you enter this old stone home you are enveloped in a country ambiance enhanced by fine antiques, heavy beams, copper pots hanging on the walls, and extravagant bouquets of flowers. The heart of the inn is its kitchen, long famous as one of Italy's finest. The food, featuring regional specialties prepared from the freshest of locally produced ingredients, is expensive, but outstanding. If you cannot overnight here, the inn is well worth a visit simply for its atmosphere and cuisine. However, if possible, plan to spend the night so you can linger over your dinner and savor the fine food and wines. Some of the guestrooms are in the main building, others are in rooms tucked around the back garden. Each of the bedrooms is nicely decorated, but with a much more modern mood than the dining rooms. Although the food and country-style furnishings are outstanding, it is the traditional Italian welcome and caring warmth of the owners, Francesca and Mario Colombani, that make the Albergo del Sole special. *Directions*: From the A1, take the Piacenza Nord exit. Go through Codogno, following signs for Maleo. Go through Maleo and just after the high watchtower, turn right on Via Travattoni.

*ALBERGO DEL SOLE*
*Owners: Francesca & Mario Colombani*
*Via Trabattoni, 22*
*20076 Maleo (MI), Italy*
*Tel: (0377) 58 142, Fax: (0377) 45 80 58*
*8 rooms, Double: Lire 260,000–290,000, Apt: Lire 360,000*
*Closed Jan & Aug, Credit cards: all major*
*Restaurant closed Sunday evenings & Mondays*
*60 km S of Milan, 23 km W of Cremona*
*Region: Lombardy, Michelin Map 428*

Clinging to the steep hillside above the beautiful coast of Basilicata, Maratea is a charming village of very old colorful houses and narrow cobbled streets. As the road loops ever-upward through the town, you soon come to the Locanda delle Donne Monache, carved into the rocky slope next to the tiny parish church of St. Maria. Originally a nunnery dating back to the early 1700s, the convent has been transformed into a deluxe small hotel. The exterior—salmon-colored stuccoed walls with white trim and rustic heavy-tiled roof—blends well with other houses in the village. Inside, the color scheme continues with sky-blue added for accent. The bedrooms are tucked throughout the hotel, each taking advantage of its special vista. The largest guestrooms are designated as suites. Number 9 is especially interesting, with a dramatic bathtub carved into the rocks and a pretty view out over the tiled rooftops. The most outstanding feature of the hotel is its garden where, located on the upper terrace next to the small church, a swimming pool seems to float in the air, romantically suspended above the jumble of village rooftops. Overlooking the garden, on balmy summer evenings, guests enjoy superb meals outside under the stars. The quiet serenity that must have appealed to the nuns so long ago greets guests each morning as the sweet fragrance of flowers, the song of birds, and the church bells cast their spell. *Directions:* Follow the road up the hill to Maratea and then continue winding up the hillside, following signs for *Centro Storico* . In the main square you will see signs pointing up the hill to the hotel.

*LA LOCANDA DELLE DONNE MONACHE*
*Owner: Bruno Raffaele*
*Via Carlo Mazzei, 4*
*85046 Maratea (PZ), Italy*
*Tel: (0973) 87 74 87, Fax: (0973) 87 76 87*
*E-mail: locdonnemonache@crosswinds.com*
*30 rooms, Double: Lire 280,000–360,000*
*Open Apr to Oct, Credit cards: all major*
*Restaurant open daily, 220 km S of Naples, 5 km W of Maratea*
*Region: Basilicata, Michelin Map 431*
*www.karenbrown.com/italyinns/donnemonache.html*

The sienna-and-cream-colored, Liberty-style Villa Cheta Elite is located on the main coastal road just south of Acquafredda. A steep path winds up through the garden to the hotel, which has a series of tall French doors opening onto a shaded terrace where glimpses of the sea can be seen through the flowers and the trees. The hotel retains the genuine warmth and charm of a private home, without any hint of the formal commercialism of a hotel. Throughout there is a comfortable lived-in, old-fashioned elegance. The exceptionally gracious owner personally supervises every detail in the operation of his small hotel and welcomes one and all as personal guests. Some of the staff speak English, but Lamberto does not need to—his smile and infectious laughter transcend any language barrier. Each bedroom is individually decorated using homey family antiques. When the weather is balmy guests eat dinner on the terrace whose white wrought-iron tables are prettily set with fresh linens and bouquets of flowers from the garden. The home-cooked meals are outstanding. If you prefer small, family-owned hotels to the sophisticated glamour of expensive resort-style hotels along this magical coast of southern Italy, the Villa Cheta Elite will definitely win your heart.

*ROMANTIK HOTEL VILLA CHETA ELITE*
*Owner: Lamberto Aquadro*
*Via Timpone, 46*
*85041 Acquafredda di Maratea (PZ), Italy*
*Tel: (0973) 87 81 34, Fax: (0973) 87 81 35*
*E-mail: villacheta@tin.it*
*18 rooms, Double: Lire 210,000–250,000*
*Open all year, Credit cards: all major*
*Restaurant open daily*
*1 km S of Acquafredda, 210 km S of Naples*
*Region: Basilicata, Michelin Map 431*
*www.karenbrown.com/italyinns/villachetaelite.html*

One of our favorite recommendations along the southern coast of Italy is the Santavenere Hotel, an ideal stopping point if you are driving south to Sicily. However, don't just consider it as a place to spend the night en route—the Santavenere is so special you will want to linger and use it as a base to explore this lovely niche of Italy. The hotel, built in 1953, is perfectly positioned on a promontory above the sea, affording unsurpassed views of the gorgeous, sparkling, turquoise water. Although the hotel is of contemporary construction, its interior radiates an old-world charm combined with a nautical flair. The living room is elegant, but not stuffy—comfortable slipcovered chairs and sofas form cozy conversation nooks, while fine antiques and beautiful ship models lend further charm. The guestrooms too are extremely attractive in their decor and, best of all, each has its own terrace or balcony with a view of the sea. The property is very large and in the meticulously groomed gardens there are gorgeous displays of flowers and lush lawns. Here you find a beautiful swimming pool from which a path leads to the edge of the cliff and then loops down through a fragrant pine forest to the sea where guests can swim in the crystal-clear water. There are a bar and a barbecue at the water's edge, so you will not need to go back up the hill for a snack or cold drink. *Directions:* Take the coastal highway N18 to Maratea. Do not go into the town, but instead follow signs for the *porto* and Fiumicello, then for the hotel.

*SANTAVENERE HOTEL*     **New**
*Manager: MaurizioPaterlini*
*85040 Fiumicello di Maratea (PZ), Italy*
*Tel: (0973) 87 69 10, Fax: (0973) 87 76 54*
*E-mail: santavenerehotel@virgilio.it*
*40 rooms, Double: Lire 270,000–860,000*
*Open Apr to Oct, Credit cards: all major*
*Restaurant open daily*
*220 km S of Naples, adjacent to Maratea Porto*
*Region: Basilicata, Michelin Map 431*
*www.karenbrown.com/italyinns/santavenere.html*

If you are intrigued with the idea of *really* getting off the beaten path, look no further than the Tenuta del Barco, a vast farming estate of over 100 hectares that sweeps right down to the sand dunes of the Ionian Sea. The extraordinary warmth and charm of your hosts, Maria Cristina and Nick Donadio, combined with their good taste and professionalism, make the Tenuta del Barco a special place to stay. Both Maria and Nick went to school in the United States and so speak fluent English—a great bonus since they can advise you how to explore this enchanting niche of southern Italy. If you are traveling with children, the Tenuta del Barco is ideal since there is a playground on the property, an excellent beach just a few minutes away, and each room has a kitchenette. The farm (which produces wine, olive oil, various fruits and vegetables, and cheeses) has been in Nick's family for over 250 years and almost everything served in the restaurant comes from the estate. You enter through a gate into a large, square courtyard bound by pure-white, Moorish-style buildings that reflect the brilliant sun. To the left are the reception and the restaurant, built into the old stables. When the weather is warm, dining is outside on the terrace. The guestrooms also face the courtyard. The buildings date back to the 16th century and great care has been taken to preserve and enhance their superb architectural features, including incredible soaring, cathedral-like stone ceilings. The decor is refreshingly simple and in perfect harmony with the architecture.

*TENUTA DEL BARCO*    **New**
*Owners: Maria Cristina & Nick Donadio*
*74026 Marina di Pulsano (TA), Italy*
*Tel & fax: (099) 53 33 051 or (059) 92 13 23*
*E-mail: teunta@iname.com*
*7 apartments, Double: Lire 160,000–220,000*
*1-week minimum in Jul & Aug—ask for rates*
*Open all year, Credit cards: all major*
*Restaurant open daily by reservation*
*22 km SE of Taranto, 5 km SE of Pulsano*
*Region: Apulia, Michelin Map 431*
*www.karenbrown.com/italyinns/tenutadelbarco.html*

Castel Labers (also called Schloss Labers) is a lovely old castle which, while dating back to the 11th century, has more of a feel of a grand Victorian home than a fortification. It has a picturesque setting on a hillside surrounded by vineyards and overlooking the beautiful Merano Valley, which is framed by dramatic mountains. Although not luxurious, this castle has character and charm. Signor Neubert told me that his great-grandfather came from Copenhagen in 1885 and bought the castle, which became so popular with his visiting friends that it soon became a prosperous hotel. The lounges and dining rooms are not fancy, but have a lived-in, comfortable atmosphere. Many fresh foods are included in the menu and both red and white wines, produced from the inn's own vineyards, are served with meals. The central staircase leads dramatically upstairs where many of the bedrooms have lovely mountain views (I loved our room 14b). After a day of sightseeing you can swim in the pool or the more energetic can enjoy a game of tennis. There is also a restored 16th-century chapel on the grounds that offers a holy mass every Saturday at 6 pm. *Directions:* Take the Merano Sud exit from the new Bolzano-Merano road. Follow signs for Hafling for 4.5 km, then turn right towards Labers and the castle is soon visible on your left.

*HOTEL CASTEL LABERS*
*Owners: Stapf-Neubert family*
*Via Labers, 25*
*39012 Merano (BZ), Italy*
*Tel: (0473) 23 44 84, Fax: (0473) 23 41 46*
*32 rooms, Double: Lire 290,000–520,000*
*Open Apr to Nov*
*Credit cards: all major*
*Restaurant open daily*
*In the countryside 3 km NE of Merano*
*28 km NW of Bolzano, 150 km N of Verona*
*Region: Trentino-Alto Adige, Michelin Map 429*
*www.karenbrown.com/italyinns/hotelcastellabers.html*

Alexander Ortner's grandfather bought this shooting lodge in 1954 and over the years the family has expanded it to become the smallest four-star hotel in Merano. It really deserves accolades, for it is a simply delightful hotel, hospitably run by the Ortners, with the most spectacular views across the vineyards of the Merano Valley. This gorgeous view is the focus of the vine-covered terrace and in warm months guests are assigned a table both here and in the dining room so that they always have a choice of where to dine. The set dinner menu ranges from five to seven courses (with a choice of main course), depending on the season and what is fresh and available. Select one of the estate's wines to accompany the meal. Relax by the pool in the shade of the old apple trees or sunbathe *au naturel* on the secluded deck. If you want the most private of rooms, choose the doll-like chalet tucked away in the woods with its terrace offering splendid valley views. This same view is enjoyed by the "new" rooms decked out in blond pine— several are spacious suites large enough for a family of four. I was very struck by the variety of nationalities among the guests. *Directions*: Take the Merano Sud exit from the new Bolzano-Merano road, follow signs for Hafling for 4 km, then turn right towards Labers. Follow this road for 5 km to the hotel.

*HOTEL FRAGSBURG*
*Owners: Ortner family*
*Via Fragsburger Strasse, 3*
*39012 Merano (BZ), Italy*
*Tel: (0473) 24 40 71, Fax: (0473) 24 44 93*
*16 rooms, Double: Lire 290,000–440,000\**
*\*Rate includes breakfast & dinner*
*Closed Nov to mid-Apr, Credit cards: none*
*Restaurant open daily*
*28 km NW of Bolzano, 150 km N of Verona*
*Region: Trentino-Alto Adige, Michelin Map 429*
*www.karenbrown.com/italyinns/hotelfragsburg.html*

The Antica Locanda dei Mercanti is an absolute treasure. Not that it has all the trappings of a deluxe city hotel—you could walk right by without knowing the hotel is there because there is no sign at all, just its name on one of the many buzzers on a brass panel beside a large green door. Inside, there is no elaborate lounge, no noisy bar, no fancy restaurant, no expensive boutiques. Instead, there is an intimate counter with a receptionist who offers a warm welcome and shows you to your room. This is where the magic begins. For the price, you would expect minimum accommodations but, instead, all of the guestrooms are outstanding. Each shows the loving touch of Paola Ora and although no two are alike, they all have a charming, tasteful, refined elegance. There are no TVs or mini bars in the rooms, but you will find direct-dial telephones, exceedingly comfortable mattresses, lots of electrical outlets, good reading lights, and marble bathrooms with hairdryers. Paola is passionate about fresh flowers and in each room there is a beautiful bouquet. The least expensive rooms are fairly small but the rooms in the next category up are extremely spacious. At the top of the list are four air-conditioned rooms with private rooftop garden terraces. Whichever room you choose, you will be astounded by the beauty and the quality for such an unbelievably reasonable price. The location too is excellent—just a five-minute walk to the Duomo, a five-minute walk to the Castello, and a few blocks to La Scala.

*ANTICA LOCANDA DEI MERCANTI*
*Manager: Paola Ora*
*Via San Tomasco, 6, 20121 Milan, Italy*
*Tel: (02) 80 54 080, Fax: (02) 80 54 090*
*E-mail: locanda@locanda.it*
*16 rooms, Double: Lire 210,000–400,000\**
*\*Breakfast not included, Open all year*
*Credit cards: all major*
*No restaurant, breakfast only*
*Heart of Milan, between the Duomo & the Castello*
*Region: Lombardy, Michelin Map 428*
*www.karenbrown.com/italyinns/anticalocandadeimercanti.html*

The Four Seasons opened its doors in 1993 to well-deserved rave reviews and instant success. The hotel (whose origins date back to a 15th-century convent) is superbly set in Milan's fantasy shopping area whose rich selection of chic designer boutiques is unrivaled anywhere in the world. For sightseeing, just a comfortable stroll through quaint cobbled streets brings you to La Scala Theatre, the Galleria, and the stunning Duomo. The hotel is an oasis of refined, understated elegance and restful tranquillity. You enter into what was originally the chapel, now a spacious, refreshingly uncluttered room decorated in muted tones of beiges and creamy whites. Fresh flowers abound, enhancing vaulted ceilings, fine contemporary furnishings, fragments of stunning frescoes (uncovered during renovation and meticulously restored), and accents of museum-quality antiques. Unfortunately, there is not enough space on this page to go into greater detail about the hotel. In essence, the two restaurants are superb, the inner courtyard garden lovely, the guestrooms have every conceivable convenience, the linens are the finest. No expense was spared to pamper the guest—as an example, the marble walls, floors, and even mirrors in the bathrooms are heated so that no fog will collect. The icing on the cake is the caring staff who pamper you shamelessly.

*FOUR SEASONS HOTEL MILANO*
*Manager: Vincenzo Finizzola*
*Via Gesù, 8*
*Milan 20121, Italy*
*Tel: (02) 77 088, Fax: (02) 77 08 50 04*
*E-mail: milano@fourseasons.com*
*118 rooms, Double: Lire 980,000–1,130,000*
*Suite: Lire 1,250,000–7,000,000*
*Breakfast: Lire 50,000–60,000 per person*
*Open all year, Credit cards: all major*
*One restaurant open daily, other closed Sundays*
*Heart of Milan, close to shopping & sightseeing*
*Region: Lombardy, Michelin Map 428*
*www.karenbrown.com/italyinns/fourseasonmilan.html*

In the first edition of our guide to Italy, the Grand Hotel et de Milan was featured as our favorite hotel in Milan. Soon after the book was in print, the hotel closed for renovation but now has reopened its doors—more beautiful than ever. There is no hotel in Milan more richly imbued with tradition. Dating back to 1863, it is located only two blocks from La Scala Theatre and has been "home" for many of the world's most famous artists, including Giuseppe Verdi who composed some of his operas while living here. From first glance you are immediately enveloped in a romantic mood of the past. The heart of the hotel is the spacious lounge, gently illuminated by a large domed skylight, with cream-colored wood paneling, marble floor accented by Oriental carpets, comfortable sofas and chairs, potted palms, and a marble fireplace completing the elegant scene. Beyond the lounge there is a nostalgic, old-fashioned bar whose mirrored walls and elegant drapes form the perfect backdrop for afternoon tea or a post-theater drink. The hotel's Don Carlos restaurant (named after one of Verdi's operas) continues the romantic theme with dark-green fabric walls almost covered with pictures of famous artists who have performed at La Scala. As you would expect, the guestrooms too are superbly decorated with fine furniture, lovely fabrics, and many antiques.

*GRAND HOTEL ET DE MILAN*
*Manager: Antonio Cailotto*
*Via Manzoni, 29*
*20121 Milan, Italy*
*Tel: (02) 72 31 41, Fax: (02) 86 46 08 61*
*E-mail: infos@grandhoteletdemilan.it*
*95 rooms, Double: Lire 792,000–942,000*
*Suite: Lire 1,067,000–3,025,000*
*Open all year, Credit cards: all major*
*Restaurant open daily*
*Heart of Milan, 2 blocks from La Scala*
*Region: Lombardy, Michelin Map 428*
*www.karenbrown.com/italyinns/grandhoteletdemilan.html*

The Hotel de la Ville is a gem of a hotel. The location just couldn't be more perfect—a few minutes' walk takes you to La Scala Theatre, the spectacular Duomo, or to the Galleria, Milan's romantic glass-domed shopping arcade. The exterior, a modern glass-and-stone façade, doesn't prepare you for the interior, which exudes a cozy, old-world charm. You enter into a lovely reception area, softly illuminated from a domed skylight. Just off the reception is a cozy lounge in a color scheme of rich green and gold where comfortable upholstered sofas and chairs are arranged in small groupings. An intimate cherry-paneled bar is tucked in one corner, discreetly available for afternoon tea or an aperitif. The ambiance is one of genteel, old-world elegance. The individually decorated guestrooms all boast of the same quality: the walls are covered with elegant Italian silk fabric that color-coordinates with the fabric on the beds and draperies. All rooms have completely modernized bathrooms, beautifully tiled in marble in tones of beige, cream, or green. The hotel's Canova Restaurant is well known for its regional cuisine and vintage wine cellar. The son and daughter of the founder, the late Count Bocca, continue his tradition of excellence and the finest hospitality. As an added bonus, in 2001 the hotel will open its new roof-top swimming pool (covered in winter). *Directions:* From the central ring road take the Corso Venezia to Piazza S. Babila, the Corso Matteotti to the Piazza Meda, and the Via Hoepli to the hotel. Public or private parking is available.

*HOTEL DE LA VILLE*
*Manager: Giuliano Nardiotti*
*Via Hoepli, 6, 20121 Milan, Italy*
*Tel: (02) 86 76 51, Fax: (02) 86 66 09*
*E-mail: delaville@tin.it*
*109 rooms, Double: Lire 530,000–580,000, Suite: Lire 1,200,000*
*Open all year, Credit cards: all major*
*Restaurant open daily*
*Heart of Milan, between the Duomo & La Scala*
*Region: Lombardy, Michelin Map 428*
*www.karenbrown.com/italyinns/delaville.html*

Hotel Villa Malpensa is less than a five-minute drive from the new Milan Malpensa airport. You can stay here for much less than staying in a fancy hotel in Milan, with the added bonus of knowing you don't have to rush to catch your early-morning flight. This stately, four-story formal mansion was once the home of the counts of Caproni (one of the wealthiest families of northern Italy). You enter into a formal hallway painted a soft-cream color, with a soaring ceiling, walls enhanced by ornate plaster sculpturing, marble floors, and Oriental carpets. Throughout the original core of the hotel, the past magnificence of this 1931 villa lives on through ornate architectural features. However, throughout the rest of the hotel there is no great flair to the decor—the contemporary furnishings are typical of a commercial hotel, but you cannot fault the amenities. All of the spacious guestrooms have built-in headboards with proper reading lights, comfortable mattresses, satellite televisions, mini bars, direct-dial telephones, hairdryers, and air conditioning. All of the superior rooms have balconies where you can watch the planes taking off and landing. *Directions*: From Milan, follow signs to the Malpensa airport. Exit at Terminal One, turn right immediately, then go straight. The hotel is on your right, about a two-minute drive.

*HOTEL VILLA MALPENSA*
*Owner: Fausto Bonini*
*Reception Manager: Giuseppe Gemmo*
*Via Don Andrea Sacconago, 1*
*21010 Vizzola Ticino (VA), Italy*
*Tel: (0331) 23 09 44, Fax: (0331) 23 09 50*
*E-mail: hotvil@malpensa.it*
*59 rooms, Double: Lire 320,000*
*6 superior: Lire 450,000*
*Open all year, Credit cards: all major*
*Restaurant open daily, 1 km SW of Malpensa Airport*
*Region: Lombardy, Michelin Map 428*
*www.karenbrown.com/italyinns/villamalpensa.html*

During the 17th and 18th centuries it was fashionable for wealthy Venetian nobles to build palatial retreats along the cool banks of the River Brenta, and so the waterway became lined with sensational villas all the way from Venice to Padua. Today villages and commerce have built up in the area, but many of the mansions still survive, filled with statues, frescos, and Murano glasswork, attesting to the opulent lifestyle of days gone by. Some mansions are now open as museums but for those who really want to experience living the noble life, there is the lovely 17th-century Villa Margherita, an elegant small hotel. It is situated across the highway from the canal, just a short stroll from one of the villa museums and a short drive from the others. Many converted villas in Italy are beautiful but faded, reflecting genteel neglect: not so with the Villa Margherita where all is beautifully maintained and every detail is perfect. From the lounges with their elegant antiques to the guestrooms with color-coordinated fabrics, each detail shows the care and involvement of the owners, Valeria and Remigio dal Corso. Far from the hubbub of Venice, yet only a 20-minute drive away, the Villa Margherita is an excellent hotel choice for those who prefer to avoid the hustle and bustle of the city. If you go into Venice, it's easiest to take the bus, thus avoiding the congestion of traffic and high cost of parking.

*ROMANTIK HOTEL VILLA MARGHERITA*
*Owners: Valeria & Remigio dal Corso*
*Via Nazionale, 416*
*30030 Mira (VE), Italy*
*Tel: (041) 42 65 800, Fax: (041) 42 65 838*
*E-mail: hvillam@tin.it*
*19 rooms, Double: Lire 260,000–480,000*
*Open all year, Credit cards: all major*
*Restaurant closed Wednesdays*
*On canal 2 km W of Mira, 16 km W of Venice*
*Region: Veneto, Michelin Map 429*
*www.karenbrown.com/italyinns/hotelvillamargherita.html*

Il Melograno is a rarity: a small, luxury hotel that is truly managed by the family—creating a warmth and cordiality seldom found in a hotel of this sophistication. Camillo Guerra oversees every detail of his hotel, ably assisted by his children. White walls enclose the large property whose core is a stunning, white, 16th-century fortified farmhouse, which for many years was the holiday retreat of the Guerra family. In 1985, Signor Guerra (an antique and fine-art dealer from Bari) decided to expand his home-away-from-home into a hotel. Taking meticulous care to preserve the hundreds of ancient olive trees (one 2,000 years old), he built a series of superbly furnished guestrooms clustered in white Moorish-style buildings facing intimate patios. The original farmhouse now houses the reception, romantic bar, beautiful dining room, and various intimate lounges. Throughout, everything is exquisitely decorated in antiques. Cheerful floral-slipcovered chairs and Oriental carpets accent stark white walls and floors. One of the inner patios is a fragrant small orange grove, watered by an ancient stone irrigation system. Breakfast is served on the poolside terrace overlooking the pomegranate and fig trees. Il Melograno makes an excellent, luxurious base for exploring the fascinating Apulia region of southern Italy. *Directions:* Located just west of Monopoli on the road to Alberobello. As you head toward Alerobelloi, there is a sign to the hotel on the right side of the road.

*IL MELOGRANO*
*Owners: Guerra family*
*Contrada Torricella, 345*
*70043 Monopoli (BA), Italy*
*Tel: (080) 69 09 030, Fax: (080) 74 79 08*
*E-mail: melograno@melograno.com*
*37 rooms, Double: Lire 460,000–680,000*
*Open mid-Mar to mid-Jan, Credit cards: all major*
*Restaurant open daily, Relais & Châteaux*
*On the heel of Italy, 70 km NW of Brindisi*
*Region: Apulia, Michelin Map 431*
*www.karenbrown.com/italyinns/ilmelograno.html*

The Castelletto di Montebenichi is an enchanting small castle in a tiny, storybook-perfect, medieval village perched on a hilltop in Tuscany, romantically facing a miniature plaza enclosed by a circle of homes built into the old tower walls. This is a sturdy, stone building with a crenellated roof, arched windows, and a row of colorful coats of armor stretching across the top. Inside, it seems as if you are truly stepping back into the past—the renovation has been so carefully accomplished that you don't realize any changes have been made at all (until, of course, you see the excellent modern bathrooms). All the fabulous murals have been meticulously restored and the floors and beamed ceilings reflect the rich patina of age. The furnishings, too, reflect another era, with rich fabrics, beautiful light fixtures, fine oil paintings, and many fine antiques. Your exceptionally personable hosts, Marco Gasparini and Arnaldo Soriani, want their guests to feel like friends. Everything possible is done to create this ambiance, including an open bar where guests can fix themselves refreshment whenever they want. Breakfast is served in a charming, sunny room with arched windows on three sides. There are also various cozy lounges, a stunning library, and beautiful guestrooms. The latest addition to the hotel is a fabulous swimming pool accompanied by a small sauna, nestled on a terrace on the lower hillside of the village. *Directions*: About midway between Siena and Arezzo. From the A1, exit at Valdarno, following signs for Montevarchi, Bucine, Ambra, and then Montebenichi.

*CASTELLETTO DI MONTEBENICHI*
*Owners: Marco Gasparini & Arnaldo Soriani*
*52020 Montebenichi-Bucine (AR), Italy*
*Tel: (055) 99 10 110, Fax: (055) 99 10 113*
*E-mail: info@castelletto.it*
*9 rooms, Double: Lire 400,000–480,000*
*Open Apr to Nov, Credit cards: all major*
*No restaurant, breakfast only, No children under 14*
*26 km NE of Siena, Region: Tuscany, Michelin Map 430*
*www.karenbrown.com/italyinns/castellettodimontebenichi.html*

For those who wish for accommodations with all the trimmings, yet still want to feel like a pampered guest in a private home, Villa Pambuffetti is an ideal choice. Situated in Umbria, the green heart of Italy, in the well-preserved hilltop town of Montefalco with its 13th-century Francescano frescoes, this splendid villa was once a private home. Although the hotel is managed with professional skill, the gracious Pambuffetti family has a magic touch that makes each guest feel very special. The decision to transform their country house into a 15-room inn seemed a natural choice when Signora Pambuffetti's daughter, Alessandra, and her husband, Mauro, returned from the United States with a wealth of experience in the hotel and restaurant business. Alessandra demonstrates her culinary skills preparing Umbrian specialties for guests. Her delicious cakes, tarts, and homemade jams are part of the full breakfast served in the elegant cream-and-dusty-rose-colored dining room. Here guests are treated to the same spectacular panoramic view taking in Assisi, Perugia, Spoleto, and Spello as described by the Nobel-prize-winning author Herman Hesse in 1907. The villa itself, with its manicured gardens (which now have a swimming pool) and centuries-old cypress trees, is also mentioned. Every small detail is tended to in the individually decorated rooms with their travertine marble bathrooms. The room in the tower, the Torre dell'Amore, with its 360-degree vistas, is a favorite.

*VILLA PAMBUFFETTI*
*Owners: Pambuffetti family*
*Via della Vittoria, 20*
*06036 Montefalco (PG), Italy*
*Tel: (0742) 37 94 17, Fax: (0742) 37 92 45*
*E-mail: villabianca@interbusiness.it*
*15 rooms, Double: Lire 285,000–420,000*
*Open all year, Credit cards: all major*
*Restaurant closed in winter*
*30 km S of Assisi, 80 km NE of Orvieto*
*Region: Umbria, Michelin Map 430*
*www.karenbrown.com/italyinns/villapambuffetti.html*

Il Borghetto Country Inn is an absolute dream and though a little hard to find, with our instructions you should have no problem. The charming owners, Rosi and Roberto Cavallini, are in the fashion promotion business in Milan. Wanting a hideaway in the countryside, they bought a long-neglected farmhouse in the heart of the exquisite Chianti district and totally renovated it. Later, they also bought the farmhouse next door, restored it to perfection, and opened a tiny hotel. Although the hotel is run in a most professional manner (their son, Antonio Cavallini, manages the property when they are in Milan) and guests have their own intimate lounge and dining room, there is nothing commercial about it—you really feel like a guest in a private home. Signora Cavallini did all the decorating and every detail is superb, with beautiful fabrics, original paintings, Oriental carpets, and fine antiques. Each individually decorated guestroom displays great taste. A lovely swimming pool is tucked into one of the gardens—a wonderful bonus. But the best I've saved for last—the view. It is incredible: a sweeping vista of vineyards and olive groves stretching as far as the eye can see. *Directions*: About 17 km south of Florence. From the Florence-Siena expressway exit at Bargino. As you exit, turn right and then almost immediately turn up the hill toward Montefiridolfi. About 2.6 km after leaving the highway, Il Borghetto is on your right. Look carefully for a tiny "Il Borghetto" sign on the left side of the green gates, then ring the bell for reception.

*IL BORGHETTO COUNTRY INN*
*Owners: Rosi & Roberto Cavallini*
*Via Collina S. Angelo, 23*
*50020 Montefiridolfi (FI), Italy*
*Tel: (055) 82 44 442, Fax: (055) 82 44 247*
*9 rooms, Double: Lire 300,000–500,000*
*Open Mar to Nov, 3-day minimum*
*Credit cards: AX, VS*
*No restaurant, lunch & dinner by special request*
*17 km S of Florence*
*Region: Tuscany, Michelin Map 430*

La Chiusa, nestled in the hills of Tuscany southeast of Siena, is an old stone farmhouse whose restaurant is so well known that guests come from far and wide to enjoy the meals where everything is fresh, homemade, and delicious. Dania and Umberto Lucherini are the gracious owners and Dania is the talented chef. Almost all the vegetables, olive oil, meats, wines, and cheeses come either from the inn's own farm or from those nearby. The original wood-burning oven still stands in the courtyard in front of the inn, emitting delicious aromas of freshly baking bread. The dining room is large and airy, with an uncluttered simple elegance enhanced by windows overlooking rolling hills. When the weather is balmy, meals are also served on the back terrace, which is ideally positioned to capture a sweeping view. The emphasis here is definitely on the exquisite meals, but there are also bedrooms for guests who want to spend the night. Like the dining room, the guestrooms are perfectly in keeping with the ambiance of the old farmhouse, lovely in their rustic simplicity yet with every modern convenience. In addition to the standard guestrooms, there are some deluxe suites—one even has an olive press in the bathroom!

*LA CHIUSA*
*Owners: Lucherini family*
*Manager: Franco Sodi*
*Via della Madonnina, 88*
*53040 Montefollonico (SI), Italy*
*Tel: (0577) 66 96 68, Fax: (0577) 66 95 93*
*14 rooms, Double: Lire 350,000–550,000*
*4 suites: Lire 690,000–850,000*
*Open Mar 2 to Nov 15, Credit cards: all major*
*Restaurant closed Tuesdays*
*60 km S of Siena, 10 km NW of Montepulciano*
*Region: Tuscany, Michelin Map 430*

Tucked inside the tiny picturesque walled village of Montefollonico, Locanda La Costa is an intimate, family-run hotel with an outstanding restaurant where you can enjoy a typical Tuscan-style meal with everything freshly prepared. When I first visited, Patrizia and Paolo Masini, your gracious hosts, had a small restaurant in Montefollonico (where Paolo was the chef) and had just expanded by opening a small hotel a few blocks away. The new venture become so successful that they increased the number of guestrooms, and Paolo moved his restaurant to a more commodious facility next to the hotel. The Locanda La Costa is built within a medieval stone house, which has been restored with loving attention to detail. You enter into a reception area and then down a few steps into a most appealing breakfast room enhanced by exposed stone walls and arches. This opens onto a wine bar. However, it is not until you step outside to the rear of the hotel that its most outstanding feature is revealed—a splendid terrace with a sweeping, 180-degree view of rolling hills and perched medieval villages—a view which cannot be surpassed at any price. For lunch and dinner, Tuscan specialties are served in the restaurant or on the panoramic terrace. The Locanda used to be very inexpensive, but with the expansion, the quality of the rooms has been upgraded and the prices increased. There are many suites, but the prize rooms are the most recently added doubles—these have terraces with stunning vistas. *Directions*: Located inside the walled village.

*LOCANDA LA COSTA*
*Owners: Masini family*
*Via Coppoli, 15*
*53040 Montefollonico (SI), Italy*
*Tel: (0577) 66 94 88, Fax: (0577) 66 88 00*
*E-mail: info@lacosta.it*
*12 rooms, Double: Lire 250,000–350,000*
*Open all year, Credit cards: all major, Restaurant open daily*
*60 km S of Siena, 10 km NW of Montepulciano*
*Region: Tuscany, Michelin Map 430*
*www.karenbrown.com/italyinns/locandalacosta.html*

The tiny medieval village of Montegridolfo, nestling on the crown of a gentle hill, seems too perfect to be real—everything looks fresh and new and all the buildings homogeneous. At first it is a bit confusing because every picture-perfect little restaurant, shop, and boutique has the same buff-colored brick façade, the same pretty red geraniums out front, and the same white embroidered curtains peeking behind brown-shuttered windows. Yes, the village is real, but was totally reconstructed at one time as one development. The Albergo Palazzo Viviani, a part of this development, is a hotel converted from a noble palace and still retains the charm of a private home. The living room with its honey-colored walls, oil paintings, opulent drapes, open fireplace, and handsome antique furnishings is extremely attractive. Upstairs are eight elegant, luxurious guestrooms. The most dramatic is the Affreschi suite, with gorgeous frescoes on the walls, ornately painted ceiling, and, best of all, windows on three sides letting light stream into the room. In a separate building in the garden there are more rooms, each named for a flower. These guestrooms are less expensive, but although smaller than those in the Palazzo, are beautifully decorated. Also in the garden there is a gorgeous swimming pool. There are also five suites in various buildings around the town. *Directions:* From A14 take the Pesaro-Urbino exit. Follow signs to Montecchio then turn right following signs to Montegridolfo.

*ALBERGO PALAZZO VIVIANI*
*Director: Giancarlo Bartolini*
*47837 Montegridolfo (RN), Italy*
*Tel: (0541) 85 53 50, Fax: (0541) 85 53 40*
*24 rooms, Double: Lire 390,000–600,000*
*Open all year*
*Credit cards: all major*
*Restaurant*
*35 km NW of Rimini*
*Region: Emilia-Romagna, Michelin Map 430*

Nestled in the tranquil Tuscan countryside between two enchanting hilltop villages (Pienza and Monticchiello), is another jewel, L'Olmo. You cannot help instantly losing your heart to this very special little hotel. It has the warmth and intimacy of a bed and breakfast, yet the service and amenities rival those of the finest deluxe hotel. This bit of paradise is owned by the Lindo family. A few years ago they left the bustling city of Turin and bought a beautiful 16th-century stone house, which they lovingly restored to perfection, down to the smallest detail, preserving original terra-cotta floors and wood-beamed ceilings. With superb taste and guests' comfort in mind, five suites were created and appointed with antique chests, locally made wrought-iron beds, and pretty floral fabrics for color. Each has its own travertine marble bathroom and two have a fireplace. The two suites on the ground floor have their own garden and whirlpool bathtubs. Francesca and her mother Loredana, your exceptionally charming hostesses, tend to guests in a warm and highly professional manner. Common rooms downstairs include two cozy sitting rooms with fireplace and invitingly soft armchairs, leading out to the stone courtyard with tables and large pots of flowers. A full buffet breakfast or gourmet candlelit dinner—upon request—is served in the luminous dining room. Outdoors is the swimming pool with a 360-degree view over the soft green countryside. *Directions*: From Pienza continue straight southward out of town and after 6 km turn left for Monticchiello. Signs indicate the bed and breakfast, on your right, before you come to Monticchiello.

*L'OLMO*
*Owners: Francesca & Loredana Lindo*
*53020 Localita: Monticchiello di Pienza (SI), Italy*
*Tel: (0578) 75 51 33, Fax: (0578) 75 51 24*
*E-mail: olmopienza@iol.it*
*5 suites, 1 room & 1 apt, Double: Lire 270,000–430,000*
*Open Apr to Nov, Credit cards: all major*
*No restaurant, dinner upon request*
*6 km S of Pienza, Region: Tuscany, Michelin Map 430*
*www.karenbrown.com/italyinns/lolmo.html*

The promontory of Argentario, facing the islands of Giglio and Giannutri, has always been a favorite seaside haven for Romans. The area is well worth a visit with its long beaches, fishing towns, spectacular panoramic coastal drive, and picturesque inland villages in the Maremma countryside. Hotels tend to be rather basic in the area so it was a surprise to come across the San Biagio right in the quaint town of Orbetello, a narrow strip of land between two lakes connecting Argentario to the mainland. The Magnosi family from Rome recently bought and restored the palazzo, originally a private residence dating back to 1851. They have recreated the feeling of a noble's home, not only in the rich furnishings, but also with the many original architectural features of the palazzo itself. Some of these wonderful features include the arched entrance hall that leads to a small courtyard where meals are served (also to non-guests), the high ceilinged rooms with ornate moldings and frescoed borders, and the central staircase leading up to the thirteen double rooms and four suites. The family's valuable antique pieces collected throughout Europe adorn both the downstairs and upstairs sitting rooms as well as the bedrooms. Very comfortable bedrooms are richly appointed and have luxurious marble travertine bathrooms (the suite has two bathrooms). Cordial manager, Sonia, is available to assist guests with area itineraries. Although the San Biagio offers no views in a seaside location, it offers top-level accommodation at exceptional comparative rates. *Directions*: From the N1, take the exit to Orbetello and go to the old part of town. Facing the church (*Duomo*), Via Dante is the street the runs to its left side.

*SAN BIAGIO*
*Owners: Gianfranco Magnosi family*
*Via Dante, 34*
*58015 Orbetello (GR), Italy*
*Tel: (0564) 86 05 43, Fax: (0564) 86 77 87*
*17 rooms, Double: Lire 240,000–380,000, Open all year*
*Credit cards: MC, VS, No restaurant, breakfast only*
*Center of Orbetello, 160 km N of Rome*
*Region: Tuscany, Michelin Map 430*

The town of Orvieto, just off the main expressway between Rome and Florence, is one of the most picturesque of all the Umbrian hilltowns. This small city is perched on the top of a hill—an intriguing sight that can be viewed from many kilometers away. Less than a ten-minute drive south of Orvieto is a 12th-century Gothic abbey that has been converted into a hotel where you can stay surrounded by the romantic ruins of yesteryear. Although there is a commercial air to La Badia, the reception is caring. The director, Ettore Pelletti, has been with the hotel for over 20 years, as has the chef. So, as you can see, there is a real continuity of management. Although this is not a cozy, small hotel, you are bound to enjoy the setting, the pool, the old-world ambiance, and the food. The dining room is one of the most attractive rooms in the hotel. It has an enormous, high-vaulted stone ceiling, wrought-iron fixtures, heavy wooden beams, eye-catching copper accents, and, at one end, a cavernous fireplace complete with a roasting spit. The standard bedrooms, although not large or with inspired decor, are comfortable and many have a stunning view up to the town of Orvieto. If you want to splurge, ask for one of the romantic suites, which have much prettier furnishings. In the meadows behind the monastery there is a pool, which makes a welcome respite from a day on the road. *Directions*: From Orvieto, follow signs for Viterro. The hotel is 4 km south of Orvieto.

*LA BADIA*
*Owner: Contessa Luisa Fiumi*
*Manager: Ettore Pelletti*
*05019 Orvieto Scalo (TR), Italy*
*Tel: (0763) 30 19 59, Fax: (0763) 30 53 96*
*26 rooms, Double: Lire 300,000–340,000*
*Suite: Lire 440,000–550,000*
*Closed Jan & Feb, Credit cards: all major*
*Restaurant closed Wednesdays*
*4 km S of Orvieto, 115 km N of Rome*
*Region: Umbria, Michelin Map 430*

The Villa le Barone was once the home of the famous Tuscan family, Della Robbia, whose beautiful terra cottas are still seen throughout Italy. Most of the estate has now been converted into a deluxe small hotel, but the present owner, Duchessa Franca Viviani Della Robbia, still maintains a charming vine-covered cottage for her own use. Although she is now in her 90s, the Duchessa comes frequently to the villa to ensure that her impeccable standards and taste prevail. Staying at the Villa le Barone is very much like being the guest in a private, elegant home set in the gorgeous Tuscan hills. The lounges are especially inviting, beautifully furnished with charming, family antiques. There are 30 guestrooms, all of which vary in size and are individually decorated with a somewhat dated charm. In addition, there is a lovely swimming pool, romantically set on a terrace looking over the vineyards and out to the mellow hills beyond. Wonderful little hideaways are found secluded in the parklike setting where guests can find a quiet nook to read or just to sit and soak in the beauty. Dinner is served in the restaurant, which formerly housed the stables. *Directions*: From the center of Panzano, follow signs to the hotel.

*VILLA LE BARONE*
*Owner: Duchessa Franca Viviani Della Robbia*
*Manager: Caterina Buonamici*
*Via San Leolino, 19*
*50020 Panzano in Chianti (FI), Italy*
*Tel: (055) 85 26 21, Fax: (055) 85 22 77*
*30 rooms, Double: Lire 390,000–500,000\**
*\*Rate includes breakfast & dinner*
*Open Apr to Nov, Credit cards: all major*
*Restaurant open daily for guests only*
*31 km S of Florence, 6 km S of Greve*
*Region: Tuscany, Michelin Map 430*

Relax in the countryside just 6 kilometers from the bustling city of Verona at the exquisite Villa del Quar where you can enjoy excellent accommodations, gourmet dining, and the warmth and charm of a family-managed hotel. The gracious owner, Leopoldo Montresor, is a talented architect who spared no expense to assure that his renovations resulted in an estate exuding charm and taste. The Montresors live in one wing of the villa, conveniently close for Evelina Acampora-Montresor who manages the hotel. The property has been in the Montresor family for many generations—ever since Leopoldo's great-great-great-grandfather won the land in a game of cards at the casino in Venice in the early 1800s. Your heart will be captivated from the moment you pass the family chapel and enter the reception lounge, elegantly decorated with finely upholstered sofas in warm shades of pinks and mellow yellows. Sunlight floods the room through a wall of windows, which open onto an inviting side terrace where guests dine in warm weather. There is also a superb 16th-century wine cellar and a most attractive beamed-ceilinged dining room where meals are served elegantly on tables set with fine linens. The guestrooms are equally appealing and furnished in antiques. A large swimming pool is set enchantingly in a meadow with vineyards stretching almost to the edge of the pool.

*HOTEL VILLA DEL QUAR*
*Owners: Evelina Acampora-Montresor & Leopoldo Montresor*
*Via Quar N12, 37020 Pedemonte (VR), Italy*
*Tel: (045) 68 00 681, Fax: (045) 68 00 604*
*E-mail: villadelquar@c-point.it*
*22 rooms, Double: Lire 480,000*
*Suite: from Lire 670,000*
*Open mid-Mar to Dec, Credit cards: all major*
*Restaurant open daily*
*Relais & Châteaux*
*6 km N of Verona, 22 km E of Lake Garda*
*Region: Veneto, Michelin Map 429*
*www.karenbrown.com/italyinns/hotelvilladelquar.html*

The Castel Pergine is a storybook castle delightfully transformed into a small hotel, perfect for the budget-minded tourist. No need to forfeit romance and glamour, for even though the Castel Pergine is good value for money, it has a fabulous location dominating a hilltop above the town of Pergine with incredible views out over the valleys and wooded hills. The Castel Pergine is more famous as a restaurant than a hotel—the dining room has an engaging medieval decor, gorgeous views, and good food. When Verena and Theo Schneider-Neff came from Switzerland and took over the hotel, they made many improvements, including installing a state-of-the-art kitchen. They also upgraded the bedrooms to add snug shower rooms, something they continue to do so that eventually all the rooms will have private shower rooms. The guestrooms range from rather simple to comfortably charming, the more expensive having en-suite showers, handsome wooden paneling, and country-style furnishings. Room 27, a corner room, is especially pretty, but the beds are shorter and narrower than in the other superior rooms. The Castel Pergine is a real bargain and its secluded hilltop setting is definitely a winner. *Directions*: Exit the autostrada at Trento Nord and follow signs for Padova to Pergine (10 km beyond Trento). Exit for *centro* and at the first roundabout take the first exit and at the second the second exit. After 1 km turn left at the chapel. Do not go into the center of Pergine.

*CASTEL PERGINE*
*Managers: Verena & Theo Schneider-Neff*
*38057 Pergine (TN), Italy*
*Tel: (0461) 53 11 58, Fax: (0461) 53 13 29*
*E-mail: verena@castelpergine.it*
*21 rooms, Double: Lire 180,000–240,000\**
*\*Rate includes breakfast & dinner*
*Open Easter to Nov, Credit cards: all major*
*Restaurant open daily in high season*
*10 km E of Trento, 2.5 km E of Pergine*
*Region: Trentino-Alto Adige, Michelin Map 429*
*www.karenbrown.com/italyinns/castelpergine.html*

I am such a romantic that, as the boat chugged across Lake Maggiore from Stresa to the medieval fishing village of Isola dei Pescatori (Fisherman's Island) and I saw the Hotel Verbano with its reddish-brown walls, dark-green shutters, and tables set on the terrace overlooking the lake, my heart was won—completely. To accommodate the many people who clamber off the excursion boats each day to visit this picturesque island, the hotel has a large dining room with arched windows overlooking the lake. However, when the weather is warm, the favorite place to dine is outside on the idyllic terrace overlooking nearby Isola Bella (Beautiful Island). In the evening, when most of the tourists have departed, the terrace becomes even more romantic—particularly with a full moon reflecting on the rippling water. The food is excellent, featuring fish fresh from the lake. The 12 bedrooms, all with a lake view, are delightful, with high ceilings, wooden floors, and modern bathrooms. Several have balconies and three share a large terrace. *Directions*: Exit the A26 at Stresa and follow signposts for the waterfront where you take the public ferry to Isola dei Pescatori (the ferry is much cheaper than the private water taxis).

*HOTEL VERBANO*
*Owners: Alberto & Roberto Zacchera, Ermano Gafforini*
*Via Ugo Ara, 2*
*28838 Isola dei Pescatori, Stresa*
*Borromee Isole, Lake Maggiore (VB), Italy*
*Tel: (0323) 30 408, Fax: (0323) 33 129*
*E-mail: hotelverbano@tin.it*
*12 rooms, Double: Lire 250,000*
*Open all year, Credit cards: all major*
*Restaurant open daily*
*80 km NW of Milan, ferry from Stresa*
*Region: Lombardy, Michelin Map 428*
*www.karenbrown.com/italyinns/hotelverbano.html*

When it comes to dining in Cortona, you find the most inventive array of Tuscan-based recipes at the famed Tonino's restaurant with its terrace overlooking the entire valley. Following a long family tradition in hospitality and exceptional fare, daughter Ilaria is the young hostess at the newly opened Alla Corte del Sole. Her family bought and completely restructured a group of five 16th-century brick houses as an elegantly rustic country lodging. No two rooms are alike in dimension, taking on the natural shape of the houses, although each has been individually decorated with fine brocade fabrics and antiques set off beautifully against the country simplicity of beams and brick floors. The delightful bathrooms have been personalized by a local artist whose whimsical designs reflect the various room names. A bountiful buffet breakfast with a table full of fresh-baked goods from grandmother's kitchen is served in its own house opposite those with rooms. A passion for flowers is evident in the surrounding garden, which leads to a large swimming pool. Bordering Umbria and Tuscany, the Corte is just the right place from which to easily explore highlights of both regions. *Directions*: Exit from the A1 autostrada at Valchiana and follow signs for Perugia. Take the second Cortona exit towards Montepulciano, driving 7 km to the turnoff for Petrignano-Pozzolo. The hotel is after Petrignano and just before I Giorgi.

*ALLA CORTE DEL SOLE*       *New*
*Owner: Ilaria Spiganti*
*Localita: I Giorni*
*06061 Petrignano (PG), Italy*
*Tel: (075) 96 89 008, Fax: (075) 96 89 070*
*E-mail: info@cortedelsole.com*
*22 rooms, Double: Lire 250,000–290,000*
*No restaurant, breakfast only*
*Open all year, Credit cards: MC, VS*
*16 km S of Cortona*
*Region: Tuscany, Michelin Map 430*
*www.karenbrown.com/italyinns/allacortedelsole.html*

It is difficult to find a hotel in Rome with windows thick enough to keep out the ever-present buzz of traffic. Less than an hour's drive from the city, the Borgo Paraelios offers the perfect solution: a luxurious country villa immersed in the lovely Tuscan-like hills of Sabina. In this splendid villa, filled to the brim with elegant antiques, rich, warm-colored tapestries, and period paintings, it is impossible to find a detail overlooked. It is a masterpiece of harmonizing old and new, with antique terra-cotta tile floors, stone fireplaces, beamed ceilings, and antique doors from castles and villas brought here and cleverly incorporated into the building. The very inviting bedrooms, each with its own character and color scheme, look out over the lush garden where guests can breakfast among flower-laden terra-cotta pots. Meandering through the gracious living room, two libraries, and billiard and bridge rooms, one has the sense of having been invited to the country home of nobility for a weekend of absolute peace and tranquillity. A nine-hole golf course (discounted for guests) and a spectacular indoor swimming pool add to the ambiance. For an additional charge, transportation is available to and from Rome. When you return from the bustle of the city, exquisite meals are served in the frescoed formal dining room. *Directions:* Go north from Rome on the A1 and exit at Fiano Romano toward Passo Corese. Go left on S.S. 313. The hotel is on your left after about 16 km.

*HOTEL BORGO PARAELIOS*     ***New***
*Owner: Adolfo Salabé*
*Localita: Valle Collicchia*
*02040 Poggio Mirteto (RI), Italy*
*Tel: (0765) 26 267, Fax: (0765) 26 268*
*18 rooms, Double: Lire 450,000–550,000*
*Open all year, Credit cards: all major*
*Restaurant closed Tuesdays*
*Relais & Châteaux*
*45 km NE of Rome, 2 km N of Poggio Mirteto*
*Region: Lazio, Michelin Map 430*

Gennarino a Mare is primarily a restaurant—one of the best-known in Ponza both for its seafood specialties and its prime location right on the waterfront. It even has a large deck that stretches out over the water, built upon sturdy wooden pilings. Gennarino a Mare is a favorite place to dine, especially in summer when boats of all shapes and sizes dock alongside at the adjacent pier and the merry yacht set comes to eat and drink. The restaurant has hosted many of the world's rich and famous, so no telling who might be sitting at the next table—unfortunately I just missed seeing Sidney Poitier. It is no wonder the restaurant is so popular: as you enjoy your dinner, you can watch the reflection of the fishing boats shimmering in the water and, behind them, the gaily painted houses of Ponza stepping up the hill like brightly painted blocks. The property's gracious owner, Francesco Silvestri, was born right in the same house where the restaurant now stands. His parents lived here and ran a small *pension*—before that, it was the home of his grandmother. The 12 simple bedrooms, located on the floors above the restaurant, are all decorated similarly with colorful matching drapes and bedspreads setting off white walls. Although small, each room has its own little step-out balcony with a romantic view. Remember, Gennarino a Mare is basically a restaurant—in no way a luxury hotel, but a real winner for a simple, reasonably priced place to stay in Ponza.

*GENNARINO A MARE*
*Owner: Francesco Silvestri*
*Via Dante, 64*
*04027 Isola di Ponza (LT), Italy*
*Tel: (0771) 80 071, Fax: (0771) 80 140*
*12 rooms, Double: Lire 220,000–380,000*
*Open all year, Credit cards: all major*
*Restaurant open daily*
*Facing harbor in heart of Ponza*
*Island of Ponza, ferry from Anzio*
*Region: Lazio, Michelin Map 430*

The Al Vecchio Convento is a real gem, offering quality accommodation for a moderate price. Its several dining rooms are brimming with rustic country charm and serve delicious meals prepared from local produce. There are 15 guestrooms, each with a private bathroom and each tastefully decorated with antiques. Portico di Romagna is, like the inn, inviting yet unpretentious—a very old village surrounded by wooded hills and clear mountain streams. A stroll through medieval pathways that twist down between the weathered stone houses leads you to an ancient stone bridge gracefully arching over a rushing stream. The inn too is very old. At first I thought its origin must have been an old convent because of its name, but the wonderfully gracious owner, Marisa Raggi, told me that the name came from a restaurant, located in a convent, that she and her husband, Giovanni (who is the chef), used to operate. Later, when they moved the restaurant to its present location and added a few guestrooms, they kept the original name, Al Vecchio Convento. The restaurant is still their main focus, featuring fine meals beautifully prepared from local produce. Due to the winding, two-lane mountain highway that leads to the village, it takes about two hours to drive from Florence, but if you enjoy the adventure of exploring Italy's back-roads, this small hotel will certainly be one of your favorites, as it is mine.

*ALBERGO AL VECCHIO CONVENTO*
*Owners: Marisa Raggi & Giovanni Cameli*
*Via Roma, 7*
*47010 Portico di Romagna (FO), Italy*
*Tel: (0543) 96 70 53, Fax: (0543) 96 71 57*
*E-mail: info@vecchioconvento.it*
*15 rooms, Double: Lire 200,000*
*Open all year, Credit cards: all major*
*Restaurant open for hotel guests*
*75 km NE of Florence, 34 km SW of Forli*
*Region:Tuscany, Michelin Map 429/430*
*www.karenbrown.com/italyinns/albergoalvecchio.html*

The Il Pellicano (one of Italy's most idyllic hotels) has been beautifully designed in the traditional villa style and, although not old, looks as though it has snuggled on its prime hillside position overlooking the Mediterranean for many years. The façade is of stucco, painted a typical Italian russet and set off by a heavily tiled roof. Vines enwrap the building, further enhancing its appealing look. You enter into a spacious, attractive lobby where the sun streams through the windows enhancing the white walls, terra-cotta floors, and wood-beamed ceilings. The cheerful ambiance continues with pretty sofas, antique accents, and enormous displays of fresh flowers enlivening every conceivable nook and cranny. The overall impression is one of light and color—and impeccable taste. Beyond the reception area is a spacious terrace where sometimes the chef prepares elaborate buffets, served out of doors overlooking the exquisite bay (the food at Il Pellicano is expensive, but truly exceptional). From the terrace, a lawn dotted with pine trees extends down the hillside to where there is a beautiful pool romantically perched at the cliff's edge. From the bluff, both steps and an elevator access a pier at the water's edge. Off the stairs, small individual terraces with lounge chairs and mats for sunning have been built into the rocks. The hotel also has a spa, beauty salon, and tennis court.

*IL PELLICANO*
*Manager: Signora Cinzia Fanciulli*
*58018 Porto Ercole (GR), Italy*
*Tel: (0564) 85 81 11, Fax: (0564) 83 34 18*
*E-mail: info@pellicanohotel.com*
*31 rooms, Double: Lire 530,000–1,345,000*
*19 suites: Lire 825,000–2,740,000*
*Open Apr to Oct, Credit cards: all major*
*Restaurant open daily, Relais & Châteaux*
*South end of peninsula, Hwy 1 exit Orbetello*
*160 km N of Rome, 4.5 km S of Porto Ercole*
*Region: Tuscany, Michelin Map 430*
*www.karenbrown.com/italyinns/ilpellicano.html*

Standing proudly on the cliffs overlooking one of Italy's most spectacular coastlines are the remains of a 13th-century Spanish watchtower. The tower has been cleverly incorporated into, and stands as the dramatic symbol for, the Hotel Torre di Cala Piccola which shares a beautiful small promontory (called Cala Piccola) with luxurious private villas discreetly hidden behind high walls. The hotel looks as though it too might be a private home. The first part of the hotel you see (which houses the reception area, lounge, and bar) is a sienna-toned building with red-tiled roof and green shutters, snuggled amongst silvery olive trees and flowering oleanders. The moderately sized, nicely decorated guestrooms are not in the main building, but instead share romantic stone cottages. Some of the accommodations are designated as one-room apartments with a divider creating a separate sitting area. However, these are a bit cut up and I much preferred the regular doubles. The cottages are strategically placed amongst the trees on the property to capture the view. And what a view! It definitely rivals some of the world's finest coastal beauties such as Italy's Amalfi Drive or California's Big Sur. High cliffs drop precipitously down to the sea, forming a series of coves where the rich blue water of the Mediterranean dances in the sunlight. Also capturing this absolutely stunning vista are a lush lawn where breakfast is served and, on a lower terrace, a dramatic swimming pool, which seems to almost float high above the sea.

*HOTEL TORRE DI CALA PICCOLA*
*Manager: Franco Borracci*
*Cala Piccola, 58019 Porto Santo Stefano (GR), Italy*
*Tel: (0564) 82 51 11, Fax: (0564) 82 52 35*
*50 rooms, Double: Lire 375,000–520,000*
*E-mail: prenotazioni@torredicalapiccola.com*
*Open mid-Mar to Nov, Credit cards: all major*
*Beach restaurant open daily*
*On the coast, 10 km SW of Porto Santo Stefano*
*Region: Tuscany, Michelin Map 430*
*www.karenbrown.com/italyinns/torredicalapiccola.html*

If money doesn't matter, when in Portofino settle in for a long stay at the incomparable Hotel Splendido. But since not everyone's travel budget can stretch to such luxury, the Hotel Eden is a welcome alternative. Although the price at the Eden might seem high for the accommodation offered, just remember that Portofino is the target of the wealthy from around the world, and rates in restaurants and places to stay reflect this popularity. If you are prepared for simplicity (tempered with the warmth of hospitality offered at family-run hotels), you will be happy to discover the Eden, tucked right in the heart of Portofino, not facing the harbor, but down a little lane, just two minutes' walk away. Wrought-iron gates open to steps leading to the front garden, a peaceful oasis of flowers and green lawn. Facing the garden is a side terrace where meals are served outside when the weather is warm. The hotel is a soft mustard-colored villa with green shutters. As you enter, to the right is a porch-like dining room. Farther on you find the registration desk where the personable Signor Osta will probably be waiting to check you in. The guestrooms we saw were simply decorated but have been refurnished since our last visit. The best rooms are on the second floor—these are larger and have better facilities.

*HOTEL EDEN*
*Owner: Ferruccio Osta*
*Via Dritto, 18*
*16034 Portofino (GE), Italy*
*Tel: (0185) 26 90 91, Fax: (0185) 26 90 47*
*E-mail: eden@ifree.it*
*12 rooms, Double: Lire 300,000–450,000*
*Open all year, Credit cards: all major*
*Restaurant closed Mondays*
*5 km S of Santa Margherita Ligure*
*35 km E of Genoa*
*Region: Liguria, Michelin Map 428*
*www.karenbrown.com/italyinns/hoteleden.html*

Located up a winding, wooded road high above the town of Portofino, the super-deluxe Hotel Splendido sits majestically above the beautiful blue Mediterranean, overlooking the boats moored in Portofino's lovely harbor. Stretching across the front of the hotel is a magnificent terrace—a favorite choice of guests who enjoy dining outside with an incredible vista of the sea. As would be expected in such a world-class hotel, the food is outstanding and beautifully served. Leading from the hotel are romantic little pathways where you can stroll through the wooded grounds and stop along the way at strategically placed benches to enjoy incomparable views. For those who would like more serious exercise, on a terrace below the hotel is an enormous swimming pool, while located in the gardens to the left of the hotel are tennis courts. The public rooms are charming, with comfortable chairs covered with floral prints and fresh flowers galore. Every detail is perfect and in excellent taste. The bedrooms too are lovely and decorator-perfect, many with balconies affording a splendid view of Portofino. The Splendido is expensive, but without a doubt one of the most special resorts in Italy.

*HOTEL SPLENDIDO*
*Manager: Maurizio Saccani*
*16034 Portofino (GE), Italy*
*Tel: (0185) 26 78 01, Fax: (0185) 26 78 06*
*69 rooms, Double: Lire 1,540,000–3,290,000\**
*\*Rate includes breakfast & dinner or lunch*
*Open Mar 24 to Jan*
*Credit cards: all major*
*Restaurant open daily*
*5 km S of Santa Margherita Ligure*
*35 km E of Genoa*
*Region: Liguria*
*Michelin Map 428*

Ask any experienced traveler to name one of the most picturesque harbors in the world, and tiny Portofino, with its cluster of colorful houses reflecting in the turquoise sea, is always right on top of the list. However, this adorable town has only a few places to stay, so it was with great excitement that we learned that one of our very favorite inns, Hotel Splendido (a dazzling jewel on the hillside overlooking Portofino), was opening an extension in the center of town. We had the privilege of being among the first to see this lovely new hotel, maneuvering from room to room as the final coats of paint were being applied. As would be expected, this new facility rates only superlatives. Everything is done in excellent taste and the quality in every detail is supreme. The ambiance and beautiful decor is much like its "sister" hotel on the hill, with a similar elegantly serene color scheme. There is a pretty, fresh quality throughout, with gleaming hardwood floors, light-colored wood furnishings, and beautiful fabrics. Nothing is heavy or formal—a refined yet happy, cheerful ambiance prevails. The food also is of the same superb standards as the Splendido, with meals served either in a charming dining room or else outside on the terrace overlooking the harbor. If you want to be at the heart of the action of picturesque Portofino, especially if you enjoy watching the glamorous yachts pull into the harbor, the Splendido Mare makes an excellent choice. An added bonus: you can use all of the facilities at the Splendido, which is just a sweet walk away along a romantic wooded path.

*SPLENDIDO MARE*
*Manager: Maurizio Saccani*
*16034 Portofino (GE), Italy*
*Tel: (0185) 26 78 02, Fax: (0185) 26 78 07*
*16 rooms, Double: Lire 870,000–1,210,000*
*Open all year, Credit cards: all major*
*Restaurant open daily*
*35 km E of Genoa*
*Region: Liguria, Michelin Map 428*

The Albergo Casa Albertina is a prime example of what a difference management can make. There is a wide choice of hotels in the picturesque little fishing village of Positano—many, like the Casa Albertina, with spectacular views, pleasant decor, and good meals. However, they don't have Michele Cinque, who is an outstanding hotelier: gracious and warmhearted—willing to do whatever is required to make each guest feel very special. It is not surprising that Michele is such a pro—he had been in the hotel business for many years, having been the manager of one of Positano's most deluxe hotels (Le Sirenuse) before deciding to help his wife and mother-in-law (who died in 2000) manage the Casa Albertina full-time. Although Michele has partially retired, his two sons extend the same warmth of welcome as their father and son Lorenzo has officially taken over the management of the hotel. All of the bedrooms have a view and are nicely decorated. Ask for one of the largest rooms—these only cost a bit more. The hotel (which is built into a 12th-century house) clings to the hillside above Positano, a position that affords superlative views, but also means a strenuous walk into town. There are also many steps from the parking area to the hotel. *Directions:* As you drive down the hill into Positano, there is a sign on the left pointing to the winding, walking-alleyway to the hotel.

*ALBERGO CASA ALBERTINA*
*Owners: Cinque family*
*Via della Tavolozza, 3*
*84017 Positano (SA), Italy*
*Tel: (089) 87 51 43, Fax: (089) 81 15 40*
*E-mail: info@casalbertina.it*
*20 rooms, Double: Lire 380,000–400,000\**
*\*Rate includes breakfast & dinner*
*Open all year, Credit cards: all major*
*Restaurant open daily for guests only*
*Amalfi Coast, 55 km S of Naples, 17 km S of Sorrento*
*Region: Campania, Michelin Map 431*
*www.karenbrown.com/italyinns/albergocasaalbertina.html*

*Hotel Descriptions*

The intimate Buca di Bacco won our hearts immediately—not that it is super-elegant or grandly deluxe, but it possesses all the ingredients that make a hotel very, very special. It has an unbeatable location directly on the beach in the center of Positano, charming decor, excellent food, and spectacular views and—most important of all—radiates a graciously warm welcome. It is no wonder that the hospitality is so genuine: the Rispoli family has been catering to guests for three generations. Grandfather Rispoli emigrated to the United States many years ago but his heart always longed for his beautiful Positano, so when he saved enough money, he returned and bought a small property right on the beach where he opened a restaurant with guestrooms. Following generations have expanded the hotel and restaurant, but have always maintained grandfather's hospitality. From the moment you enter, you will be impressed by the tasteful decor. The lobby has a tiled floor in a beautiful green, yellow, and white design. The greens and yellow are picked up in the various fabrics used throughout. Salvatore Rispoli is often at the front desk, but the entire family is busy behind the scenes. Salvatore's sister is responsible for the glorious flower arrangements, while Carla and Nicodemo Rispoli are often in the kitchen overseeing the excellent meals. Almost all of the rooms have either a balcony or a terrace with a view. If you really want to splurge, ask for the most deluxe room, number 10, an exceptional corner room with an enormous terrace and the best view in Positano.

*BUCA DI BACCO*     **New**
*Owners: Rispoli family*
*Via Rampa Teglia, 4*
*84017 Positano (SA), Italy*
*Tel: (089) 87 56 99, Fax: (089) 87 57 31*
*E-mail: bacco@starnet.it*
*47 rooms, Double: Lire 350,000–570,000*
*Closed Nov to Mar, Credit cards: all major*
*Restaurant open daily*
*Amalfi Coast, 55 km S of Naples, 17 km S of Sorrento*
*Region: Campania, Michelin Map 431*
*www.karenbrown.com/italyinns/bucadibacco.html*

For those who want to in the heart of the colorful fishing village of Positano, the Palazzo Murat, a charming, family run hotel, makes an excellent choice. It is superbly located—surrounded by shops and only steps down to the beach. The hotel consists of two parts: the original building (a 200-year-old palace) plus an attached new wing that stretches to the side. The palace has a faded-pink patina whose charm is accented by wonderful arched alcoves, intricately designed windows, and magenta bougainvillea clinging to the walls and cascading from the wrought-iron balconies. The entrance to the hotel is through a sun-drenched patio, a favorite gathering spot for guests. In the evening, tables are beautifully set on the patio where guest can dine under the stars with the scent of jasmine perfuming the air. Within, the old-world feeling is maintained with tiled floors, white walls, and formal settings of antique sofas and chairs. My favorite bedrooms are the five upstairs in the palace section: especially appealing are those with shuttered French doors opening onto small balconies that capture a view of the bay. All the rooms are comfortable and have television, radio, and mini bar. The hotel has its own boat that takes guests for excursions along the coast five times a week. *Directions:* Follow signs from the center of the village (located in the pedestrian area).

*HOTEL PALAZZO MURAT*
*Owners: Attanasio family*
*Manager: Carlo Attanasio*
*Via dei Mulini, 23*
*84017 Positano (SA), Italy*
*Tel: (089) 87 51 77, Fax: (089) 81 14 19*
*30 rooms, Double: Lire 350,000–600,000*
*Open Mar to Nov, Credit cards: all major*
*Restaurant open for dinner only*
*Amalfi Coast, 55 km S of Naples, 17 km S of Sorrento*
*Region: Campania, Michelin Map 431*

The Villa Franca, with a commanding position overlooking the sea, is one of Positano's classic villas transformed into a well-priced hotel. The management is extremely friendly and there is an immediate warmth and charm as soon as you walk into the redesigned and redecorated villa. The Russo family wanted to create an attractive full-service hotel combined with the friendliness and service of a small inn, and it is just that. The fresh Mediterranean decor is most appealing, with royal-blue slip-covered armchairs, a profusion of plants, lacquered terra-cotta vases, white-tiled floors and walls, and arched windows everywhere, so that you don't miss a second of the mesmerizing views of the sea. The elegant glassed-in restaurant with floral-tapestry chairs and blue tablecloths specializes in fresh local seafood. The food is exceptional: Mario Russo is himself a talented chef and personally oversees both the food and impeccable service. In the winter, the hotel sponsors a cooking school where Diana Folonari teaches her pupils the art of Italian-Mediterranean specialties. The bedrooms follow the same cheerful theme with colorful ceramic-tiled floors, cream bedspreads with green-and-yellow-striped trim and exquisite views. On the rooftop is a swimming pool surrounded by yellow chaise lounges and palms with a 360-degree panoramic view over the world's most beautiful coastline. A sauna, massage room, and solarium are recently added amenities. *Directions:* Follow the road leading down into Positano and the Hotel Villa Franca is on the left.

*HOTEL VILLA FRANCA*
*Owner: Mario Russo*
*Viale Pasitea, 318*
*Positano 84017 (SA), Italy*
*Tel: (089) 87 56 55, Fax: (089) 87 57 35*
*E-mail: hvf@starnet.it*
*28 rooms, Double: Lire 320,000–480,000*
*Open Apr to Oct, Credit cards: all major*
*Restaurant open daily*
*Amalfi Coast, 55 km S of Naples, 17 km S of Sorrento*
*Region: Campania, Michelin Map 431*
*www.karenbrown.com/italyinns/hotelvillafranca.html*

The spectacular, family-run Il San Pietro di Positano is claimed to be one of the most beautiful, deluxe hotels in the world. It is—there is no question about it. From the moment you approach the hotel, class is evident: no large signs; no gaudy advertising; just an ancient chapel along the road indicates to the knowledgeable that an oasis is hidden below the hill. After parking in the designated area near the road, you take an elevator, which whisks you down to the lounge and lobby. You walk out of the elevator to a dream world—an open, spacious oasis of sparkling white walls, tiled floors, colorful lounge chairs, Oriental rugs, antique chests, flowers absolutely everywhere, and arches of glass through which vistas of greenery and sea appear. To the right is a bar and to the left is a marvelous dining room—again with windows of glass opening to the view, but with the outdoors appearing to come in, with the walls and ceilings laced with plants and vines. The bedrooms too seem to be almost a Hollywood creation—more walls of glass, bathrooms with views to the sea, and balconies on which to sit and dream. If you can tear yourself away from your oasis of a bedroom, an elevator will whisk you down the remainder of the cliff to the small terrace at the water's edge. If all this sounds ostentatious, it isn't. It is perfect. *Directions:* Follow the coastal highway south from Positano. Soon after town, a small chapel on the hillside to your right marks the entrance to the hotel.

*IL SAN PIETRO DI POSITANO*
*Owners: Virginia Attanasio Cinque & sons Vito and Carlo*
*84017 Positano (SA), Italy*
*Tel: (089) 87 54 55, Fax: (089) 81 14 49*
*61 rooms, Double: Lire 700,000–800,000*
*Suite: Lire 980,000–1,500,000*
*Closed Nov to Apr, Credit cards: all major*
*Restaurant open daily, Relais & Châteaux*
*2 km S of Positano on Amalfi Drive*
*Amalfi Coast, 62 km S of Naples*
*Region: Campania, Michelin Map 431*

Le Sirenuse is a superb luxury hotel tucked in the picturesque ancient fishing village of Positano. It is no wonder that so many writers and artists have been attracted to this colorful town of brightly hued houses clinging to the precipitous hillside as it drops down to its own small bay. And it is also no wonder that so many of these famous people have found their way to the oasis of Le Sirenuse, a favorite hideaway for discerning travelers seeking discreet, understated elegance. From the moment you enter the hotel lobby the mood is set with fresh white walls, tiled floors, oil paintings on the walls, accents of antiques, and an abundance of colorful flowers everywhere. The hotel is built on terraces cut into the hillside and so almost all the rooms capture a wonderful view out over the quaint rooftops and the tiled domed cathedral to the shimmering blue waters of the bay. It is only a short walk through the perpendicular streets until you are on the beach. The dining room has walls of glass that allow the maximum enjoyment of the vista below, but most diners prefer the splendor of eating outdoors on the terrace, surrounded by flowers and views of the sea. On another level of the hotel there is a swimming pool. The hotel also has a new spa and its own parking area (rare for Positano). *Directions:* Located near the center of town, on the right side of the road as you drive up the hill.

*LE SIRENUSE HOTEL*
*Manager: Antonio Sersale*
*Via C. Colombo, 30*
*84017 Positano (SA), Italy*
*Tel: (089) 87 50 66, Fax: (089) 81 17 98*
*E-mail: info@sirenuse.it*
*60 rooms, Double: Lire 462,000–1,100,000*
*Suite: Lire 1,265,000–2,970,000*
*Open all year, Credit cards: all major*
*Restaurant open daily*
*Amalfi coast, 55 km S of Naples, 17 km S of Sorrento*
*Region: Campania, Michelin Map 431*
*www.karenbrown.com/italyinns/lesirenuse.html*

The Hotel Poseidon, owned and lovingly managed by the Aonzo family, is a member of the Romantik Hotels group, an affiliation of small hotels with charm and family management. The hotel is not in the center of town, but perched above the main road as it winds down from the highway. However, it is just an easy few minutes' walk when you want to browse through Positano's maze of romantic cobbled alleyways, shop in the attractive boutiques, or walk along the beach where the colorful fishing boats are moored. As you walk into the hotel there is a reception desk on the first level, but the main part of the hotel is reached up a flight of stairs. Here you find a series of intimate, small rooms that open up one after another through a series of arched doorways. It looks like a private home with many potted plants, Oriental carpets enhancing tiled floors, whitewashed walls, and cozy sitting niches with comfortable, white-slipcovered chairs. There is even a grand piano next to the bar. However, the nicest feature of the hotel is the terrace that sweeps across the front, perched above the street with a lovely view of the town. This terrace is truly the heart of the hotel, for being outside is the essence of Positano. Here, surrounded by cascades of colorful bougainvillea and many plants, guests take most of their meals and also enjoy a large swimming pool. For those who like to truly pamper themselves on vacation, the hotel has the Laura Elos Beauty Center where guests can enjoy various beauty treatments or maintain fitness in the gym.

*ROMANTIK HOTEL POSEIDON* **New**
*Owners: Aonzo family*
*Via Pasitea, 148*
*84017 Positano (SA), Italy*
*Tel: (089) 81 11 11, Fax: (089) 87 58 33*
*E-mail: poseidon@starnet.it*
*50 rooms, Double: Lire 470,000–780,000*
*Open Apr 14 to Jan 8, Credit cards: all major*
*Restaurant open daily*
*Amalfi Coast, 55 km S of Naples, 17 km S of Sorrento*
*Region: Campania, Michelin Map 431*
*www.karenbrown.com/italyinns/hotelposeidon.html*

The Relais Fattoria Vignale is a very charming, delightful small hotel located in the heart of the Chianti wine region. It enjoys the enviable honor of having the best of both worlds—it feels as if you are in the countryside, yet is right in town. The hotel was the manor house of a large Chianti estate: the family's wines are still produced and are sold in the wine shop next to the hotel. The front of the hotel faces the main street, but magically, the back of the hotel opens onto splendid views of rolling hills laced with vineyards and dotted with olive trees. Some of the guestrooms are in the annex across the street and these also have a pretty view looking over the valley. The swimming pool also has a gorgeous view. The guestrooms and the cozy lounges are beautifully decorated with a combination of authentic antiques and excellent reproductions. Care has been taken in the restoration to preserve many of the enticing architectural features of the manor such as heavy beams, arched hallways, decorative fireplaces, and painted ceilings. The wine cellars have been transformed into a tavern with wine-tasting and a rustic-style restaurant serving simple meals. Only 300 meters from the hotel is the Ristorante Vignale, which is under the same ownership as the hotel.

*RELAIS FATTORIA VIGNALE*
*Manager: Silvia Kummer*
*Via Pianigiani, 15*
*53017 Radda in Chianti (SI), Italy*
*Tel: (0577) 73 83 00, Fax: (0577) 73 85 92*
*34 rooms, Double: Lire 280,000–400,000*
*Suite: Lire 500,000–700,000*
*Open Apr 1 to Dec 8 & Dec 26 to Jan 6*
*Credit cards: all major, Tavern with light meals*
*In the heart of Chianti wine region*
*52 km S of Florence, 31 km N of Siena*
*Region: Tuscany, Michelin Map 430*

The Ansitz Heufler Hotel, built in 1578 by Count Heufler, is actually a castle, but not one of the large, foreboding castles sometimes found high on mountain peaks. This is a little, friendly castle, located in a sunny mountain valley in northeastern Italy within a short drive of dramatic Dolomite vistas. Inside its thick walls are some absolutely delightful rooms. The smoke-blackened bar where drinks are enjoyed is the place where meat was once smoked. The charming dining rooms with their old paneled walls, planked wooden floors, and tables set with crisp linens are popular places to dine. The broad staircase leads up to a wide hallway off which you find a cozy television room (no TVs in rooms) and a magnificent pine-paneled room with intricate inlayed designs. It is also here that you find the chalet-style bedrooms. Some have sitting nooks set in the towers and several have accent pieces that were made for the castle in the 16th century. Half of the first (second in the US) floor is a lovely suite that can accommodate a family of four. In winter there is skiing nearby and in summer walking trails beckon in every direction. *Directions:* Leave the 49 (Bressanone to Lienz road) at Rasun di Sotto and go through the village to the adjacent village of Rasun di Sopra where you find the castle.

*ANSITZ HEUFLER HOTEL*
*Owner: Hannes Oberhammer*
*Valle di Anterselva*
*39030 Rasun di Sopra (BZ), Italy*
*Tel: (0474) 49 85 82, Fax: (0474) 49 80 46*
*9 rooms, Double: Lire 150,000–220,000*
*Closed May & Nov, Credit cards: VS*
*Restaurant closed Tuesdays*
*90 km NE of Bolzano, 12 km E of Brunico*
*Region: Trentino-Alto Adige, Michelin Map 429*

The Hotel Palumbo is a 12th-century palace, owned since 1875 by the Vuilleumier family. The location is perfect—high in the clouds overlooking terraced vineyards and beyond to the brilliant blue Mediterranean, which dances in and out of the jagged rocky coast. The romance begins when you enter the richly hued, ceramic-tiled lobby with its ancient atrium of arched colonnades, green plants flowing from every nook, masses of fresh flowers, and gorgeous antiques. Each small corner is an oasis of tranquillity, from the intimate bar to the cozy antique-filled tiny lounges. There is a lovely dining room with a crystal chandelier, bentwood chairs, and a fireplace, but usually meals are served on the terrace, which perches like a bird's nest in the sky. Wherever you dine, the food is expensive, but excellent. There is a stunning garden in the rear featuring a vine-covered terrace overlooking the Amalfi coast. Another tiny patio capturing both the sun and the view is tucked onto the roof of the villa. There are only 21 bedrooms—the size varies since this was an old villa, but all are individually decorated and have their own charming personality. A few guestrooms are located in an annex. The Hotel Palumbo exudes a romantic ambiance and a wealth of old-world character. *Directions:* Located on the upper edge of the village on a pedestrian street. Ask for directions to the hotel garage.

*HOTEL PALUMBO*
*Owners: Vuilleumier family*
*Manager: Marco Vuilleumier*
*Via S. Giovanni del Toro, 16*
*84010 Ravello (SA), Italy*
*Tel: (089) 85 72 44, Fax: (089) 85 81 33*
*E-mail: palumbo@amalfinet.it*
*21 rooms, Double: Lire 920,000–1,550,000\**
*\*Rate includes breakfast & dinner*
*Open all year, Credit cards: all major*
*Restaurant open daily*
*66 km S of Naples, 6 km N of Amalfi*
*Region: Campania, Michelin Map 431*
*www.karenbrown.com/italyinns/hotelpalumbo.html*

The Marmorata Hotel was converted into a hotel from the shell of an old paper mill. Today, only a few of these old paper mills are still in operation in Italy, but at one time the Amalfi area was famous for its production of fine paper. The official address of the Marmorata is Ravello; however, the hotel is not located in the famous cliff-top town of Ravello, but rather perched on a low, rocky ledge on the edge of the sea. As you enter the hotel you notice the nautical theme carried throughout the decor from the chairs in the dining room to the mirrors on the walls. The interior has comfortable leather lounge chairs and accent Oriental rugs. There is a sun terrace on a lower level, and snuggled into the rocks, a small swimming pool overlooking the sea. The compact bedrooms maintain the ship-like motif: the beds seem to be built into captains' sea chests, small windows, and nautical prints hang on the walls. The bathrooms are also small, but modern and attractive. All of the bedrooms have radios, color televisions, telephones, air conditioning, and small refrigerators. Many of the rooms have an excellent view of the water and rugged coast. For those on a budget, the Marmorata Hotel provides good value: *Directions:* On the right side of the coastal highway, driving south Ravello toward Salerno.

*MARMORATA HOTEL*
*Owners: Camera d'Afflitto family*
*Strada Statale, 163*
*84010 Ravello (SA), Italy*
*Tel: (089) 87 77 77, Fax: (089) 85 11 89*
*E-mail: marmorata@starnet.it*
*40 rooms, Double: Lire 250,000–400,000*
*Open all year, Credit cards: all major*
*Restaurant open daily*
*On the coast below Ravello*
*62 km S of Naples, 23 km N of Salerno*
*Region: Campania, Michelin Map 431*
*www.karenbrown.com/italyinns/marmorata.html*

The Palazzo Sasso, a stunning hotel that opened in 1997, is located in the spectacular village of Ravello with its spellbinding views of the sea. It is built within the Sasso family's private 12th-century villa, which was a favorite romantic hideaway of Ingrid Bergman and Roberto Rossellini. Richard Wagner too loved the Villa Sasso and in 1880 wrote part of the *Parsifal* while a guest here. The villa had lain empty for many years before being converted by Richard Branson (creative entrepreneur of Virgin Airlines, music, and hotels) into an opulent, world-class, luxury hotel. Many architectural features—such as vaulted ceilings, marble patterned floors, and Moorish-shaped windows—are enhanced by the predominantly white and gold surroundings, and accented by priceless antique pieces. Most of the white-tiled bedrooms, appointed with neo-classical furnishings, offer the famed sea views through large windows and have compact bathrooms with every amenity imaginable. Rosellini's is the elegant restaurant that looks out onto a flower-laden terrace where breakfast is served. Here top-rated chef, Antonio Genovese, insists on the freshest of local seafood and produce for his innovative creations, based on true Italian recipes. The latest enhancement is a beautiful swimming pool with an underwater window positioned on a terrace below the hotel. *Directions:* Located on the upper edge of the village on a pedestrian-only street. *NOTE*: the Palazzo Sasso is so discreet that only a tiny brass plaque designates its location (close to Hotel Palumbo).

*PALAZZO SASSO*
*Manager: Attilio Marro*
*Via San Giovanni del Toro, 28*
*84010 Ravello (SA), Italy*
*Tel: (089) 81 81 81, Fax: (089) 85 89 00*
*E-mail: info@palazzosasso.com*
*43 rooms, Double: Lire: 550,000–1,500,000*
*Closed Nov to Feb, Credit cards: all major*
*Restaurant open daily*
*66 km S of Naples, 6 km N of Amalfi*
*Region: Campania, Michelin Map 431*
*www.karenbrown.com/italyinns/palazzosasso.html*

The Villa Cimbrone is not only a hotel: its gardens are one of Ravello's most famous attractions. The tourist office proclaims, "The Villa Cimbrone, essence of all the enchantment of Ravello, hangs like a swallow's nest on the cliffs." The villa is reached by a delightful ten-minute walk from Ravello's main square (the signs are well marked to this favorite sightseeing prize); then, once you pass through the gates, the villa and its magnificent gardens open up like magic. The gardens are truly superb—if you have ever received a postcard from Ravello, chances are it showed the view from the terrace of the Cimbrone. Most dramatic of all is the belvedere with its stately Roman statues accenting the dazzling view. Luckily, this outstanding villa is also a small hotel. The rooms are of museum quality with furniture fit for a king. We toured through the marvelous old building, which is not open to the public—only to the guests. This fabulous villa was once the prized possession of an English lord. Later it was sold to the present owner, Marco Vuilleumier, who told us the following romantic tale: toward the end of World War II, the English nobleman, who owned Villa Cimbrone, landed with the Allied troops in Salerno. Somehow he was able to find a jeep, and—you guessed it—wound up the twisting road to see his beloved villa once again. *Directions:* Because its gardens are open to the public, the hotel is signposted from the center of town. Pedestrian-only area.

*VILLA CIMBRONE*
*Owners: Vuilleumier family*
*Manager: Giorgio Vuilleumier*
*84010 Ravello (SA), Italy*
*Tel: (089) 85 74 59 or 85 80 72, Fax: (089) 85 77 77*
*20 rooms, Double: Lire 400,000–650,000*
*Suite: Lire 600,000*
*Open Apr to Nov, Credit cards: all major*
*No restaurant, 10-minute walk to parking in town*
*66 km S of Naples, 6 km N of Amalfi*
*Region: Campania, Michelin Map 431*

The Villa Maria is perhaps best known for its absolutely delightful terrace restaurant, which has a bird's-eye view of the magnificent coast. Whereas most of the hotels in Ravello capture the southern view, the Villa Maria features the equally lovely vista to the north. The Villa Maria is easy to find because it is on the same path that winds its way from the main square to the Villa Cimbrone. Park your car in the main square of Ravello (or at the Hotel Giordano, which is under the same ownership) and look for the signposts for Villa Maria. After about a two-minute walk, you find the hotel perched on the cliffs to your right. The building is a romantic old Roman villa with a garden stretching to the side where tables and chairs are set—a favorite place to dine while enjoying the superb view. Inside, there is a cozy dining room overlooking the garden. The bedrooms have old-fashioned brass beds and antique furniture. The bathrooms have been freshly remodeled, some with Jacuzzi tubs. The hotel is owned by Vincenzo Palumbo. His staff speaks excellent English, which is very helpful if you call for a reservation. Vincenzo Palumbo also owns the nearby Hotel Giordano with its heated pool, which can be used free by guests at the Villa Maria. A recent enhancement is a private garden just down the road where guests may relax. Many readers have written to us saying how gracious and warm a welcome they receive at the Villa Maria. *Directions*: Follow signs along the path to the Villa Cimbrone. The hotel is on the right.

*VILLA MARIA*
*Owner: Vincenzo Palumbo*
*Via S. Chiara, 2*
*84010 Ravello (SA), Italy*
*Tel: (089) 85 72 55, Fax: (089) 85 70 71*
*24 rooms, Double: Lire 300,000–480,000, Suite: to Lire 680,000*
*Open all year, Credit cards: AX, VS*
*Restaurant open daily*
*66 km S of Naples, 6 km N of Amalfi*
*Region: Campania, Michelin Map 431*
*www.karenbrown.com/italyinns/villamaria.html*

The northeastern corner of Italy, south of Venice, offers such splendid cities as Ferrara, Mantova, Rovigo, and Ravenna. The latter has gained worldwide recognition for its stunning gold and brightly-colored mosaics preserved from Byzantine times and shown off in eight of the city's churches and basilicas. Since the city is surrounded by flat marshland near the Adriatic Sea, most of its population gets around by bicycle, which makes its historical center a pleasant place to walk. Accommodation in general is limited, so it was a great discovery to come across the newly opened Albergo Cappello, a truly unique hotel. After the death of one of Italy's foremost industrialists who had spent great sums of money on restoring the 14th-century palazzo, it was taken over by young and enthusiastic entrepreneurs Francesca and Filippo. In order to give the exquisite property back to the citizens of Ravenna, they came up with the concept of a cultural center/art gallery/restaurant/hotel. The three double rooms and four suites are located on the upper floors off a high-ceilinged, frescoed hall (identical to the downstairs entrance hall) where artwork is displayed. The guestrooms, with all amenities and luxurious marble bathrooms, are purposely decorated in minimalist style, using contemporary lighting and soft hues so as not to distract from the original architectural features. Light lunches are served in the *cantina*, while dinners are served out in the courtyard. This is not a hotel in the standard sense—keys are given to the front door in the evening and breakfast is eaten at the café across the street.

*ALBERGO CAPPELLO*
*Owners: Francesca Fronzoni & Filippo Donati*
*Via IV Novembre, 41*
*48100 Ravenna, Italy*
*Tel: (0544) 21 98 13, Fax: (0544) 21 98 14*
*7 rooms, Double: Lire 200,000–350,000*
*Open all year, Credit cards: all major*
*Restaurant open daily, In the heart of Ravenna*
*74 km E of Bologna, 136 km NE of Florence*
*Region: Emilia-Romagna, Michelin Map 429/430*

The Villa Rigacci, once a private residence, now an inviting small inn, is only about a half-hour's drive from Florence, easily accessible from the A1 to Rome. This 15th-century building is a picture-perfect example of a Tuscan villa with its creamy-white stucco façade, thick walls, heavy, weathered, red-tile roof, green-shuttered windows, and parklike gardens. Federico Pierazzi and his sister, Fiorenza, take great care to see that all guests receive personal attention and are made to feel "at home." In summer, after a day of sightseeing, guests relax in the back garden where a large pool, surrounded by lounge chairs and umbrellas, stretches out on a terraced lawn. Inside, handsome antiques adorn the sitting rooms and library. The dining room is especially appealing and, according to the guests staying at the inn, the chef is excellent. In summer guests usually choose to take their meals outside on the terrace. All of the bedrooms have air conditioning, direct-dial telephone, color television, small bar, and bathroom. Each is individually decorated with very attractive country-style antiques and lovely fabrics creating rooms that blend beautifully with the old-world ambiance of the villa. Although I personally prefer the area of Tuscany that stretches directly south of Florence where the villages seem more secluded, the conveniently located Villa Rigacci offers easy access to the expressway and accommodation with charm, hospitality, and warmth. *NOTE:* Vaggio is a small town southwest of Reggello.

*VILLA RIGACCI*
*Owners: Fiorenza & Federico Pierazzi*
*50066 Vaggio-Reggello (FI), Italy*
*Tel: (055) 86 56 718, Fax: (055) 86 56 537*
*25 rooms, Double: Lire 260,000–310,000*
*Suite: Lire 350,000*
*Open all year, Credit cards: all major*
*Restaurant open daily*
*30 km SE of Florence, 5 km SW of Reggello*
*Region: Tuscany, Michelin Map 430*

The Villa Luppis property, with its rich historical past, was originally an 11th-century monastery restored in 1500 after a devastating war and bought by the Luppis family in 1800. In order to be able to maintain and share the vast estate with visitors, Stefania and Giorgio Ricci Luppis opened its doors as a hotel in 1993. Their intention was to maintain the flavor of their original home by keeping the family's period antiques and precious paintings intact. The effect is just that—true old-world charm exudes within the beamed dining room with enormous fireplace, various frescoed sitting rooms, and arched front hall overlooking the garden. Bedrooms and suites within two wings of the villa are in theme with matching bedspreads and draperies, antique pieces, gilded mirrors, and stenciled bordered or beamed ceilings. In order to lure guests up to its off-the-track location bordering Veneto and the foothills of the Friuli region, on-site activities such as a large swimming pool, tennis courts, and bikes for touring the surrounding park are offered. The excellent restaurant, where Chef Antonino Sanna works wonders with fresh seafood, organizes a three- to five-day cooking school and wine lessons—the classes even include visits to local *cantinas* and cheese producers. A variety of fascinating local itineraries are suggested to the Villas of Palladio on the Brenta canal, or to the Pordenone, Udine, and Gorizia castles. A shuttle is available every day to/from Venice (40 minutes). Transportation to/from Marco Polo airport is available on request.

*VILLA LUPPIS*
*Owners: Stefania & Giorgio Ricci Luppis*
*Via S. Martino, 34*
*33080 Rivarotta (PN), Italy*
*Tel: (0434) 62 69 69, Fax: (0434) 62 62 28*
*E-mail: hotel@villaluppis.it*
*28 rooms, Double: Lire 350,000–420,000*
*6 suites: Lire 410,000–550,000, Open all year*
*Credit cards: all major, Restaurant open daily*
*15 km SW of Pordenone, 50 km NE of Venice*
*Region: Friuli, Michelin Map 429*
*www.karenbrown.com/italyinns/villaluppis.html*

How could one possibly write about hotels in Rome and leave out one of the most historical places to stay in the city—the Albergo del Sole? Dating back to 1467, this is the oldest hotel in Rome—possibly one of the longest-operating hotels in the world. In addition to being of great historical interest, the hotel has the blessing of holding a prime location: looking across the ancient Piazza della Rotonda to one of Rome's masterpieces, the Pantheon, which was standing before the birth of Christ. The Albergo del Sole has been meticulously restored, faithfully reflecting its 15th-century heritage. You enter into an attractive long, narrow lobby with arched ceiling, red-tiled floor, whitewashed walls, and a very large, ornately framed antique oil painting over the reception desk. From the lobby, doors lead into the various lounges, which maintain the same elegantly simple, uncluttered look with white walls, white upholstered chairs and sofas, and antique accent pieces. One floor up is a lovely interior garden-patio, which opens onto an intimate breakfast room where the tables are invitingly set with pretty floral-print tablecloths. The bedrooms are each individual in decor, but similar in mood, with color-coordinating bedspreads and draperies. The suite is especially attractive, with a beautiful antique wooden headboard. There are also five suites in an adjacent building.

*ALBERGO DEL SOLE*
*Manager: Giancarlo Piraino*
*Piazza della Rotonda, 63*
*00186 Rome, Italy*
*Tel: (06) 67 80 441, Fax: (06) 69 94 06 89*
*E-mail: hotsole@flashnet.it*
*30 rooms, Double: Lire 600,000–800,000 (suite)*
*Open all year, Credit cards: all major*
*No restaurant, breakfast only*
*In the center of old Rome*
*Region: Lazio, Michelin Map 430*
*www.karenbrown.com/italyinns/delsole.html*

For location, the Gregoriana is superb: it is situated on Gregoriana Street which runs into the Piazza Trinita dei Monti at the top of the Spanish Steps. In spite of the perfect location, when I first saw the Gregoriana I just did not see how I could include it in our book because it has no antique ambiance: in fact, the decorating style might be classified as Chinese with a mish-mash of art deco. However, after staying at this hotel, I just did not see how I could *not* include it—it is such a well-run small hotel and has such a sparkle of personality that it brightens the otherwise often impersonal city of Rome. As a guest here, you will not be just one of the thousands of tourists in Rome—upon arrival, the concierge will probably already know you by name and will continue to greet you personally as you come and go. Instead of feeling like a face that goes with a key hanging on the wall, you will experience a warmth and intimacy—as if you were a guest in a private home. The bedrooms are simple and spotlessly clean. Those at the rear are especially quiet and some enjoy a balcony with a view over the rooftops of Rome. Only breakfast is served. However, there is a concierge on duty 24 hours a day to cater to your special needs. *NOTE:* If you are traveling with a family, ask about the exceptionally spacious suites.

*HOTEL GREGORIANA*
*Owner: Maria Novella Panier-Bagat*
*Manager: Aldo Basso Bondini*
*Via Gregoriana, 18*
*00187 Rome, Italy*
*Tel: (06) 67 94 26 9, Fax: (06) 67 84 25 8*
*19 rooms, Double: Lire 380,000–800,000*
*Open all year, Credit cards: none accepted*
*No restaurant, breakfast only*
*Near the top of the Spanish Steps*
*Region: Lazio, Michelin Map 430*

The Hassler, located at the top of the Spanish Steps, is a landmark in Rome. Here guests have no need of taxis since the majority of the monuments and elegant boutiques are within walking distance. Complimentary bikes are available to guests who would like to have a ride in the park of Villa Borghese. This small, superb hotel (in days-gone-by a wealthy Medici palace) stands out as Rome's premier deluxe establishment—the only one in Rome still privately owned and personally managed by the family. The fact that the owners are on the premises shines forth: you almost feel like a guest in a private home with a staff on hand to pamper you. There is a formality to the lounges that is offset by an inner garden courtyard—a superb oasis with stone walls covered with vines, statues, flowers, cozy little tables, and a bar. You can linger in the garden, take refreshment in the afternoon, or perhaps meet a friend for an aperitif in the evening. The rooftop restaurant at the Hassler is also spectacular, boasting one of the finest views in Rome: the entire panorama of the city surrounds you as you dine. As the evening deepens and the city lights begin to flicker, the scene becomes one of utter romance. The individually decorated bedrooms are lovely. If money is no object, reserve one of the Hassler's magnificent suites, some with enormous terraces and a view so spellbinding that you will never want to set foot from this beautiful hotel.

*HOTEL HASSLER*
*President & Manager: Roberto E. Wirth*
*Owners: Wirth family*
*Trinita Dei Monti, 6*
*00187 Rome, Italy*
*Tel: (06) 69 93 40, Fax: (06) 67 89 991*
*E-mail: hasslerroma@mclink.it*
*85 rooms, Double: Lire 890,000–1,370,000*
*Suite: Lire 1,668,000–3,368,000*
*Open all year, Credit cards: all major, Restaurant open daily*
*At the top of the Spanish Steps, Region: Lazio, Michelin Map 430*
*www.karenbrown.com/italyinns/hotelhassler.html*

The Hotel Lord Byron is owned by a superb hotelier, Amedeo Ottaviani, who believes "Hospitality is like an exquisite flower, it must be surrounded by a thousand delicate attentions"—a concept which transforms each of his hotels into far more than just a place to spend the night. Each is designed to be a home away from home—a quiet sanctuary, well run and full of character. Ottaviani's chain of small, unique hotels includes the Lord Byron, which is tucked on a tiny lane across the Villa Borghese Park from the historic center of Rome. Surrounded by glamorous homes, it is much more like a private townhouse than a commercial establishment. The reception desk is discreetly located in the foyer that opens onto an elegant lounge. An elevator takes guests to the bedrooms, each individually decorated: fabrics, carpets, and the materials used on the custom-built pieces of furniture are carefully chosen to suit the personality of the room. Most of the furniture is new—modern yet traditional in feel. The colors used in fabrics, wall coverings, and carpets are mostly strong, bold colors—frequently with large, bright floral prints, consistently of excellent quality. On the lower level is an intimate drawing room-bar where guests can relax before or after dining. Next door is an elegant restaurant, the Relais Le Jardin, serving some of the finest cuisine in Rome.

*HOTEL LORD BYRON*
*Owner: Amedeo Ottaviani*
*Via G. de Notaris, 5*
*00197 Rome, Italy*
*Tel: (06) 32 20 404, Fax: (06) 32 20 405*
*E-mail: info@lordbyronhotel.com*
*37 rooms, Double: Lire 440,000–660,000*
*Suite: Lire 1,200,000–1,650,000*
*Open all year, Credit cards: all major*
*Restaurant closed Sundays to non-residents*
*On the edge of Villa Borghese Park*
*Region: Lazio, Michelin Map 430*
*www.karenbrown.com/italyinns/lordbyron.html*

The Hotel Majestic Roma, located on the famous Via Veneto, exudes a refined, tasteful, old world ambiance. As with other luxury hotels in Rome, the rates are high, but so is the outstanding ambiance and the service. From the moment you enter through the circular revolving doorway into the spacious, high-ceilinged lobby with a few well-chosen antiques and bouquets of fresh flowers, the mood of quiet elegance is established. Instead of one large lounge, there is a series of intimate parlors where guests can gather. In each room there are beautifully upholstered chairs and opulent fabrics on the walls and richly draped windows. Be sure to peek in and see the fabulous frescoed ceiling of the 19th-century *Salone Verdi*, which is used for special banquets. A wonderful old-fashioned wrought-iron elevator with polished brass trim takes guests to the bedrooms, each with its own personality, as in a private home. All are elegant in decor and traditionally furnished in an old-world, opulent style. On warm days, an outdoor terrace with a view of the city is a perfect place to pause for a cool drink. There is also a beautifully decorated, formal dining room, La Veranda, where guests enjoy typical Mediterranean dishes, as well as Continental cuisine.

*HOTEL MAJESTIC ROMA*
*Manager: Franco Sestini*
*Via Veneto, 50*
*00187 Rome, Italy*
*Tel: (06) 42 14 41, Fax: (06) 48 80 984*
*96 rooms, Double: Lire 788,000–950,000\**
*\*Breakfast not included*
*Open all year, Credit cards: all major*
*Restaurant open daily*
*In the heart of Rome on Via Veneto*
*Region: Lazio, Michelin Map 430*

La Residenza was recommended to us by several readers who claimed it to be their favorite place to stay in Rome. And, after a personal visit, I can certainly understand why they like it so much. This former villa really is quite different—appearing to be more like a private residence (which once it was) than a hotel. Its façade looks very Italian, with typical brown-shuttered windows, greenery, and flowers behind a small paved courtyard where guests may park their cars (based on availability of space). As for location, it just couldn't be better—just off the Via Veneto with Rome's poshest hotels for neighbors. The front hall has been converted into a reception area flanked by several guest lounges. On our original visit, these public rooms lacked much style, but on our last inspection we were amazed at the changes. Now, instead of dated grass cloth, the walls in the lounges are splendidly covered with traditional striped fabric in rich pinks, creams, and greens. To complement the newly covered walls, the overall decor has also been upgraded and the ambiance is one of comfortable sophistication with lovely antiques, potted plants, and handsome paintings. The breakfast room has also had a face-lift and it is much prettier than before. This four-star hotel is one of the best buys in Rome.

*LA RESIDENZA*
*Manager: Casaburo Vincenzo*
*Via Emilia, 22*
*00187 Rome, Italy*
*Tel: (06) 48 80 789, Fax: (06) 48 57 21*
*27 rooms, Double: Lire 325,000–350,000*
*Suite: Lire 375,000–390,000*
*Open all year, Credit cards: all major*
*No restaurant, breakfast only*
*Between Via Veneto and the Spanish Steps*
*Region: Lazio, Michelin Map 430*

The Romantik Hotel Barocco is one of Rome's finest small hotels in the moderate price range. The location is excellent—although the address is shown as being on the busy Piazza Barberini, just a tantalizing narrow portion of the pretty hotel peeks onto the square. The entrance, marked by a row of potted shrubbery, is discreetly tucked around the corner. You enter into an intimate lobby where there is no frenzy of activity, just a reception counter tended by a gracious staff happy to assist you, whether it is with reservations for dinner or transportation to the airport. Beyond the reception area is a lounge which opens onto a cute little bar. The decor features a series of handsome murals depicting scenes of Rome, below which the walls are covered with a rich cherry wood. Nothing is flamboyant or fussy, just a fresh, uncluttered look. The breakfast room (where—except on Sundays—sandwiches, salads, and even pasta are available for guests who want a light meal) has the same decor with scenes of Rome on the wall. The guestrooms (all similar in decor, but different in shape) continue the same smart tailored look, featuring an abundant use of cherry wood in the built-in headboards, wainscoting, desks, chairs, and bedside tables. Deep-blue drapes accent the beautiful wood, giving a sophisticated, refreshing, almost nautical look. The rooms are good sized, but seem larger by the placement of enormous mirrors that cover the walls behind the beds.

*ROMANTIK HOTEL BAROCCO*
*Manager: Franco Caruso*
*Via della Purificazione 4, Piazza Barberini, 9*
*00187 Rome, Italy*
*Tel: (06) 48 72 001, Fax: (06) 48 59 94*
*E-mail: hotelbarocco@hotelbarocco.it*
*37 rooms, Double: Lire 400,000–630,000*
*Open all year, Credit cards: all major*
*No restaurant, breakfast & snacks only*
*Heart of city, facing Piazza Barberini*
*Region: Lazio, Michelin Map 430*
*www.karenbrown.com/italyinns/romantikhotelbarocco.html*

A welcome recent discovery in Rome is the divine Inn at the Spanish Steps. Surprisingly, even though the Jubilee Year has brought many improvements, there are few exceptional accommodation choices in the historic center, but this property, at half a block from the world's most famous staircase, is truly remarkable. The dream of the Di Rienzo brothers, owners of several large hotels in Rome, was to create an intimate, almost club-like ambiance with all the trimmings for a few privileged guests in an unbeatable location, so they took over an historical, 17th-century private residence (Hans Christian Anderson lived here for years), striving to maintain its origins as a home. The inn now offers a minuscule reception room on the ground floor, 24 bedrooms spread out among the three upper floors, and a marvelous rooftop garden where guests can have an ample buffet breakfast or sunset drink, either in the cozy veranda or out on the flower-laden terrace, complete with bird's eye view of the steps and the fashionable Via Condotti. Doubles are divided into two categories: superiors at the back and luxury doubles and junior suites at the front. Rooms with wood floors and antique furnishings include every possible amenity including air conditioning and Jacuzzi tubs in some of the smart marble bathrooms. Upholstered walls and coordinated drapes accent original features such as frescoed or beamed ceilings. Guests who remain more than three nights receive the bonus of an airport transfer or guided tour of the city. Nothing else compares.

*THE INN AT THE SPANISH STEPS*     **New**
*Manager: Silvio Catalano*
*Via dei Condotti, 85*
*00187 Rome, Italy*
*Tel: (06) 88 45 896, Fax: (06) 84 13 929*
*E-mail: info@atspanishsteps.com*
*24 rooms, Double: Lire 400,000–1,000,000*
*Open all year, Credit cards: all major*
*No restaurant, breakfast only*
*At the Spanish steps, Region: Lazio, Michelin Map 430*
*www.karenbrown.com/italyinns/spanishsteps.html*

Sarah Townsend, artist, painter, decorator, landscape designer, and overall connoisseur of life's best offerings, can only be described as the Renaissance woman. She has astounded everyone with the magnificent restoration project of Palazzo Terranova, her greatest challenge after selling her previous bed and breakfast, Il Bacchino. Accessed by a steep, winding road, the 18th-century rectangular palazzo, which dominates the northern Tiber valley and seemingly all of Umbria, is softened by surrounding terraced gardens filled with roses, lavender, cascading geraniums, and magnolia trees. The stylish home is a showplace for the family's own precious heirlooms and paintings brought over from England, combined with the best artisans' creations that Umbria has to offer. Each masterpiece of a bedroom, with its stenciled and painted designs, holds some enchanting feature and, just as in the creation of a painting, utmost attention has been given to color scheme, composition, and lighting. The palatial Traviata suite, on a floor of its own, off one of the many sitting rooms open to guests, has it all—a king-sized wrought-iron poster bed, custom lace linens, solid marble bath, and stunning views. Delightful staff is on hand to satisfy any whim. If you cannot get a room, do reserve a meal prepared by skilled chef, Patrizio. The food is beyond paradise! *Directions*: Palazzo Terranova is in Ronti, a tiny village located on the Città del Castello—Castiglion Fiorentino road. To find the inn, you need more information than we have space to provide, but don't worry: Sarah can send you detailed directions.

*PALAZZO TERRANOVA*
*Owners: Sarah & Johnny Townsend*
*Localita: Ronti*
*06010 Morra (PG), Italy*
*Tel: (075) 85 70 083, Fax: (075) 85 70 014*
*7 rooms, 1 suite, Double: Lire 670,000–1,500,000*
*Open all year, Credit cards: all major*
*Restaurant open daily, 80 km N of Perugia*
*Region: Umbria, Michelin Map 430*

Finding the appealing Romantik Golf Hotel brought us an unexpected bonus: we discovered a niche of Italy that hugs the border north of Trieste, an absolutely gorgeous region of wooded hills, rolling fields, and vineyards. The Castello Formentini, superbly positioned on a hillock overlooking the countryside, has belonged to the Counts of Formentini since the 16th century. For many years there has been a restaurant within the castle which serves excellent meals and a medieval banquet on select Saturdays. Just outside the castle walls, one of the historic buildings of the castle complex has been converted into a small, charming luxury inn. The attractive, gracious owner, Isabella Formentini, says that all of the magnificent antique furnishings in the hotel are family heirlooms: in fact, she says the furniture is more valuable than the castle. Everything is authentic, even the wonderful prints and paintings. From the intimate lobby to each of the spacious guestrooms, everything is decorator-perfect and exudes a delightful country-manor ambiance. Only four of the rooms are within the castle, but all guests can stroll through the gate and into the castle grounds where the swimming pool lies invitingly in the shaded lawn. There are also a tennis court and a nine-hole pitch-and-putt golf course.

*ROMANTIK GOLF HOTEL*
*Owner: Contessa Isabella Formentini*
*San Floriano del Collio*
*34070 Gorizia (GO), Italy*
*Tel: (0481) 88 40 51, Fax: (0481) 88 40 52*
*14 rooms, Double: Lire 290,000–355,000*
*Suite: Lire 450,000–530,000*
*Open Mar to Nov, Credit cards: all major*
*Restaurant closed January & Mondays*
*40 km N of Trieste, 7 km N of Gorizia*
*Region: Friuli-Venezia Giulia, Michelin Map 429*

Without a doubt, San Gimignano is one of the most picturesque places in Tuscany: a postcard-perfect hilltop village punctuated by 14 tall towers. During the day, the town bustles with activity, but after the busloads of tourists depart, the romantic ambiance of yesteryear fills the cobbled streets. For the lucky few who spend the night, there is a jewel of small inn, the Hotel L'Antico Pozzo. What a pleasure to see a renovation with such excellent taste and meticulous attention to maintaining the authentic character of the original building. The name of the hotel derives from an antique stone well (*pozzo*) which is softly illuminated just off the lobby. The fact that only the most affluent families could afford the luxury of a private well indicates that this 15th-century townhouse was at one time a wealthy residence. A timeworn stone staircase leads up to the air-conditioned bedrooms, tucked at various levels along a maze of hallways. Each one of the quietly elegant rooms has its own personality with frescoes, thick stone walls, terra-cotta floors, and beautifully framed antique prints, plus satellite television. One of my favorites, number 20, has the palest of pastel-peach-colored walls, windows opening onto the terrace, and a fabulous domed ceiling painted with ancient Roman designs. Number 14 is also really outstanding—a very large room with a canopy bed. Another advantage of L'Antico Pozzo is that this is a long-time family-run hotel.

*HOTEL L'ANTICO POZZO*
*Manager: Emanuele Marro*
*Via San Matteo, 87*
*53037 San Gimignano (SI), Italy*
*Tel: (0577) 94 20 14, Fax: (0577) 94 21 17*
*E-mail: info@anticopozzo.com*
*18 rooms, Double: Lire 220,000–280,000*
*Open all year, Credit cards: all major*
*No restaurant, breakfast only*
*55 km SW of Florence, 38 km N of Siena*
*Region: Tuscany, Michelin Map 430*
*www.karenbrown.com/italyinns/anticopozzo.html*

San Gimignano is one of the most fascinating of the medieval Tuscany hilltowns. As you approach, this looks like a city of skyscrapers: come even closer and the skyscrapers emerge as 14 soaring towers—dramatic reminders of what San Gimignano must have looked like in all her glory when this wealthy town sported 72 giant towers. Most tourists come just for the day to visit this small town, but for those lucky enough to be able to spend the night, San Gimignano has a simple but very charming hotel, La Cisterna. The hotel is located on the town's main square and fits right into the ancient character of the surrounding buildings with its somber stone walls softened by ivy, arched shuttered doors, and red-tile roof. Inside La Cisterna, the medieval feeling continues with lots of stone, vaulted ceilings, leather chairs, and dark woods. The bedrooms are not fancy, but pleasant, and some have balconies with lovely views of the valley. Renovations added air conditioning in the restaurant and satellite TV (for European channels). La Cisterna is probably more famous as a restaurant than as a hotel and people come from far and wide because not only is the food delicious, but the dining rooms are delightful. Especially charming is the dining room with the brick wall, sloping ceiling supported by giant beams, and picture windows framing the gorgeous hills of Tuscany.

*LA CISTERNA*
*Owners: Salvestrini family*
*Piazza della Cisterna, 24*
*53037 San Gimignano (SI), Italy*
*Tel: (0577) 94 03 28, Fax: (0577) 94 20 80*
*50 rooms, Double: Lire 165,000–235,000*
*Open Mar 10 to Jan 10, Credit cards: all major*
*Restaurant closed Tuesdays & lunch on Wednesdays*
*55 km SW of Florence, 38 km NW of Siena*
*Region: Tuscany, Michelin Map 430*

La Collegiata is the perfect choice for those who want to explore the wonders of the Tuscan countryside beginning with the medieval town of San Gimignano. Celebrating 400 years of existence, the stone convent was transformed into a private residence by the Contessa Guicciardi one hundred years ago, then after a six-year restoration project it recently opened as a hotel. Achieving a masterpiece of architectural engineering, all possible efforts were made to conserve original features while incorporating modern conveniences. On the main road just outside town, the fortress-like structure is surrounded by a botanical park, a rose garden, and a heated swimming pool. The downstairs sitting rooms, library, and elegant dining rooms are situated around a stone courtyard with a stone well that is a miniature of the famous *cisterna* in the piazza of San Gimignano. The hotel features vaulted or paneled ceilings, unique antique pieces, portrait paintings, and terra-cotta floors. Individually styled bedrooms, all with views, have antique furnishings, rich blue or green draperies, and beautiful travertine marble bathrooms. The bi-level suite within the tower has the only element out of context with the rest of the Renaissance ambiance—a large Jacuzzi right in the middle of the room surrounded by windows taking in the magnificent views.

*LA COLLEGIATA*
*Manager: Silva Perko*
*Localita: Strada 27*
*53037 San Gimignano, Italy*
*Tel: (0577) 94 32 01, Fax: (0577) 94 05 66*
*20 rooms, Double: Lire 600,000–1,500,000*
*Closed Jan*
*Credit cards: all major*
*Restaurant open daily*
*2 km W of San Gimignano*
*Region: Tuscany, Michelin Map 430*

Staying at the Villa Arceno is truly like staying with friends in a sumptuous Italian villa. Although a luxurious property with stunning decor and impeccable service, the hotel exudes the warmth and charm of a small inn. The manager, Gualtiero Mancini, makes everyone feel at home, even dropping by each table to personally greet his guests at dinner. The mood of grandeur is set as you approach by a seemingly endless private road that winds through lovingly tended vineyards to a classic, three-story, ochre-colored villa. At one time the summer home of royalty, this 17th-century Palladian villa has been masterfully restored, both outside and within. The public rooms are more like lounges in a private home with a sophisticated, yet comfortable, elegance. The individually decorated guestrooms in the main villa are gorgeous—even the standard rooms are enormous and splendidly decorated. All the rooms are so outstanding it is difficult to choose, but I think my favorites are suites 104 and 204, both with sweeping vistas of vine-covered fields. In addition to just reveling in the utter peace and quiet, sightseeing in nearby Siena, or exploring the wonders of Tuscany, you can enjoy bicycles, a swimming pool, a tennis court, and, best of all, a park. Here you can stroll for hours along romantic lanes shaded by imposing rows of centuries-old cypress trees or meander on paths through the forest, passing almost-hidden statues and small temples, down to an idyllic, secluded lake.

*HOTEL VILLA ARCENO*
*Manager: Gualtiero Mancini*
*53010 San Gusmè (SI), Italy*
*Tel: (0577) 35 92 92, Fax: (0577) 35 92 76*
*16 rooms, Double: Lire 560,000*
*Suite: 720,000–800,000*
*Open mid-Mar to mid-Nov, Credit cards: all major*
*Restaurant open daily*
*22 km NE of Siena, 9 km NW of Castelnuovo*
*Region: Tuscany, Michelin Map 430*
*www.karenbrown.com/italyinns/hotelvillaarceno.html*

If you are looking for a place to stay in the heart of Tuscany that is moderately priced, yet does not sacrifice one ounce of charm or quality of accommodation, the family-run Hotel Belvedere di San Leonino is unsurpassable. Ceramic pots of geraniums, trellised grapevines, and climbing roses soften and add color to the weathered stone buildings, which were originally a cluster of 15th-century farmers' cottages. Off the central patio area is a small reception area, a living room blandly decorated with contemporary furniture, and an attractive dining room with tiled floors, rustic beamed ceiling, and appropriately simple wooden tables and chairs. When the weather is warm, meals are served outside in the garden. Because the rooms are tucked into various parts of the old farmhouses, they vary in size and shape. They also differ in decor, but all have an antique ambiance with wrought-iron headboards, beautiful old armoires, and pretty, white curtains. What adds the icing to the cake is the setting of the Belvedere, nestled in the very heart of the Chianti wine region, surrounded by stunning scenery—in every direction you look there are idyllic, sweeping vistas of rolling hills dotted with vineyards, olive groves, and pine forests. Hotel Belvedere is conveniently located only a short drive from the freeway.

*HOTEL BELVEDERE DI SAN LEONINO*
*Manager: Signora C. Orlandi*
*Localita: San Leonino*
*53011 Castellina in Chianti (SI), Italy*
*Tel: (0577) 74 08 87, Fax: (0577) 74 09 24*
*Fax after midnight: (0577) 74 09 24*
*E-mail: info@hotelsanleonino.com*
*28 rooms, Double: Lire 180,000–200,000*
*Open mid-Mar to mid-Nov, Credit cards: all major*
*Restaurant for guests only, closed Tuesdays*
*16 km N of Siena, 65 km S of Florence*
*Region: Tuscany, Michelin Map 430*
*www.karenbrown.com/italyinns/hotelbelvedere.html*

The Residence San Sano is a very special small hotel in San Sano—a picturesque hamlet in the center of the Chianti wine-growing region. We were charmed by the hotel, which is incorporated into a cluster of 16th-century stone houses. The exceptionally gracious owners, Giancarlo Matarazzo and his German wife, Heidi, were both schoolteachers in Germany prior to returning to Italy to open this small hotel. They have done a splendid job in the renovation and in the decor. A cozy dining room serves guests excellent meals featuring typically Tuscan-style cooking. Each of the bedrooms is delightfully furnished in antiques and each has a name incorporating some unique feature of the hotel—the name evolving from the time during reconstruction when Heidi and Giancarlo remembered each room by its special feature. One is called the Bird Room: here birds had claimed the room for many years and had nested in holes that went completely through the wall. With great imagination, the holes were left open to the outside, but on the inside were covered with glass. Another room is named for a beautiful, long-hidden Romanesque window that was discovered and incorporated into the decor and another for an antique urn uncovered during renovation. On our latest visit, a swimming pool and several spacious new rooms overlooking the vineyards had been added.

*HOTEL RESIDENCE SAN SANO*
*Owners: Heidi & Giancarlo Matarazzo*
*Localita: San Sano*
*53010 Lecchi in Chianti (SI), Italy*
*Tel: (0577) 74 61 30, Fax: (0577) 74 61 56*
*E-mail: hotelsansano@chiantinet.it*
*14 rooms, Double: Lire 200,000–250,000*
*Open mid-Mar to Nov, 5-night minimum*
*Credit cards: all major*
*Restaurant for guests only, closed Sundays*
*60 km S of Florence, 9 km S of Radda*
*Region: Tuscany, Michelin Map 430*
*www.karenbrown.com/italyinns/residencesansano.html*

The 16th-century Locanda San Vigilio is truly special: our favorite among the tiny luxury inns along the shores of the picturesque lakes in northern Italy. Although the hotel is expensive, it costs less to stay here than at many of the famous queens along the lake. The Locanda has been in Guarienti Di Brenzone's family for over 400 years! Not only is this an impeccably managed hotel, but the location is unsurpassed: romantically positioned fronting the water on an exquisite, parklike peninsula that juts out into Lake Garda with a private beach for hotel guests. There is not much action here. If you want to see and be seen by the rich and famous, choose the glamorous Villa d'Este as your hub, but if you desire utter tranquillity and beautiful accommodations, go to the San Vigilio. Here you will find understated luxury, nothing commercial at all—in fact, hardly a sign marks the tree-lined entrance just a few kilometers north of the town of Garda. After parking your car in the designated area, you walk past the family's villa and then down a path to the hotel, a sturdy stone building so close to the water that waves gently lap the walls. The dining room is lovely and if you are lucky, you can eat at one of the cozy tables overlooking the lake. The food is outstanding and the decor is faultless. Upstairs, the prize guestrooms overlook the lake. If traveling with your family, ask about the fabulous suites. You won't be surprised to learn that Winston Churchill came here to paint—the beauty of San Vigilio is truly inspiring.

*LOCANDA SAN VIGILIO*
*Owners: Agostino & Guariente Di Brenzone*
*Manager: Christine Kössler*
*37016 San Vigilio, Lake Garda (VR), Italy*
*Tel: (045) 72 56 688, Fax: (045) 72 56 551*
*E-mail: sanvigilio@gardanews.it*
*14 rooms, Double: Lire 340,000–1,200,000*
*Open end of Mar to Nov 10, Credit cards: AX, VS*
*Restaurant open daily for guests only*
*154 km W of Venice, 3 km N of Garda*
*Region: Veneto, Michelin Map 428/429*
*www.karenbrown.com/italyinns/locandasanviglio.html*

Santa Maria di Castellabate is a picturesque village hugging the sea at the southern tip of the Bay of Salerno. I fell in love with this exceptionally colorful, unspoiled, fishing hamlet several years ago and thought how wonderful it would be if one of the quaint buildings nestled along the water's edge housed a hotel. Happily, now one does—the Hotel Villa Sirio. The villa had been in the Tortora family for many generations, but was sold early in the 20th century. Luckily for you and me, Alfonso Tortora bought back his family home and with his wife, Rosalinda, took several years restoring the building, opening it in 1997 as a charming, small hotel. They are fantastic hosts who treat guests as friends, extending their hearts to all who come through the door. The handsome building is painted a rich yellow with white trim around the windows and dark-green shutters. The mood is set as you enter the intimate reception area where oil paintings decorate the walls and give a welcoming, homelike ambiance. The color scheme throughout is a happy one and all of the guestrooms are lovingly decorated in fine taste. The rooms facing the sea are in pretty hues of blue and yellow, while those facing the village are in green and yellow. Ask for one of the rooms facing the sea with a balcony— these are especially romantic. What fun to sleep with the waves lapping beneath your window! The food is excellent and served in a beautiful dining room under a coved ceiling with giant arches where the fishing boats used to be brought into the house for safekeeping.

*HOTEL VILLA SIRIO*    **New**
*Owners: Rosalinda & Alfonso Tortora*
*Via Lungomare de Simone*
*84072 Santa Maria di Castellabate (SA), Italy*
*Tel: (0974) 96 01 62 or 96 10 99, Fax: (0974) 96 05 07*
*E-mail: villasirio@costacilento.it*
*14 rooms, Double: Lire 340,000–420,000\**
*\*Rate includes breakfast & dinner*
*Closed mid-Jan to mid-Mar, Credit cards: all major*
*Restaurant open daily, 72 km S. of Salerno, in center of village*
*Region: Campania, Michelin Map 431*
*www.karenbrown.com/italyinns/villasirio.html*

Sardinia's lovely beaches and inlets of turquoise water are outstanding, but not to venture inland from the coast means missing wonderful scenery and rich archeological sites. The perfect solution is to combine the two—after a holiday by the sea, plan to stay for several days at the Hotel Su Gologone. Here you can experience all the best the countryside has to offer: delightful rural landscape, rustic country charm, excellent meals featuring Sardinian specialties, and even sightseeing excursions. The Hotel Su Gologone is set in a high valley among gently rolling hills dotted by grazing sheep. Adding drama to the tranquil scene is a backdrop of granite mountains whose jagged peaks reach to the sky. The exterior of the hotel exudes a country charm with stark white walls accenting Mediterranean-blue shutters and doors, red-tiled roof, and flowers, flowers, flowers. Inside, the ambiance of a country hotel is set from the moment you enter the lobby. All of the furnishings have a rustic flair with the extensive use of local handicrafts including hand-woven rugs, pretty fabrics, and simple wooden furniture. Although there are 65 guestrooms, the hotel seems much smaller because many of the rooms are in small cottages scattered about the property. Although the room rate is amazingly low, the Su Gologone offers many of the amenities of a resort hotel with a large swimming pool, tennis courts, mini golf, sightseeing excursions, bikes, horseback riding, and a new spa!

*HOTEL SU GOLOGONE*
*Manager: Luigi Crisponi*
*Sorgente Su Gologone*
*08025 Oliena (NU), Sardinia, Italy*
*Tel: (0784) 28 75 12, Fax: (0784) 28 76 68*
*E-mail: gologone@tin.it*
*65 rooms, Double: Lire 240,000–430,000*
*Open Christmas & Mar to Nov, Credit cards: all major*
*Restaurant open daily, 6 km NE of Oliena, on road to Dorgali*
*Island of Sardinia, closest airport Olbia*
*Region: Sardinia, Michelin Map 433*
*www.karenbrown.com/italyinns/hotelsugologone.html*

The Pitrizza is a tiny jewel of a hotel located on the Emerald Coast of the island of Sardinia—the playground of the Aga Khan and the jet set of the world. From the moment you enter through the front gate, marked only with a discreet sign, you are in a world of tranquillity and absolute beauty. There is a central clubhouse that has a beautiful lounge, a delightful dining room with hand-hewn wooden chairs, a card room, and a bar. A small protected patio extends from the dining room where meals are served when the weather is warm. French doors from the lounge open onto the terrace, which leads down to a most unusual swimming pool, cleverly designed into the natural rock. Once in this outstanding pool, you have the impression that you are swimming in the sea, not a pool, because the water level matches that of the bay. The bedrooms are all spacious and beautifully decorated—everything is of the very finest quality. They are tucked away in small cottages whose sod roofs covered with flowers blend into the landscape. If your idea of a vacation is a frenzy of activity and things to do, then the Pitrizza is definitely not for you. There are no planned activities, no sports director, no loud music—only lovely peacefulness, food, a beautiful pool, a beauty and fitness spa, and a delightful small white-sand beach. Although extremely expensive, the Pitrizza is truly special and lives up to every expectation of excellence.

*HOTEL PITRIZZA*
*Manager: Pierangelo Tondina*
*07020 Porto Cervo, Sardinia, Italy*
*Tel: (0789) 93 01 11, Fax: (0789) 93 06 11*
*51 rooms, Double: Lire 1,540,000–2,728,000\**
*\*Rate includes breakfast & dinner*
*Open early May to mid-Oct*
*Credit cards: AX, MC*
*Restaurant open daily*
*NE tip of Sardinia*
*Island of Sardinia, closest airport Olbia*
*Region: Sardinia, Michelin Map 433*

Sardinia is a large island, making it difficult to settle in just one place and visit all the sights. Therefore, we felt it important to find a hotel recommendation for those who want to explore in depth the area around Alghero. After looking without success for a charming place to stay in the city itself, we chose instead the Hotel El Faro, a large hotel situated 12 kilometers away on the tip of a small peninsula. Both an ancient round stone tower and a lighthouse mark the strategic spot. The hotel too has a mock lighthouse as a symbol of its name "El Faro." The white-stuccoed hotel spreads out over the peninsula and because there is water on three sides, all of the guestrooms have a sea view (and a balcony from which to enjoy it). Some of the vistas are more spectacular than others, so ask for a room in front overlooking the bay, such as number 159 or one of its neighbors. The mattresses are a bit soft for our taste, but the large bathrooms are top notch, and the furniture attractive—mostly good-quality wicker with fabric-covered cushions. Terraced below the hotel are a large sun deck, then on a still lower level, a circular swimming pool, and lower still (snuggled in the rocks) a third pool. The ambiance is of a modern, first-class resort-style hotel—not much to distinguish it from those you would find anywhere in the world, but a friendly, well-kept place to stay.

*HOTEL EL FARO*
*Manager: Yvan Bezzi*
*07041 Porto Conte-Alghero (SS)*
*Sardinia, Italy*
*Tel: (079) 94 20 10, Fax: (079) 94 20 30*
*98 rooms, Double: Lire 280,000–480,000*
*Suite: Lire 580,000–820,000*
*Open May to end of Sep, 3-night minimum*
*Credit cards: all major, Restaurant open daily*
*12 km from Alghero, Island of Sardinia*
*Closest airport Alghero*
*Region: Sardinia, Michelin Map 433*
*www.karenbrown.com/italyinns/hotelelfaro.html*

The Is Morus Relais has a truly superb setting on the southern coast of Sardinia. The low-rise, white-stuccoed hotel with traditional red-tiled roof is set in 14 acres of park where towering pines and mature eucalyptus trees gently shade the flagstone paths that weave through the estate. The grounds are exceptionally attractive, but the most outstanding feature of the hotel is its private beach, where a cove of creamy sand is picturesquely sheltered on one side by a smooth, natural slab of white rock. Above the beach are terraces where guests can relax on lounge chairs, enjoy the solitude of the sea, and order a drink and a snack from the bar. Or they can swim in the large pool nestled in the garden. Also set out spaciously in the parklike grounds are separate cottages which are favorites for families since many contain two-bedroom suites. About half of the guestrooms are located in the main part of the hotel. All of the bedrooms are individually decorated but have a similar ambiance, with white walls accented by pretty cotton fabrics. Throughout, the hotel has a fresh, uncluttered, restful appeal. Although this is a deluxe resort, a friendly, homelike ambiance prevails—a refined, understated quality of excellence. A bonus—the Is Molas golf course is nearby. *NOTE:* The hotel has new management since our last visit.

*IS MORUS RELAIS*
*Manager: Maurizio Maffei*
*Santa Margherita di Pula (CA)*
*09010 Sardinia, Italy*
*Tel: (070) 92 11 71, Fax: (070) 92 15 96*
*85 rooms, Double: Lire 240,000–680,000*
*Half Pension Double: Lire 750,000–1,490,000\**
*\*Rate includes breakfast & lunch or dinner*
*Open Apr 24 to mid-Oct, Credit cards: all major*
*Restaurant open daily*
*37 km SW of Cagliari, 7 km W of Pula*
*Island of Sardinia, closest airport Cagliari*
*Region: Sardinia, Michelin Map 433*
*www.karenbrown.com/italyinns/ismorusrelais.html*

Having heard about a lovely little chalet tucked among the pines high in the Italian Alps near the French border, I was beginning to wonder what awaited me as the road wound through the ski town of Sauze d'Oulx with its unattractive jumble of modern concrete ski hotels. However, the road soon left the resort town and continued as a track, twisting higher and higher into the mountains until suddenly Il Capricorno came into view, nestled in the forest and surrounded in winter by ski runs. This is a wonderful place to enjoy a skiing holiday or perfect for summer walking along mountain trails. Just as you enter the hotel there is a tiny bar and, beyond, a cozy dining room enhanced by dark wooden chalet-style chairs, rustic wooden tables, and a stone fireplace with logs stacked neatly by its side. The bedrooms, too, are simple but most pleasant, with dark-pine handmade furniture, neat little bathrooms, and, for a lucky few, balconies with splendid mountain views. However, the greatest assets of this tiny inn are the owners, Mariarosa and Carlo Sacchi. Carlo personally made most of the furniture and will frequently join the guests for skiing. Mariarosa is the chef, a fabulous gourmet cook. *Directions:* Exit the A32 at Oulx (signpost Sauze d'Oulx) and follow the road up into the mountains and through the town. In winter you are collected by snowmobile from the town.

*IL CAPRICORNO*
*Owners: Mariarosa & Carlo Sacchi*
*Les Clotes*
*10050 Sauze d'Oulx (TO), Italy*
*Tel: (0122) 85 02 73, Fax: (0122) 85 00 55*
*7 rooms, Double: Lire 300,000*
*Open Dec 1 to May 1 & mid-May to mid-Sep*
*Credit cards: VS, Restaurant open daily for guests only*
*2 km E of Sauze d'Oulx via small lane*
*5 km from autostrada*
*60 km W of Turin, 28 km W of Susa*
*Region: Piedmont, Michelin Map 428*
*www.karenbrown.com/italyinns/ilcapricorno.html*

After five years of renovation, the Masseria San Domenico opened its doors to guests in the spring of 1996. Not that the building is new—quite the contrary—the lovely old farmhouse (*masseria*) dates back to the 17th century. The age is immediately reconfirmed as you drive up to the hotel—both sides of the lane are bordered by groves of centuries-old olive trees whose thick gnarled trunks and silvery-green leaves contrast splendidly with the red soil. Typical of the region, the large farm complex has a Moorish look, with white walls gleaming in the sunlight. However, the fact that this is no longer a rustic farm is quickly apparent: an enormous, lake-like swimming pool lies snuggled next to the hotel; there are two tennis courts; the food is outstanding; the beautifully decorated guestrooms are all spacious, with large tiled bathrooms. The decor in all the bedrooms is similar, with marble floors, crisp-white walls, cheerful floral drapes and matching bedspreads, stenciled designs accenting the ceilings, and fanciful, painted wrought-iron headboards. The sea is 200 meters from the hotel and some of the rooms capture the bright blue of the Adriatic sparkling in the sun across an expanse of olive trees. The Masseria San Domenic makes the perfect choice if you are looking for a hotel offering every amenity, yet so superbly managed by Luigi Anfosso that you feel like a pampered guest in a small, family-run hotel. *Directions:* Drive south from Savelletri di Fasano. The hotel is signposted on the right side of the road.

*MASSERIA SAN DOMENICO*
*Manager: Luigi Anfosso*
*72010 Savelletri di Fasano (BR), Italy*
*Tel: (080) 482 79 90, Fax: (080) 482 79 78*
*E-mail: masseriasandomenico@puglianet.it*
*52 rooms, Double: Lire 420,000–580,000*
*Closed May 1–5, Credit cards: MC, VS*
*Restaurant open daily*
*2 km S of Savelletri on coastal road*
*Region: Apulia, Michelin Map 431*
*www.karenbrown.com/italyinns/masseriasandomenico.html*

The Maremma, a beautiful area in the coastal foothills of southern Tuscany, quite undiscovered by tourists, offers a wealth of sightseeing possibilities: walled villages, Etruscan ruins, archaeological sites, and lovely landscapes. Until recently there were few places to stay that offered much charm, but happily this problem was solved when the Pellegrini family converted a 200-year-old stone farmhouse into a small hotel. Here you will find true Tuscan hospitality. The dining room is the heart of the inn and has tables set in a beamed-ceilinged room, which is filled with sunlight from large French doors opening onto a terrace where meals are served on warm days. The bedrooms in the original house are quite small, but 16 new, very spacious guestrooms with terraces are being built in an annex. Another real bonus is the food: it is wonderful—everything is homemade under the direction of Signora Pellegrini, including marvelous pastas prepared by local housewives, and the hotel even produces its own wines which are served with the meals. A specialty of the inn is trekking (horseback riding). In the corral below the hotel, horses are groomed each day for guests' use: in fact, special room rates are offered which include riding in the Maremma countryside. *Directions*: From Scansano, take S.S. 322 toward Manciano. The hotel is on your left.

*ANTICO CASALE DI SCANSANO*
*Owners: Massimo Pellegrini & family*
*58054 Castagneta-Scansano (GR), Italy*
*Tel: (0564) 50 72 19, Fax: (0564) 50 78 05*
*E-mail: antico.casale@tiscalinet.it*
*32 rooms, Double: Lire 200,000–320,000*
*Open Mar to mid-Jan*
*Credit cards: all major*
*Restaurant open daily*
*30 km S of Grosseto, 2 km E of Scansano*
*Region: Tuscany, Michelin Map 430*
*www.karenbrown.com/italyinns/anticocasale.html*

The Villa Soranzo Conestabile is a splendid, three-story, 16th-century mansion that was built as a summer residence by one of the wealthiest Venetian families who were direct descendants of the powerful Doge, Giovanni Soranzo (the genius who originated the concept of Venice as a great sea power). Although located in the center of Scorzè, a small agricultural and commercial town, the house is secluded within its own 3-hectare park, which is especially romantic with a small pond, a stream, lovely gardens, centuries-old trees, and seven spectacular magnolias, which must be some of the largest in the world. Today the Villa Soranzo Conestabile is owned by the Martinelli family. The property was bought by the grandfather whose restaurant in Cortina was a favorite hangout for Hemingway (you will probably notice wonderful old photos of Hemingway and granddad on the wall). My favorite guestroom, number 2, is a spacious, high-ceilinged corner room with antique furniture and windows capturing lovely views of the park. If you are on a budget, choose one of the less expensive bedrooms on the top floor. Although smaller and less grand, they are also decorated with antiques and are very attractive (my favorite again is a corner room, number 18). The Villa Soranzo Conestabile is an excellent value—especially when compared with hotel prices in Venice. It is possible to commute to the city center by the frequent bus service from in front of the house (a 45-minute trip).

*VILLA SORANZO CONESTABILE*
*Owners: Martinelli family*
*Via Roma, 1*
*30037 Scorzè (VE), Italy*
*Tel: (041) 44 50 27, Fax: (041) 58 40 088*
*E-mail: vsoranzo@tin.it*
*20 rooms, Double: Lire 200,000–300,000, Suite: Lire 500,000*
*Open all year, Credit cards: all major*
*Restaurant open Mar to Oct, Mon to Fri, for guests only*
*Region: Veneto, Michelin Map 429*
*www.karenbrown.com/italyinns/villasoranzo.html*

This is one of the most scenic areas of the Dolomites and Sesto is one of the most attractive of the mountain towns. Just beyond town you find the delightful Berghotel Tirol, a lovely hotel built in typical Dolomite chalet style. Inside, the tasteful decor continues the delightful Alpine style, with one lovely room with beams and light-pine furniture leading to another. However, the special features of the Berghotel Tirol are its marvelous location on the hillside looking over this lovely valley with towering mountains as a backdrop and the warmth of welcome from Kurt Holzer, his wife Resi, and their son Walter. Many of the rooms have large balconies, which capture the view and the warmth of the mountain sun. The adjacent "residence" has lovely apartments (for two to four persons) with tiny kitchens, which can be rented for weekly stays or on a half-board basis. A network of trails in every direction tempts everyone into the crisp mountain air. When you return at night to the hotel, it is rather like a house party: table-hopping is prevalent as guests share their day's adventures. Below the hotel are a fitness center with sauna, whirlpool, and massage rooms, a children's room with billiards and football, and a large parking garage. *Directions:* Arriving in Sesto from Dobbiaco, go through town to the suburb of Moos where you turn left for the hotel.

*BERGHOTEL TIROL*
*Owners: Holzer family*
*39030 Sesto (Sexten) (BZ), Italy*
*Tel: (0474) 71 03 86, Fax: (0474) 71 04 55*
*E-mail: info@berghotel.com*
*46 rooms, Double: Lire 200,000–380,000\**
*\*Rate includes breakfast & dinner*
*Open Christmas to Easter & late May to Oct*
*Credit cards: none accepted, Restaurant open daily*
*2 km SE of Sesto toward Moos, 44 km NE of Cortina*
*116 km E of Bolzano*
*Region: Trentino-Alto Adige, Michelin Map 429*
*www.karenbrown.com/italyinns/berghoteltirol.html*

When you wake up at the Hotel Helvetia and look out your window at the tiny crescent bay where colorful houses reflect in the still waters and fishing boats bob in the harbor, you might think for a moment you are in Portofino. Sestri Levante is not quite as picture-perfect—but almost—and here you will find less congestion and much more reasonable prices. In the beautiful section called *Baia del Silenzio* sits a jewel of a small hotel, the Helvetia, pressed snugly into the hillside, at the far end of the bay with a stunning view. This appealing small hotel is not fancy or pretentious, but just exactly right, and its prices provide an exceptional value. The decor is bright and pretty, with a few antiques for accent and masses of fresh flowers. All the rooms have been renovated and have excellent modern bathrooms. Opt for one of the lovely deluxe rooms with a view of the sea and a balcony—these are worth every penny. The final touch of perfection to this delightful establishment is that the owners, Signor and Signora Pernigotti, personally manage the property. *Directions*: Exit the A12 at Sestri Levante, following signs to the town center. At the roundabout in the center of town, go around the circle and take the road that runs along the park. Turn left when you come to the beach, left in front of the white church with tall columns, then immediately left again. At this point, follow signs to Hotel Helvetia.

*HOTEL HELVETIA*
*Owner: Signor L. Pernigotti*
*Via Cappuccini, 43*
*16039 Sestri Levante (GE), Italy*
*Tel: (0185) 41 175, Fax: (0185) 45 72 16*
*24 rooms, Double: Lire 220,000–250,000*
*Open May to Nov, Credit cards: all major*
*No restaurant, breakfast only*
*34 km SE of Portofino, 59 NW of La Speziz*
*Region: Liguria, Michelin Map 428*

The Foresteria Baglio della Luna is a charming hotel within a few minutes' drive of Agrigento's jewel—the Valley of the Temples. The oldest part of the complex is a 13th-century square tower. Later, more buildings were added, and in the 18th century the property became a private countryside estate, which today has been cleverly converted into an appealing inn. You enter from a quiet lane through high walls into an attractive inner courtyard with an ancient well in the center, colorful potted plants, and pretty, lacy trees. At the far end of the courtyard a doorway through the stone wall leads down to beautiful terraced gardens. The spacious, deluxe suites (all with Jacuzzi tubs) are located in the tower, but even the standard guestrooms are very comfortable and prettily furnished with antique headboards, tiled floors, handmade rugs, and attractive, color-coordinated fabrics on the drapes and bedspreads. Along one side of the courtyard are the public rooms: a cozy bar, a pretty lounge with lots of paintings on the walls and comfortable leather sofas, and the restaurant, which specializes in regional Sicilian and Italian dishes. The attractive, formal restaurant opens onto one of the most outstanding features of this intimate hotel—a delightful indoor-outdoor dining room with walls of glass that fold back completely so that the room is totally open to the cool breezes. Here you can dine and enjoy a romantic view across the valley to the Temple of Concordia in the distance.

*FORESTERIA BAGLIO DELLA LUNA*     **New**
*Manager: Ignazio Altieri*
*Contrada Maddalusa–Valle de'Templi*
*92100 Agrigento, Sicily, Italy*
*Tel: (0922) 51 10 61, Fax: (0922) 59 88 02*
*24 rooms, Double: Lire 420,000–900,000\**
*\*Rate includes breakfast & dinner*
*Open all year, Credit cards: all major*
*Restaurant open daily*
*128 km SE of Palermo, 212 km SW of Taormina*
*Region: Sicily, Michelin Map 432*

Agrigento is home to Valle dei Templi, justifiably the most visited archeological site in Sicily. To savor these stunning Greek temples to their fullest, be sure to plan ahead so that you can secure a room at the Villa Athena whose location is absolute perfection. Behind the hotel, the gardens (where a large swimming pool is nestled) extend to the very edge of the archeological site. If you enjoy walking, there is no need for a car—just steps from the hotel a path leads in one direction to the temples and in the other to the museum where many of the fabulous artifacts from the site are beautifully displayed. In front of the hotel, in a separate building opposite the parking area, is the hotel's restaurant—a popular luncheon stop for tour groups. In the summer, dinner is served outside on an incredible terrace where you dine under the stars with the Greek temples softly illuminated on the nearby hill. As you enter the hotel, there is a reception area which opens onto a contemporary-style bar and lounge with black leather sofas and chairs. The modern bedrooms are all similar in style with comfortable, simple furnishings. What is special about the Villa Athena is not the decor, but the ambiance of the 18th-century villa, and, above all, the awesome views. This is one place you must splurge: request one of the rooms overlooking the ruins. And, if you really want to go all out, ask for a balcony! To wake up in the morning and watch the sun's first rays cast their glow on the marvelous temple of Concordia is magical. *Directions:* The Villa Athena adjoins Valle dei Templi. Follow signs to the archeological site—the hotel is on the same road.

*VILLA ATHENA*
*Owners: d'Alessandro family*
*Via dei Templi, 33*
*92100 Agrigento, Sicily, Italy*
*Tel: (0922) 59 62 88, Fax: (0922) 40 21 80*
*40 rooms, Double: Lire 350,000*
*Open all year, Credit cards: all major, Restaurant open daily*
*128 km SE of Palermo, 212 km SW of Taormina*
*Region: Sicily, Michelin Map 432*
*www.karenbrown.com/italyinns/villaathena.html*

Hugging the crest of a rocky coastal mountain rising 750 meters above Trapani, Erice's authentic testimony to yesteryear is broken only by several tall communication towers just outside the ancient walls. This appealing town of twisting cobbled streets makes a convenient overnight stop when visiting the Greek temple and theater at Segesta. As you wind up the hill toward Erice, watch for the parking area near Porta Trapani: park here and walk through the arched stone entrance and up the Via Vittorio Emanuele to the Hotel Moderno. The intimate reception area is very inviting, with fresh flowers and attractive prints on the walls. A hallway leads to a lounge accented by chairs grouped around small round tables where guests can just relax or enjoy a cold drink from the adjacent bar. A stone staircase leads up to the guestrooms, all of which are immaculately clean and fresh with whitewashed walls and white-tiled floors. Some bedrooms are decorated with light knotty-pine furniture; others have an antique motif. One of my favorites, room 35, has a handsome king-sized iron bed with brass trim and an antique armoire. About half of the rooms are located just across the street in another very old building which has been renovated—these rooms are similar and equally pleasant. My favorite in the annex is number 71, an especially spacious room with a king-sized bed with a handsome French-style headboard.

*HOTEL MODERNO*
*Owner: Giuseppe Catalano*
*Via Vittorio Emanuele, 63*
*91016 Erice, Sicily, Italy*
*Tel: (0923) 86 93 00, Fax: (0923) 86 91 39*
*41 rooms, Double: Lire 200,000*
*Open all year, Credit cards: all major*
*Restaurant closed Mondays*
*15 km NE of Trapani, 96 km SW of Palermo*
*Region: Sicily, Michelin Map 432*

Tenuta Gangivecchio is far off the beaten path. Not only will you discover a jewel of a small inn, but the adventure of finding Gangivecchio leads you through Sicily's beautiful Madonie region. The Tornabene family began by converting a room in their home (a characterful 13th-century Benedictine monastery) into a restaurant, serving a set-menu lunch based upon fresh produce from the farm. The excellence of the simple, yet delicious meals soon brought guests from as far away as Palermo, a two-hour drive away. Happily for the traveler who loves to stay in the countryside, the enterprising Tornabene family have now renovated the stables of the monastery into ten tastefully decorated guestrooms, appealing in their simplicity, with rustic red-tile floors, fresh whitewashed walls, hand-loomed scatter rugs, dark-wood accents, rough-hewn beamed ceilings, attractively framed old prints on the walls, and sweet cotton floral bedspreads. Delicious home-cooked meals are served to guests in a pretty dining room on the ground floor of the inn. Plan to arrive on a weekend for a lunch prepared by Signora Wanda and her daughter Giovanna, served in the dining room of the monastery. *Directions:* Drive east through Gangi on S.S. 120. Just outside town, turn right at a small signpost for Gangivecchio. Go for about a kilometer and turn left at a tiny yellow sign. Continue up the hill for about 5 kilometers: Tenuta Gangivecchio is on your right.

*TENUTA GANGIVECCHIO*
*Owners: Paolo Tornabene*
*C. da Gangivecchio*
*90024 Gangi, Sicily, Italy*
*Tel & fax: (0921) 68 91 91*
*10 rooms, Double: Lire 220,000\**
*\*Rate includes breakfast & lunch or dinner*
*Closed 1 or 2 weeks end of Jun, Credit cards: AX, VS*
*Restaurant open daily*
*130 km SE of Palermo, 127 km NW of Catania*
*Region: Sicily, Michelin Map 432*

The more adventurous traveler will be greatly rewarded with a stay at the Eremo, a 15th-century convent-turned-inn near the sea, conveniently located for exploring the baroque cities of Ragusa, Noto, and Modica. The noble Nifosi family restored the historic building with the desire to carry on the tradition of offering unique accommodation to travelers (during the 16th century it was an oasis for the Knights of St. John en route to the island of Malta). The combination of professions in the family (antique collector, architect and chef) made the project a natural. The typical *baglio* fortress with white-stone courtyard dominates the flat plain. An arched reception area was once part of the church and is striking with its contrast of white stone walls and black tiled floors, guarded by a knight in armor. The refined decor throughout is soothingly simple, in keeping with the building's medieval origins, and bedrooms, fashioned from friars' cells, are appointed with wrought-iron beds, white bedspreads, and antique armoires. Particular attention has been given to the traditional Sicilian cuisine, accompanied by a long list of local wines and served in either what was once the vaulted refectory or the crypts below. Fascinating itineraries are organized by horseback, bike, jeep, or even by the owner's private plane, including overnight trips to the islands or Tunisia. Shuttle service is available from cities or airports. *Directions:* From N115, turn southwest toward the coast. Approximately 9 km before you reach Marina di Ragusa, turn right and follow the signs to the Eremo della Giubilliana.

*EREMO DELLA GIUBILIANA*
*Manager: Elena Restuccia*
*S.P. per Marina di Ragusa Km 7.5*
*97100 Marina di Ragusa, Sicily, Italy*
*Tel: (0932) 66 91 19, Fax: (0932) 62 38 91*
*9 rooms, 2 suites, Double: 352,000–532,000*
*Open all year, Credit cards: all major*
*Restaurant open daily*
*On the southern coast of Sicily*
*Region: Sicily, Michelin Map 432*

If you want to stay in the heart of Palermo, the Centrale Palace Hotel has an absolutely superb location—on one of Palermo's most colorful main streets with the city's prime sightseeing targets just steps away. Within minutes you can be at the spectacular cathedral, or the museums, or the theater. However, it is not location alone that makes the Centrale Palace so special—this well-run, friendly hotel would be a winner anywhere. The building dates back to the 17th century, at which time it was the home of a noble family. Its grand past is still alive in the soaring ceilings, beautiful polished tile floors, marble columns, ornate chandeliers, frescoed ceilings in the conference rooms, handsome mirrors, fine oil paintings, and many precious antiques. The attractive guestrooms maintain the old-world ambiance with traditional furnishings and color-coordinating fabrics. One of the most endearing features of the hotel is its lovely roof garden overlooking the city, where breakfast and dinner are served in warm weather. Palermo is such an impossibly congested metropolis that our suggestion is to pick up a rental car as you leave the city. However, if you do drive, ask the hotel to send you directions, then mark the location on your map. Happily, once you arrive, the receptionist will have a porter take your car to their parking area—this, I assure you, is a blessing. The hotel has plans underway to add more bedrooms in the near future.

*CENTRALE PALACE HOTEL*     **New**
*Manager: Salvatore Schifano*
*Corso Vittorio Emanuele, 327*
*90134 Palermo, Sicily, Italy*
*Tel: (091) 33 66 66, Fax: (091) 33 48 81*
*E-mail: cphotel@tin.it*
*63 rooms, Double: from Lire 355,000*
*Open all year, Credit cards: all major*
*Restaurant open daily*
*On the northern coast of Sicily*
*Region: Sicily, Michelin Map 432*
*www.karenbrown.com/italyinns/centralepalace.html*

The Villa Igiea Grand Hotel is an oasis of blissful tranquility, insulated from the frantic traffic and congestion of Palerno. With all the fabulous archaeological sites, quaint towns, and outstanding cathedrals in the area, it is wonderful to have such a splendid hotel to come home to at night. The approach to the villa is not scenic, but from the moment you enter the gates you are in another world: a world of spacious lobbies, sweeping verandas, formal dining rooms, handsome antiques, and generously sized, well-furnished bedrooms with large modern bathrooms. Many of the bedrooms have private balconies overlooking the gardens to the sea. There is a museum-like quality to the hotel, yet it has all the comforts of a deluxe hotel. It is called a villa, but has more of the ambiance of a small castle. The hotel, situated on a low bluff overlooking the sea, is surrounded by greenery. In addition to tennis courts, a lovely free-form swimming pool nestles on a ledge that overhangs the water. Next to the pool the hotel has its very own ancient Greek temple—now how many hotels can top that? The most outstanding attributes of the hotel are its gardens that envelop the building in a nest of beautiful pines and masses of gorgeous flowerbeds intertwined with twisting pathways. Altogether, a most delightful spot. *Directions:* The Villa Igiea is situated on the bay at the western edge of town, just before the mountain.

*VILLA IGIEA GRAND HOTEL*
*Manager: Maurizio Viviani*
*Salita Belmonte, 43 (Acquasanta)*
*90142 Palermo, Sicily, Italy*
*Tel: (091) 63 12 11, Fax: (091) 54 76 54*
*115 rooms, Double: Lire 370,000–610,000*
*Open all year, Credit cards: all major*
*Restaurant open daily*
*On the northern coast of Sicily*
*Region: Sicily, Michelin Map 432*

Although often missed by tourists (which makes the city refreshingly uncrowded), Syracuse has a fascinating ancient center, *centro historico*, located on the island of Ortigia, where the Greeks founded the city of Syracuse. However, you hardly realize you are on an island since it is linked to the modern town by just a short bridge. This historic old part of Syracuse is definitely where you want to be and, without a doubt, the Grand Hotel Siracusa is the place you want to stay. The hotel has a ideal setting: across the street from the dock where colorful fishing boats are pulled up and just a pleasant stroll away from the beautiful Duomo, the Piazza Archimede, and the Temple of Apollo. The Grand Hotel Siracusa, housed in a handsome yellow building with white trim, has a pleasing old-world ambiance. Inside, you are greeted by an old-fashioned elegance with marble columns, polished marble floors, high ceilings, potted plants, portraits on the walls, huge Venetian-glass chandeliers, and accents of antique furniture. The bedrooms are tastefully decorated with traditional-style furniture, pretty, muted wallpapers, and color-coordinating bedspreads and draperies. Ask for one of the rooms with a view to the sea—it is fun to look out your window and watch the fishing boats reflecting in the clear blue water. A glass-enclosed elevator takes you up to the attractive rooftop restaurant where you dine romantically in front of walls of windows overlooking the waterfront and the town.

*GRAND HOTEL SIRACUSA      **New***
*Manager: Nicola Calandruccio*
*Viale Mazzini, 12*
*96100 Syracuse, Sicily, Italy*
*Tel: (0931) 46 46 00, Fax: (0931) 46 46 11*
*58 rooms, Double: Lire 380,000–580,000*
*Open all year, Credit cards: all major*
*Restaurant open daily*
*On the eastern coast of Sicily*
*Region: Sicily, Michelin Map 432*

There is no doubt that the Timeo is the new shining star of Taormina. The spectacular luxury hotel just reopened in 1999 after a 14-year closing period and is truly a dream. Its location alone is worth special mention, being positioned just under the main attraction of Taormina's historical center, the Greek-Roman amphitheater, dramatically illuminated at night. Since there is no street traffic it is a particularly peaceful spot as well. The discreet entrance and reception lead to the veranda living room, with parquet floors and highlighted by selected antiques. A cozy winter-garden bar with painted trellis is found off a long hallway lined with windows leading to the restaurant. Two contrasting dining rooms, one with arches and original dark mahogany panels and the other luminous and airy with surrounding full-length windows, are where exquisite meals based on fresh seafood are served. The true center of the hotel is the expansive terrace which all the common rooms overlook, divided into outdoor dining area and sitting areas with plump wicker sofas from which to enjoy the breathtaking sea views. An elegant, neo-classical style prevails throughout the bedrooms, which are situated above and below the main building and in the adjacent peach-colored villa, most with terraces or balconies. As an added bonus to perfection, there is a splendid swimming and surrounding gardens. A shuttle service down to a private beach is provided. *Directions:* Follow signs to the *Teatro Greco*—the hotel is on the way.

*GRAND HOTEL TIMEO*
*General Manager: Ninni Occhipinti*
*Via Teatro Greco, 59*
*98039 Taormina, Sicily, Italy*
*Tel: (0942) 23 801, Fax: (0942) 62 85 01*
*56 rooms, Double: Lire 680,000–1,800,000*
*Open all year, Credit cards: all major*
*Restaurant open daily*
*On the eastern coast of Sicily*
*Region: Sicily, Michelin Map 432*

With a glorious, unobstructed view to the sea, the Hotel Belvedere can definitely lay claim to one of the prime positions in the picturesque town of Taormina. Of course this location is not just luck because, undoubtedly, the site was carefully chosen when the Belvedere (one of the first hotels in town) was constructed at the turn of the century. The gentleman who originally built the hotel is the grandfather of the present owners—a continuity that adds greatly to the care and warmth of welcome given to the guests. From first glance, the hotel is immediately appealing—a pale ochre-colored villa laced with ivy and accented by wrought-iron balconies. Flowers abound on the walkways and a romantic garden terraces down below the hotel, providing quiet shady nooks for guests to enjoy the view. On one of the lower terraces, a large swimming pool is practically hidden by a lush blanket of shrubs, shade trees, and towering palms. This cool oasis is a favorite gathering spot for guests, and although there is no formal restaurant, light refreshments including pasta, sandwiches, and cold drinks are available by the pool. The lounges of the hotel are pleasantly decorated with contemporary furniture accented by some family antiques. The guestrooms are modern, with built-in beds. However, it is not the decor that captures the hearts of guests who return each year, but rather the friendliness of the staff and the superb setting.

*HOTEL BELVEDERE*
*Owner: Claude Pecaut*
*Via Bagnoli Croci, 79*
*98039 Taormina, Sicily, Italy*
*Tel: (0942) 23 791, Fax: (0942) 62 58 30*
*E-mail: info@villabelvedere.it*
*47 rooms, Double: Lire 180,000–290,000*
*Open mid-Mar to Nov & Christmas, Credit cards: MC, VS*
*Poolside snack bar open daily*
*On the eastern coast of Sicily*
*Region: Sicily, Michelin Map 432*
*www.karenbrown.com/italyinns/belvederesicily.html*

The Villa Sant'Andrea is a deluxe hotel snuggled along a tiny bay that lies below Taormina, our favorite, very old, Sicilian town, which has a breathtaking position on a cliff above the sea. A cable car (within an easy walk of the hotel) can swiftly whisk you up the hill to Taormina to see its splendid Greek theater, browse through the quaint streets, or have lunch in a *trattoria*. Then, when your excursion is over, you can take the cable car back to the tranquillity of the beautiful Villa Sant'Andrea, which exudes the ambiance of an English home—which is not surprising as the hotel was originally built in 1830 as a private residence for a wealthy English family. Of course, the building has been added on to over the years, but it still has an intimate appeal. Commanding a superb waterfront setting, the villa is built in levels that step down the hill, ending right on the beach where, surrounded by palm and banana trees, the hotel has its own section with lounge chairs reserved exclusively for guests. On a level just above the beach there is a charming terrace—a favorite nook for breakfast. The decor of the public rooms has a refined, homelike elegance with many lovely antiques and period paintings. Good taste also prevails in the guestrooms, some of which have a lovely view of the sea, enhanced by the dramatic rocks that jut above the clear blue waters. *Directions:* On S114, the road that runs along the sea below Taormina.

*VILLA SANT'ANDREA*    **New**
*Manager: Stefano Alfio Scalia*
*Via Nazionale, 137*
*98030 Taormina Mare, Sicily, Italy*
*Tel: (0942) 23 125, Fax: (0942) 24 838*
*67 rooms, Double: Lire 220,000–395,000*
*Open all year, Credit cards: all major*
*Restaurant open daily*
*On the eastern coast of Sicily*
*Region: Sicily, Michelin Map 432*

If you are looking for a place to stay within the walls of Siena, the Hotel Antica Torre is an excellent choice. Be aware that this is a simple hotel, so if you want luxurious accommodations, it will not suit you. However, the Antica Torre exudes a charm and gentle sophistication that far exceed the quality usually offered for such reasonable room rates. The hotel is located near the Porta Romana. After entering through the gates, walk straight ahead and you will soon see a sign to your right directing you to the hotel, a narrow, five-story stone building. Just a wrought-iron lamp and discreet hotel sign mark the entrance. You enter into an intimate little lobby from which a stone staircase winds upstairs where there are two guestrooms per floor. All are individually decorated but very similar in size and ambiance. Although quite small, each bedroom is tastefully decorated in a simple manner that reflects the owner's (Patrizia Landolfo) excellent taste—the walls white, the curtains of white embroidered cotton, the beds of wrought iron. Wooden armoires and desks and attractively framed prints on the walls complete the pleasing picture of refreshing, uncluttered simplicity. All the rooms have their own private bathrooms which, like the bedrooms, are small but perfectly satisfactory.

*HOTEL ANTICA TORRE*
*Owner: Patrizia Landolfo*
*Via di Fiera Vecchia, 7*
*53100 Siena, Italy*
*Tel & fax: (0577) 22 22 55*
*8 rooms, Double: Lire 248,000–268,000*
*Open all year, Credit cards: all major*
*No restaurant, breakfast only*
*Inside Porta Romana—follow signs from gate*
*Region: Tuscany, Michelin Map 430*
*www.karenbrown.com/italyinns/hotelanticatorre.html*

The Locanda dell'Amorosa, a charming small hotel with great warmth and excellent management, makes a super base for exploring Tuscany and Umbria. From the Locanda dell'Amorosa it is an easy drive to such sightseeing delights as Siena, Pienza, Orvieto, Todi, and Assisi. The Locanda dell'Amorosa is actually a tiny town located a few kilometers south of Sinalunga. You approach along a cypress-lined road that cuts through fields of grapes. Park your car and enter through the gates into the walled 14th-century medieval village where you are greeted by an enormous courtyard with its own little church—exquisite inside with its soft pastels and its lovely fresco of the Madonna holding the Christ child. A rustic wine bar next to the church features a selection of the estate's wines and can provide guests a light meal when the restaurant is closed. On the right side of the courtyard are the stables, which have been converted to a stunning restaurant whose massive beams and natural stone-and-brick walls are tastefully enhanced by arched windows, thick wrought-iron fixtures, and wooden tables. The hotel also has a swimming pool. The guestrooms, located in a separate building, are tastefully appointed with a few antiques and matching bedspreads and draperies. The rest of this tiny village spreads out behind the main square and the buildings are used for other purposes—including the production of wine. *Directions*: Exit the A1 at Sinalunga. Just before you come into town, turn left toward Torrita. After 2 km, the hotel is on your right.

*LOCANDA DELL'AMOROSA*
*Managers: Carlo Citterio & Alessandra Chervatin*
*53048 Sinalunga (SI), Italy*
*Tel: (0577) 67 94 97, Fax: (0577) 63 20 01*
*20 rooms, Double: Lire 410,000–640,000*
*Closed Jan 6 to Mar 6, Credit cards: all major*
*Restaurant closed Mondays & lunch on Tuesdays*
*80 km S of Florence, 45 km E of Siena*
*Region: Tuscany, Michelin Map 430*

There are several hotels within Sirmione's walled city, but most of the moderately priced ones lack any traditional charm in their decor. One exception is the Albergo Sirmione, which occupies a characterful 200-year-old building in the heart of town. As you enter the attractive yellow building with green shutters, you first see the reception area, which has a contemporary feel with a modern reception desk and blue walls, but a far more traditional mood is established in the lounge to the left of the entrance. This is a particularly inviting, extremely cheerful room with windows on three sides draped in a yellow-and-blue-flowered fabric that color-coordinates with pretty blue-and-yellow-plaid material on the slipcovered chairs. The lounge opens onto a sweet terrace, which is shaded in summer with a vine-covered trellis. The dining room, which is large and bright with many windows, has bentwood-style chairs set around tables dressed with crisp linens and fresh flowers. The guestrooms are small and simply furnished, but all have a private bathroom, satellite TV with CNN, radio, and mini bar. My favorite rooms are the "Imperial Rooms" in the original hotel. These rooms are worth their slightly higher price—they have lovely terraces overlooking the lake. Since our last visit, the annex building has been remodeled and contains 54 completely new rooms, a wellness center with sauna, whirlpool, thermal swimming pool, and bar overlooking the marina.

*ALBERGO SIRMIONE*
*Manager: Brigitte Bosschaart*
*Piazza Castello, 19*
*25019 Sirmione, Lake Garda (BS), Italy*
*Tel: (030) 91 63 31, Fax: (030) 91 65 58*
*101 rooms, Double: Lire 324,000–494,000*
*Open Mar to Nov, Credit cards: AX, VS*
*Restaurant open daily*
*In historic center, adjacent to ferry dock*
*127 km E of Milan, 35 km W of Verona*
*Region: Lombardy, Michelin Map 428/429*

There is no better budget-priced hotel in our guide than the Hotel Grifone, and happily it is nestled idyllically on the edge of Lake Garda in Sirmione, one of Italy's fairy-tale villages. Naturally, you cannot expect luxury in this officially rated two-star hotel, but if you are searching for a simple, clean bedroom with a world-class location—look no further! The Hotel Grifone and Restaurant Grifone share the same quaint stone building facing the castle and the lake. Both have been run for many years by the Marcolini family and just recently the operation has been taken over by the younger generation of the family—Nicola oversees the hotel operation while his charming sister, Christina, manages the restaurant. The lovely small restaurant has a beautiful outdoor terrace above the lake where guests love to dine when the weather is warm. The entrance to the hotel is on the street behind the restaurant. There is a simple lobby where you check in and to the left is a little sitting room, which opens onto a private patio overlooking a miniature sand beach. The guestrooms are all upstairs. These are small but immaculately clean and tidy, and each has a private bathroom with a shower in the corner. Best of all, every room has a view and a few (such as 26) even have a small balcony. *Directions*: Turn right immediately after coming through the gates of Sirmione. After a short walk, you will see the restaurant facing the castle.

*HOTEL GRIFONE*
*Owner: Nicola Marcolini*
*Via Bocchio, 4*
*25019 Sirmione, Lake Garda (BS), Italy*
*Tel: (030) 91 60 14, Fax: (030) 91 65 48*
*16 rooms, Double: Lire 100,000*
*Open Easter to Oct, Credit cards: none accepted*
*Restaurant closed Wednesdays*
*In historic center, near gate*
*127 km E of Milan, 35 km W of Verona*
*Region: Lombardy, Michelin Map 428/429*
*www.karenbrown.com/italyinns/hotelgrifone.html*

What a sense of impending grandeur you experience as you wait for the giant iron gates of the Villa Cortine Palace to swing open. Inside, the road winds and curves impressively past fountains and statues, flower gardens and mighty trees, until it reaches the summit where the Villa Cortine Palace majestically reigns. This beautifully situated villa has been expanded so that it now boasts a new section which appears to have more than doubled the original size. Throughout the hotel, the guestrooms are undergoing well-deserved renovation. The newly upgraded rooms have much more charm than those that still retain the rather dated rattan furniture. Some of the rooms are in the original part of the villa, which is to the left as you enter the lobby. This section displays a truly old-world grandeur with incredibly ornate furniture, soaring ceilings, and stunning paintings. What leaves absolutely nothing to be improved upon are the gardens—they are awe-inspiring. The villa is surrounded by graveled walkways that wind in and out amongst the fountains, ponds, statues, and glorious rose gardens, all overlooking the lovely Lake Garda. A path leads down to the lake where there is a private pier for swimming. The hotel also has a swimming pool and tennis court.

*VILLA CORTINE PALACE HOTEL*
*Manager: Roberto Cappelletto*
*25019 Sirmione, Lake Garda (BS), Italy*
*Tel: (030) 99 05 890, Fax: (030) 91 63 90*
*54 rooms, Double: Lire 550,000–900,000*
*Suite: Lire 1,000,000–1,380,000*
*3-night minimum*
*Open Apr 5 to Oct 21, Credit cards: all major*
*Restaurant open daily*
*Park setting—overlooks Lake Garda*
*127 km E of Milan, 35 km W of Verona*
*Region: Lombardy, Michelin Map 428/429*

The sleepy village of Solomeo, located between Perugia and Lake Trasimeno, had been almost completely abandoned until a well-known cashmere company bought and restored most of the town to its original charm, using the individual houses and apartments for offices and workshops. Pier Luigi Cavicchi, an import/export consultant, and his friendly wife Donatella (who runs the family's not-so-distant farm) inherited a turn-of-the-century villa, located right in the heart of town. Pier Luigi (who had spent many happy summers at the villa) and his wife thoroughly renovated the property and opened it as an inn. Their wish was to maintain the original character of the beloved residence while adding all possible amenities (including air conditioning). The result is a compact and quaint hotel that has it all. The 12 English-style country bedrooms are named after flowers and this theme is followed through in stenciled borders, bedspread fabrics, and bathrooms. Preserved stencil work on walls and ceilings in the entrance, tea room, and upstairs sitting room were done by the same artist who decorated the town's church across the street. The bright breakfast room downstairs has stone walls and beams and leads to terraces overlooking the countryside where a garden, swimming pool, exercise room, meeting room, and two garden bedrooms are situated. In the immediate area are a golf club and horseback-riding facilities.

*LOCANDA SOLOMEO*
*Owners: Pier Luigi & Donatella Cavicchi*
*Piazza Carlo Alberto dalla Chiesa, 1*
*06070 Solomeo (PG), Italy*
*Tel: (075) 52 93 119, Fax: (075) 52 94 090*
*E-mail: solomeo@tin.it*
*12 rooms, Double: Lire 220,000*
*Open all year, Credit cards: all major*
*Restaurant by reservation only*
*10 km W of Perugia*
*Region: Umbria, Michelin Map 430*
*www.karenbrown.com/italyinns/locandasolomeo.html*

Located about an hour's drive south of Milan's Linate airport, the Locanda del Lupo makes a convenient stop if you plan to drive directly south toward Florence. Soragna is a sleepy little town in the countryside whose main point of interest is a walled, medieval fortress. Around the central plaza buildings of great character are interspersed with modern construction. The Locanda del Lupo, built in the 18th century by the noble Meli Lupi family, is easy to find—just a block off the plaza. The inn is best known as a gourmet restaurant: there is a series of beautiful dining rooms with gleaming copper hanging from whitewashed walls, terra-cotta floors, dark-beamed ceilings, antique clocks, and 17th-century oil paintings. To the left of the reception area is a cozy bar and, beyond, a formal living room furnished in antiques. A flight of stairs leads to the guestrooms whose old-world ambiance is enhanced by beamed ceilings, tiled floors, and thick walls. Each bedroom is individually decorated and exudes a refined, country-house atmosphere. Authentic antique furnishings (including fine wooden chests and wrought-iron bedsteads) impart a feeling of quality. *Directions:* From the Milan-Bologna A1 expressway, take the Fidenza exit and follow signs to Soragna. Go to the central square (Piazza Garibaldi) where you find Via Garibaldi running off the square.

*LOCANDA DEL LUPO*
*Manager: Elisabetta Dioni*
*Via Garibaldi, 64*
*43019 Soragna (PR), Italy*
*Tel: (0524) 59 71 00, Fax: (0524) 59 70 66*
*E-mail: info@locandadellupo.com*
*46 rooms, Double: Lire 230,000, Suite: Lire 300,000*
*Closed Christmas, Credit cards: all major*
*Restaurant open daily*
*100 km S of Milan, 118 km N of Bologna*
*Region: Emilia-Romagna, Michelin Map 429*
*www.karenbrown.com/italyinns/locandadellupo.html*

The Grand Hotel Excelsior Vittoria has a superb location high on the cliff overlooking the port and bay of Sorrento and surrounded by an orange grove and park of about 4 acres with a swimming pool. You enter the hotel, a grand old villa with a real old-world atmosphere, through a formal gate, which is just a short stroll from the center of town. The furnishings, for the most part, continue the antique mood. The Excelsior Vittoria is a good place to splurge and reserve one of the superior rooms with a view of the sea. The ceilings in some of the reception rooms and in the marvelous airy dining room have gorgeous frescoed designs. The terraces and gardens surrounding the hotel offer wonderful views, as do the bedrooms that face the bay. When we first saw the Grand Hotel Excelsior Vittoria, there was a gracious, though faded, elegance to the hotel, giving it a slightly worn look. However, this magnificent villa has since been lovingly restored under the guidance of Lidia Fiorentino, the owner's wife, carefully retaining the unique turn-of-the-century mood alongside modern air conditioning. Staying here will certainly delight anyone who loves the feeling of reliving the grandeur of days gone by in a villa by the sea.

*GRAND HOTEL EXCELSIOR VITTORIA*
*Owners: Fiorentino family*
*Manager: Mario Damiano*
*Piazza Torquato Tasso, 34*
*80067 Sorrento (NA), Italy*
*Tel: (081) 80 71 044, Fax: (081) 87 71 206*
*E-mail: exvitt@exvitt.it*
*107 rooms, Double: Lire 490,000–695,000*
*Suite: Lire 932,000–2,265,000*
*Open all year, Credit cards: all major*
*Restaurant open daily*
*48 km S of Naples, 250 km S of Rome*
*Region: Campania, Michelin Map 431*
*www.karenbrown.com/italyinns/excelsiorvittoria.html*

It was love at first sight as I drove up the long graveled road through forest and vineyard and suddenly caught my first glimpse of the Borgo Pretale, a tiny cluster of weathered stone buildings nestled next to their medieval watchtower. My first impression was more than justified—this small inn is truly paradise. There are absolute serenity and beauty here with nothing to mar the perfection. Civilization seems far away as the eye stretches over a glorious vista of rolling hills forested with oaks, juniper, and laurel, interspersed with square patches of vineyards. But although this small village is seemingly remote, it is only a short drive south of Siena, thus a perfect hideaway from which to enjoy the magic of Tuscany. The rooms in the tower are showplaces of fine country antiques and splendid designer fabrics, blended together with the artful eye of a skilled decorator. Every piece is selected to create a sophisticated yet rustic elegance. The rooms in the surrounding cottages are furnished in a more "country" style, though maintaining standards of elegance and comfort. The lounge beckons guests to linger after dinner by the roaring fire. A path leads to a groomed tennis court and farther on to a swimming pool on a hillside terrace. *NOTE:* The closest town on most maps is Rosia, which is about 5 kilometers southeast of Borgo Pretale. To reach the hotel, go through Rosia and follow signs to Borgo Pretale.

*BORGO PRETALE*
*Manager: Daniele Rizzardini*
*53018 Localita: Pretale-Sovicille (SI), Italy*
*Tel: (0577) 34 54 01, Fax: (0577) 34 56 25*
*E-mail: info@borgopretale.it*
*35 rooms, Double: Lire 370,000–450,000*
*Open Apr to Nov, Credit cards: all major*
*Restaurant open daily*
*18 km SW of Siena on Rte 73*
*Region: Tuscany, Michelin Map 430*
*www.karenbrown.com/italyinns/borgopretale.html*

The walled hilltown of Spoleto is a must on any trip to Umbria. What Spoleto has that is so outstanding is its Bridge of Towers (*Ponte delle Torri*), an absolutely awesome feat of engineering. Built in the 13th century on the foundations of an old Roman aqueduct, this bridge, spanning a vast crevasse, is supported by ten Gothic arches that soar into the sky. The Hotel Gattapone (a mustard-yellow building with dark-green shutters) is built into the hillside and provides a box-seat location to admire this architectural masterpiece. As you enter, there is a cozy reception area. To the left is a bright, sunny lounge with modern black-leather sofas, a long black-leather bar, very pretty deep-blue walls, large pots of green plants, an antique grandfather clock, and, best of all, an entire wall of glass which provides a bird's eye view of the bridge. To the right of the reception area, steps sweep down to another bar and lounge where breakfast is served. This room is even more starkly modern, with deep-red wall coverings. The newer wing of the hotel houses the superior-category bedrooms, each with a sitting area and large view windows. In the original section of the hotel the bedrooms are smaller, but also very attractive and every one has a view. Tucked below the hotel is a sunny terrace. Although most of the hotels in this guide have more of an antique ambiance, the Gattapone is highly recommended—a special hotel offering great warmth of welcome and superb vistas.

*HOTEL GATTAPONE*
*Owner: Dr. Pier Hanke Giulio*
*Via del Ponte, 6*
*06049 Spoleto (PG), Italy*
*Tel: (0743) 22 34 47, Fax: (0743) 22 34 48*
*E-mail: gattapone@mail.caribusiness.it*
*15 rooms, Double: Lire 270,000–420,000*
*Open all year, Credit cards: all major*
*No restaurant, breakfast only*
*130 km N of Rome, 48 km S of Assisi*
*Region: Umbria, Michelin Map 430*
*www.karenbrown.com/italyinns/hotelgattapone.html*

Spoleto is always a favorite with tourists, not only during the music festival (which takes place from the end of June until mid-July), but throughout the year. Due to its popularity, there used to be a shortage of charming places to stay within the walled city but happily that problem was solved with the opening of the Hotel San Luca in 1995. The family-owned San Luca is a splendid small hotel—very polished, very sophisticated, yet exuding great personal warmth and friendliness. Built within a 19th-century tannery, the hotel (which is painted yellow and has a traditional red-tiled roof) only hints at its past. The renovation has been so extensive that much of what you see today is of new construction, but the ambiance is old-world. From the moment you enter, there is a fresh, luminous atmosphere with pastel walls reflecting light streaming in through large arched windows opening onto a central courtyard. The reception lounge is especially appealing, with comfortable chairs upholstered in cheerful peach fabric grouped around a large fireplace and a few choice antiques adding greatly to the homelike feeling. A pair of canaries in an antique birdcage repeats the color scheme. The spacious, pastel-colored, completely soundproofed guestrooms are all equally attractive and well equipped with lots of closets, excellent lighting, and large, exceptionally modern bathrooms. And the surprise is that the price for such high quality is amazingly low.

*HOTEL SAN LUCA*
*Manager: Daniela Zuccari*
*Via Interna delle Mura, 21*
*06049 Spoleto (PG), Italy*
*Tel: (0743) 22 33 99, Fax: (0743) 22 38 00*
*E-mail: sanluca@hotelsanluca.com*
*35 rooms, Double: Lire 250,000–520,000*
*Open all year, Credit cards: all major*
*No restaurant, breakfast only*
*In historic city center*
*130 km N of Rome, 48 km S of Assisi*
*Region: Umbria, Michelin Map 430*
*www.karenbrown.com/italyinns/hotelsanluca.html*

As you twist up the steep narrow road from Spoleto toward Monteluco, you will see on your left an appealing, ochre-colored villa just peeking out from a dense cloak of trees. The setting looks so fabulous that you will hope this is your hotel. It is, and you won't be disappointed. The Eremo delle Grazie is an astounding property—truly a living museum, with history simply oozing from every nook and cranny. The property has been the home of the Lalli family for many years, but its roots hark back to the 5th century when a small grotto where religious hermits came to live occupied the site. The grotto still exists, but now serves as a wine cellar behind the bar. From its humble beginnings the importance of this grotto grew, becoming so well known that one of Italy's important cardinals, Camilla Cybo, lived here (his bedroom is now one of the guestrooms). The cardinal enjoyed his comfort so instead of residing in the small damp grotto, he slept in a lovely bedroom, which he had painted to look like a cave. One of my favorite places in Eremo delle Grazie is the tiny, incredibly beautiful, vaulted chapel with beautifully preserved 15th-century paintings of the life of Mary. Another favorite is the splendid terrace with a sweeping view of the glorious Umbrian landscape. Just below the hotel, a swimming pool is tucked onto a terrace. According to Signor Lalli, Michelangelo was once a guest here. In his letter to Vasari, Michelangelo wrote that he left part of his heart at Eremo delle Grazie—as you will, too.

*EREMO DELLE GRAZIE*
*Owner: Professor Pio Lalli*
*06049 Monteluco, Spoleto (PG), Italy*
*Tel: (0743) 49 624, Fax: (0743) 49 650*
*11 rooms, Double: Lire 350,000–500,000*
*Open all year, Credit cards: VS*
*Restaurant open daily during high season*
*3.5 km E of Spoleto, 124 km N of Rome*
*Region: Umbria, Michelin Map 430*
*www.karenbrown.com/italyinns/eremodellegrazie.html*

The Cinque Terre—a string of five isolated hamlets dotting the coast—is a popular target for walkers, but offers a meager choice of good hotels. An outstanding alternative is to spend a few days at the Locanda Miranda, a most appealing small inn, in the tiny village of Tellaro, which is more picturesque than most along the more famous Cinque Terre. In front of the hotel you can hop on a bus for a 15-minute ride to the dock in Lerici. Here you board the ferry that plies the coastline, getting off and on at whichever of the five Cinque Terre villages catches your fancy (our choice for the most appealing is Vernazza). However, it is not just its convenient location that makes Locanda Miranda a super choice for accommodation: this simple, yet sophisticated, family-run hotel has many other merits. Basically a "restaurant with rooms," the Miranda offers such outstanding cuisine that it has earned a coveted Michelin star. Your host, Angelo Cabani, is in charge of the kitchen (specializing *exclusively* in fresh seafood and delicious homemade pasta), while his wife, Giovanna, serves the meals. They were born in Tellaro and can trace their heritage there to the 14th century. Their son, Alessandro (who speaks excellent English), works side by side with his parents. The genuine warmth of welcome of the Cabani family, the outstanding meals, and the excellent taste of Signora Cabani (who has decorated all the rooms in a refreshingly pretty, uncluttered style) make the Locanda Miranda a real winner. *Directions*: From A12 take the Sarzana exit. Go to Lerici, then follow signs to Tellaro.

*LOCANDA MIRANDA*
*Owners: Cabani family*
*Via Fiascherino, 92*
*19030 Tellaro (SP), Italy*
*Tel: (0187) 96 40 12, Fax: (0187) 96 40 32*
*E-mail: locandamiranda@libero.it*
*7 rooms, Double: Lire 400,000\**
*\*Rate includes breakfast & dinner, Closed Dec 1 to Jan 15*
*Credit cards: all major, Restaurant closed Mondays*
*4 km SE of Lerici, Region: Liguria, Michelin Map 428/430*
*www.karenbrown.com/italyinns/locandamiranda.html*

The road to the Pensione Stefaner winds up a tiny mountain valley in the heart of the Dolomites. The road is spectacular. As we rounded the last curve before San Cipriano (St. Zyprian), the valley opened up and there spread before us was a sweeping vista of majestically soaring mountains. Across soft-green meadows painted with wildflowers and dotted with tiny farm chalets soared an incredible saw-toothed range of gigantic peaks. A tiny church with a pretty steeple added the final touch of perfection to the already idyllic scene. There are many places to stay in this region—none are glamorous resorts, but generally small, family-run pensions. One of our favorites is the Pensione Stefaner, an attractive, chalet-style hotel with flower-laden balconies—easily found as it is on the main highway through town. There is a smattering of antiques, but most of the furniture is new. The hotel is efficiently and warmly managed by the attractive Villgrattner family. Mathilde is a gracious hostess and her husband Georg creates wonderful home-cooked meals for the guests (everyone also loves their friendly German Shepherd). The simple bedrooms (very '60s in their decor) all have en-suite shower rooms, while some have balconies with mountain views. *Directions*: From the Verona-Brennero autostrada, exit at Bolzano Nord and follow signs for Tires. Go through town to the adjacent little village of San Cipriano where you find the Pensione Stefaner on your left.

*PENSIONE STEFANER*
*Owners: Mathilde & Georg Villgrattner*
*39050 Tires-San Cipriano (BZ), Italy*
*Tel: (0471) 64 23 02, Fax: (0471) 64 21 75*
*15 rooms, Double: Lire 150,000–198,000\**
*\*Rate includes breakfast & dinner*
*Closed mid-Nov to mid-Dec, Credit cards: none accepted*
*Restaurant open daily for guests only*
*NE Italy in Dolomites, 17 km E of Bolzano, 3 km E of Tires*
*Region: Trentino-Alto Adige, Michelin Map 429*

Tucked into the hills above Rome where cool breezes freshen the air, Tivoli has been a retreat for Roman nobility since the 2nd century and today tourists flock here each day by the busload to visit the gardens at Villa d'Este. Until 1995, when the Hotel Sirene opened its doors after total renovation, there was no good place to spend the night in Tivoli but that has definitely changed. Now you can stay in the Sirene, just a pleasant ten-minute walk to the Villa d'Este. The hotel's most outstanding feature is its breathtaking view of the Temple of Vesta, a tiny, romantic, Corinthian-columned temple, so perfect it looks like a stage set across the ravine. Hotel Sirene was built in 1865 as a private villa by an English lady, Isabelle (the restaurant is named in her honor). The villa was later converted into a hotel and at the time was truly up to date—it was the first hotel in Italy to have electric lights. Today, the hotel not only has electric lights but they come on magically by automatic eye as you walk down the halls. The lobby of the hotel is dramatic, with marble floors and a galleried, two-story atrium highlighted by a large crystal chandelier. The guestrooms are all pleasant with color-coordinated drapes, upholstered headboards, and matching bedspreads. The ambiance is not antique, but rather of a modern, well-run, family-owned hotel. Splurge and request a room (such as 405) with a terrace overlooking the temple.

*HOTEL SIRENE*
*Owner: Lady Nadia Faroni*
*Piazza Massimo, 4*
*00019 Tivoli (RM), Italy*
*Tel: (0774) 33 06 05, Fax: (0774) 33 06 08*
*E-mail: hotel.sirene@travel.it*
*40 rooms, Double: Lire 250,000*
*Open all year, Credit cards: all major*
*Restaurant open daily*
*36 km NE of Rome, facing Temple of Vesta*
*Region: Lazio, Michelin Map 430*
*www.karenbrown.com/italyinns/hotelsirene.html*

Tivoli is best known for the gardens of Villa d'Este where hundreds of fountains lure travelers from far and near. However, in our estimation, Tivoli's most astounding attraction is 6 kilometers away where Hadrian built the most awesome villa in the ancient world. Set in a garden to the right of the entrance to Hadrian's villa is the pretty sienna-colored Hotel Restaurant Adriano. The emphasis here is definitely on the restaurant, which serves some of the finest food in Italy. The kitchen serves wonderful hand-made pasta dishes, recipes that have been passed down through the family for generations. The restaurant has hosted such notables as President Kennedy and Queen Elizabeth! The Adriano is run by the young Cinelli family (Umberto, Patrizia, and Gabriella) who personally supervise both the kitchen and the hotel. Patrizia is also an artist whose watercolors decorate the walls and whose flair for design is evident in the lovely fresh flower displays and pretty decor. The Adriano is basically a restaurant, with just a few guestrooms—*not* a fancy hotel. However, the bedrooms, although simple, are attractively decorated and each has its private bathroom. If you are looking for deluxe accommodations, this might not suit you, but if the charm and friendliness of a wonderful "restaurant with rooms" appeals to you, this is truly a winner.

*HOTEL RESTAURANT ADRIANO*
*Owners: Cinelli family*
*Adriana, 194*
*00010 Villa Adriana, Tivoli (RM), Italy*
*Tel: (0774) 38 22 35, Fax: (0774) 53 51 22*
*10 rooms, Double: Lire 270,000–380,000*
*Open all year, Credit cards: all major*
*Restaurant open daily*
*6 km S of Tivoli, 30 km NE of Rome*
*Region: Lazio, Michelin Map 430*
*www.karenbrown.com/italyinns/hotelrestaurantadriano.html*

The elegant Le Tre Vaselle is located in Torgiano, a small wine village not far from Assisi. The interior reflects the ambiance of a graceful country manor with sophisticated furnishings and exquisite taste displayed in every detail. The hotel belongs to the Lungarotti family who are famous for their production of superb wines and who own all of the vineyards surrounding Torgiano for as far as the eye can see. Excellent meals, accompanied by fine Lungarotti wines, are served in the beautiful dining room. The guestrooms are attractively decorated and offer every amenity of a deluxe hotel. Le Tre Vaselle also has outstanding conference rooms furnished in antiques with adjacent dining rooms. The Lungarotti family has thought of everything—to keep the wives happy while their husbands are in meetings, cooking classes are sometimes offered. Other diversions include an outdoor swimming pool, an indoor pool with whirlpool and jet-tech swimming, a sauna, a gym, and even a small outdoor amphitheater. The Lungarottis also have a private wine museum that would be a masterpiece anywhere in the world. Not only do they have an incredible and comprehensive collection of anything pertaining to wine throughout the ages, but the display is a work of art. If you are interested in the production of wine, the museum alone would be worth a detour to Le Tre Vaselle. The hotel is well marked in the center of town.

*LE TRE VASELLE*
*Owners: Lungarotti family*
*Manager: Giovanni Margheritini*
*Via Garibaldi, 48*
*06089 Torgiano (PG), Italy*
*Tel: (075) 98 80 447, Fax: (075) 98 80 214*
*E-mail: backoffice@3vaselle.it*
*61 rooms, Double: Lire 340,000–450,000*
*Open all year, Credit cards: all major*
*Restaurant open daily*
*17 km SW of Assisi, 158 km N of Rome*
*Region: Umbria, Michelin Map 430*
*www.karenbrown.com/italyinns/letrevaselle.html*

When the Porto Pirgos first opened its doors to guests in 1999, it redefined the meaning of luxury. You cannot help falling in love with this superb small hotel built on a slope of a hill that stretches down to a pristine white sand beach gently lapped by the crystal sea. Built upon the foundations of a private villa, the hotel today continues to exude the ambiance of an exquisite, fine home. A refined, intimate elegance reigns supreme, with cozy nooks, comfortable chairs, soft lighting, awesome antiques, bouquets of fresh flowers, wrought-iron fixtures, beamed ceilings, thick walls, oil paintings, gorgeous antiques, and richly hued Oriental carpets accenting antique terra-cotta floors. Adding to the romance are the sea views framed by every window. The guestrooms are also furnished with antiques and, like the rest of the hotel, everything is of the highest quality and good taste. A large swimming pool is set in the garden by the hotel and a second pool nestles under towering pine trees next to the beach. Breakfast and dinner are included in the price of the room and not only is the food exceptionally delicious, but the setting is outstanding. The main dining room has a stunning mosaic floor that looks as if it came straight out of an old Roman villa. When the weather is balmy, guests eat out on the terrace where, as the sun sets and the stars begin to peek through the darkness, you can see the volcano of Stromboli on the horizon.

*PORTO PIRGOS*      ***New***
*Owner: Adolfo Salabe*
*Manager: Caterina Messina*
*Localita: Marina di Bordila, S.S. 522*
*89861 Parghelia–Tropea (CZ), Italy*
*Tel: (0963) 60 03 51, Fax: (0963) 60 06 90*
*18 rooms, Double: Lire 900,000 (Jul & Aug)\**
*\*Rate includes breakfast & dinner*
*Open mid-May to Oct, Credit cards: all major*
*Restaurant open daily*
*5 km E of Tropea, Southern Italy–near tip of toe*
*Region: Calabria, Michelin Map 431*
*www.karenbrown.com/italyinns/portopirgos.html*

The deluxe Borgo di Basti Creti is not a hotel at all, but a 13th-century hamlet with just a tiny cluster of stone buildings which have been meticulously restored and now offer refined, exclusive accommodations in five cottages, each with a living room, dining room, fully-equipped kitchen, and from one to three bedrooms. There is an alluring tranquillity to this remote (yet easily accessible) hamlet that crowns a knoll overlooking the glorious Umbrian countryside. Nothing commercial intrudes upon the senses. As you drive up the hill to the property, it appears to be a private estate. Once inside the gates everything is perfect—beautiful swimming pool, meticulous gardens, lush lawns, giant trees, and birds who seem to sing on cue. Even when all the cottages are occupied, there is utter serenity. It is not surprising that Borgo di Basti Creti is so outstanding: it belongs to the Wirth family, who also own the Hassler in Rome, one of the finest hotels in the world. What makes the Borgo di Basti Creti even more special is that Carmen Wirth has poured her love and talent into every detail, personally selecting just the right elegantly rustic furnishings and tasteful materials, imbuing everything with her impeccable taste and eye for detail. *Directions*: Take the A1 towards Florence, exit at Orte and take the E45 towards Cesena. Exit at Umbertide and continue north for about 4 km to Niccone. Turn left at Niccone, then just before you come into Spedalicchio, turn left and follow the signs to Borgo di Basti Creti.

*BORGO DI BASTI CRETI*
*Owner: Carmen B. Wirth*
*Spedalicchio*
*06019 Umbertide (PG), Italy*
*Reservations: Tel: (06) 69 90 576, Fax: (06) 67 88 472*
*5 cottages, from Lire 2,450,000 per week\**
*\*1-week minimum (Saturday to Saturday)*
*Open all year, Credit cards: none accepted*
*Dinner available for guests Apr to Nov*
*3 km S of Spedalicchio, 15 km NW of Umbertide*
*Region: Umbria, Michelin Map 430*
*www.karenbrown.com/italyinns/borgodibasti.html*

The moderately priced Stella d'Italia is located in San Mamete, a tiny, picturesque village nestled along the northern shore of Lake Lugano, just a few minutes' drive from the Swiss border. Mario and Dolores Ortelli are the most cordial of hosts and son Franco, the fourth generation of the family to run the Stella d'Italia, works in the restaurant. The heart of the hotel is a 17th-century villa with thick-walled rooms, painted ceilings, and large French windows opening to views of the lake. The same panoramic lake view is enjoyed by all the guestrooms. Equally spacious rooms are found in the wing renovated in 1999—these have not only space and views but also terraces and top-of-the-line bathrooms. Quite the nicest feature of the hotel is the superb little lakefront garden—a green lawn, fragrant flowers, lacy trees, and a romantic vine-covered trellised dining area make this an ideal spot for wiling away the hours. Steps lead down to a small pier from which guests can swim. Another interesting feature for golf enthusiasts is that there are several golf courses within an easy drive of the hotel—one of these (near the town of Grandola) is among the oldest in Italy. The ferry dock for picking up and dropping off passengers is adjacent to the hotel. *Directions:* From Lugano (Switzerland) head east towards St. Moritz. Cross the border in Valsolda and San Mamete is the next little village. Park beside the hotel or in the large car park at the entrance to the village.

*STELLA D'ITALIA*
*Owners: Ortelli family*
*San Mamete*
*Lake Lugano, 22010 Valsolda (CO), Italy*
*Tel: (0344) 68 139, Fax: (0344) 68 729*
*E-mail: info@stelladitalia.com*
*35 rooms, Double: Lire 215,000–255,000*
*Open Apr to Oct, Credit cards: all major*
*Restaurant open daily*
*8 km E of Lugano, 100 km N of Milan*
*Region: Lombardy, Michelin Map 428*
*www.karenbrown.com/italyinns/stelladitalia.html*

Like most of my favorite hotels, the Concordia is a family operation. Your hostess is the charming Marina Suppiej Caputo. It was her grandfather who established the business many years ago when he bought a 17th-century house and opened a very basic hostelry with a few guestrooms, all identically decorated with characterless, store-bought furniture, and just one bathroom per floor. Although granddad might not have had the resources to begin in a grand style, he had a flair for business and the gift of knowing how to please guests, and passed on this extraordinary legacy. After he died his daughter continued to run the Hotel Concordia (today a deluxe hotel) and his son opened another outstanding small hotel in Venice, the Metropole. Although both are sophisticated properties, they still exude the charm and the genuine warmth of hospitality traditional to the family. The Concordia has a fabulous location, facing directly onto the Piazzetta dei Leoncini, a picturesque corner of Saint Mark's Square—the views of the lacy spires of Saint Mark's Cathedral are stunning. As you enter the hotel and walk up the marble staircase and into the sleek reception area, you might think the decor is quite contemporary, but the comfortable lounge and pretty breakfast area have a traditional ambiance and most of the guestrooms have wonderful, Venetian-style painted furniture. And, what would really make grandfather smile—each of the bedrooms has its very own splendid marble-tiled bathroom.

*HOTEL CONCORDIA*
*Owner: Marina Suppiej Caputo*
*Calle Larga San Marco, 367*
*30124 Venice, Italy*
*Tel: (041) 52 06 866, Fax: (041) 52 06 775*
*57 rooms, Double: from Lire 600,000 (high season)*
*Open all year, Credit cards: all major*
*Restaurant for light lunch (pasta & salad)*
*Vaporetto stop: San Marco*
*Region: Veneto, Michelin Map 429*

The Hotel Flora is reached down a tiny lane, just off one of the main walkways to St. Mark's Square: a secluded hideaway, protected from the bustle of the city yet conveniently close to all the action. At the end of the tiny alley the doors open into a small lobby, beyond which is an enchanting small garden, an oasis of serenity with white wrought-iron tables and chairs surrounding a gently tinkling fountain. Potted plants, small trees, and lacy vines complete the idyllic scene. The hotel encloses the garden on three sides: doors open to the right to a dear little bar and the breakfast room. The lounges are Victorian in mood with dark furniture. The bedrooms vary greatly in their size and decor, but all have antique furnishings and Victorian-style wallpaper covers many of the walls. There is definitely an old-world atmosphere. There is no restaurant at the hotel, which is absolutely no problem since Venice abounds with wonderful places to dine. Breakfast, of course, is served to guests. Signor Romanelli, who owns this small hotel, personally sees that his guests are well taken care of. The Hotel Flora is a favorite of many travelers to Venice. Although it is a relatively simple hotel and would not appeal to those looking for deluxe accommodations, the Hotel Flora is a rare find for those who want a relatively inexpensive place to stay in the heart of Venice that combines a superb location, warmth of welcome, and charm.

*HOTEL FLORA*
*Owner: Ruggero Romanelli*
*Calle Larga 22 Marzo, 2283/a*
*30124 Venice, Italy*
*Tel: (041) 52 05 844, Fax: (041) 52 28 217*
*E-mail: info@hotelflora.it*
*44 rooms, Double: Lire 400,000*
*Open all year, Credit cards: all major*
*No restaurant, breakfast only*
*Vaporetto stop: Vallaresso*
*Region: Veneto, Michelin Map 429*
*www.karenbrown.com/italyinns/hotelflora.html*

If you love opulent elegance, and if cost is of no consequence to you, the Gritti Palace is an excellent choice for your hotel in Venice. The location is marvelous—just a short walk from St. Mark's Square yet far enough removed to miss the city's noise and summer mob of tourists. With careful planning, you can be entirely insulated in a private and very special world from the moment you arrive until you reluctantly depart. If you take a private motor launch from the airport or the Piazza Roma, you can descend stylishly at the deluxe little private pier in front of the hotel where porters will be waiting to whisk you to your room to be pampered and spoiled. All at a price, of course. The Gritti Palace is expensive—but then what would you expect when staying in the 15th-century palace of the immensely wealthy Venetian Doge, Andrea Gritti? The Gritti Palace has a charming terrace on the bank of the Grand Canal where you dine in splendor and watch the constant stream of boat traffic. The lobby and lounge areas open off the terrace and are grandly decorated with antiques. The bedrooms are large and very fancy in decor, and those that face the canal are presented with a 24-hour show. *NOTE:* The Gritti Palace offers cooking courses—each lasting from Monday through Friday and specializing in a particular aspect of the preparation fine food. If you are interested, contact the hotel for details.

*HOTEL GRITTI PALACE*
*Manager: Massimo Feriani*
*Campo Santa Maria del Giglio, 2467*
*30124 Venice, Italy*
*Tel: (041) 79 46 11, Fax: (041) 52 00 942*
*93 rooms, Double: Lire 1,100,000–1,600,000\**
*\*Breakfast not included*
*Open all year, Credit cards: all major*
*Restaurant open daily*
*Vaporetto stop: Santa Maria del Giglio, also private dock*
*Region: Veneto, Michelin Map 429*

The Hotel La Fenice et Des Artistes, although not inexpensive, costs less than many other hotels in Venice that do not offer nearly its ambiance. This is a family-run hotel, which undoubtedly adds to its charm (the hotel was opened by the owner's mother). The lobby is small, but seems spacious since there are two small garden patios that open from it. Here guests sit in the late afternoon for a cup of tea or an aperitif before dinner. Doors to the right lead to a club-like lounge and an intimate bar. The reception area is a triangle connecting the original building on the right with a newer wing on the left. Both sections are nice and all of the rooms are air-conditioned—a welcome relief on a hot day. The bedrooms are not large, but adequate, and each room is color-coordinated with different wallpaper setting the theme. In addition to the guestrooms within the hotel, there are also five family apartments available. These are located in a separate building just a short walk away. Taverna La Fenice, one of the oldest and most elegant restaurants in Venice, is incorporated into the hotel. The hotel is located near the fabulous La Fenice theater, which burned down, but is now under reconstruction.

*HOTEL LA FENICE ET DES ARTISTES*
*Owner: Michele Facchini*
*Campiello de la Fenice, San Marco, 1936*
*30124 Venice, Italy*
*Tel: (041) 52 32 333, Fax: (041) 52 03 721*
*E-mail: fenice@fenicehotels.it*
*75 rooms, Double: Lire 260,000–390,000*
*Suite: Lire 420,000–550,000*
*Open all year, Credit cards: all major*
*Restaurant (separate management) open daily*
*Near La Fenice theater*
*Vaporetto stop: San Marco*
*Region: Veneto, Michelin Map 429*
*www.karenbrown.com/italyinns/lafeniceetdesartistes.html*

The Hotel Lisbona, a small, rose-colored villa with brown shutters, is tucked down an arcaded walkway in a quiet setting, yet only a hundred meters from Saint Mark's Square. The location is excellent and we had stopped by many times, but thought the decor too simple. However, in 1998 we had a pleasant surprise: the Lisbona had just completed a total renovation—all new carpets, wall coverings, and draperies. Everything is now fresh and pretty. The intimate reception area, which also serves as the lounge, has an old-fashioned look with a terrazzo floor accented by an Oriental carpet, chairs covered in turquoise velvet, brocade walls, and a Venetian glass chandelier. The bedrooms too have had a total face-lift. Each is now similarly decorated, with either a pastel-pink or light-blue damask material covering the walls, matching draperies, and color-coordinating bedspreads. Each room has air conditioning, a mini bar, satellite TV, direct-dial phone, and even a safe deposit box. The side of the hotel faces onto the San Moisé Canal, and from most of the bedrooms you can watch the action of gondolas and small boats as they ply the waterway. Like many of the smaller hotels in Venice, the Lisbona is managed by the owner, the gracious Cristiano Fogliata, who is usually at the front desk to personally greet his guests. The Hotel Lisbona is not a deluxe hotel, but a good-value, moderately priced place to stay in the heart of expensive Venice.

*HOTEL LISBONA*
*Owner: Cristiano Fogliata*
*San Marco, 2153*
*30124 Venice, Italy*
*Tel: (041) 52 86 774, Fax: (041) 52 07 061*
*15 rooms, Double: Lire 450,000*
*Open all year*
*Credit cards: all major*
*No restaurant, breakfast only*
*Vaporetto stop: San Marco*
*Region: Veneto, Michelin Map 429*

The Locanda Ai Santi Apostoli is housed on the third floor of the 15th-century Michiel Palace, the ancestral home of your charming host, Stefano Bianchi-Michiel. Today you would hardly realize there is a hotel in the building, most of which is leased out to various businesses. A double door faces directly onto the street with only a discreet brass plaque on the wall and the name *Locanda Ai Santi Apostoli* to give confidence that you have found the right address. Ring the bell, pass through the courtyard and into the building on the far side, turn left, and take the elevator to the third floor. Until you arrive, everything looks rather nondescript, but once you step into the intimate hotel, you see that indeed this building was at one time a proper patrician mansion with a prime location facing the Grand Canal. The living room (the favorite nook for guests to gather) is especially appealing, with comfortable sofas, fine oil paintings, antique furniture, and three tall windows overlooking the canal. If you want to splurge, the deluxe bedrooms (numbers 8 and 9) are outstanding—both capture the same romantic view of the canal. However, you can't go wrong with any of standard bedrooms. All are attractively decorated using some family antiques, and have good bathrooms and twin beds which can convert into kings. The Locanda Ai Santi Apostoli offers not only a genteel, old-fashioned elegance, but also the great bonus of your charming host, who graciously welcomes guests into his family's once-grand palace that still exudes a rich heritage of the past.

*LOCANDA AI SANTI APOSTOLI*
*Owner: Stefano Bianchi-Michiel*
*Strada Nova, 4391*
*30131 Venice, Italy*
*Tel: (041) 52 12 612, Fax: (041) 52 12 611*
*11 rooms, Double: Lire 400,000–530,000*
*2-bedroom, 1-bath suite for 4: Lire 620,000–720,000*
*Closed mid-Dec to Mar, Credit cards: all major*
*No restaurant, breakfast only*
*Vaporetto stop: Ca d'Oro, also private dock*
*Region: Veneto, Michelin Map 429*

Readers frequently share a discovery in some remote hideaway, but we rarely receive recommendations for well-known hotels in popular tourist spots. However, we heard from many readers who urged us to include the Londra Palace in our guide, and they were right—the Londra Palace is indeed very special. It enjoys a choice location, just a few minutes' walk from Saint Mark's Square, right on the waterfront, and boasts of 100 windows facing the lagoon. In addition, there is a snug rooftop terrace, which captures an incredible panorama of magical Venice. The guestrooms are splendidly decorated, each with at least one authentic, 19th-century piece of Biedermeier furniture. In addition to antiques, each room has fine original paintings and sumptuous fabrics, creating an ambiance of refinement and elegance. The bathrooms too are special—all are tiled with pink Carrara marble and equipped with Jacuzzis. Since 1992 the hotel has undergone a total renovation and the final phase of this eight-million-dollar renovation was completed in March 1999. During this final phase, the hotel's lobby, restaurant, bar, public areas, and façade have been brilliantly transformed. The hotel is gorgeous. The extra seating in the restaurant will be a bonus for chilly days, but when the weather is balmy, there is no more romantic spot to dine than the excellent Do Leoni, a terrace restaurant in front of the hotel, facing the lagoon.

*LONDRA PALACE*
*Manager: Lorenzo Righi*
*Riva degli Schiavoni, 4171*
*30122 Venice, Italy*
*Tel: (041) 52 00 533, Fax: (041) 52 25 032*
*E-mail: info@hotelondra.it*
*53 rooms, Double: Lire 468,000–785,000*
*Suite: Lire 660,000–1,097,000*
*Open all year, Credit cards: all major*
*Restaurant open daily*
*Vaporetto stop: San Zaccaria*
*Region: Veneto, Michelin Map 429*
*www.karenbrown.com/italyinns/londrapalace.html*

The Pensione Accademia is enchanting—a romantic Venetian villa with charming gardens and an idyllic setting on a small piece of land that is nestled between two canals. You enter into a sweet "secret garden," enclosed by walls that are heavily draped with ivy. If you look closely, you will discover black iron gates that open to steps leading down to the villa's private dock. As you leave the garden and enter the wisteria-covered palazzo, you come into a spacious lobby, which opens at the other end onto another garden. A staircase leads to some of the guestrooms that are located in the original villa. Other bedrooms are connected by a hallway to a portion of the hotel borrowed from an adjacent building. In 1998 all of the rooms throughout the villa were renovated. Some of the bedrooms have canal views, but from these you can hear some of the noise of passing motor boats. If you want a quiet room, ask for one overlooking over the rear garden. The only hitch to this picture of perfection is that your chances are slim of snaring a room in this romantic hideaway—the hotel is so special that loyal guests reserve their own favorite room for the following year as they leave. Spring and fall are most heavily booked—your chances are better in July and August when the prices are even a little lower.

*PENSIONE ACCADEMIA*
*Owner: Giovanna Salmaso*
*Manager: Massimo Dinato*
*Dorsoduro, 1058*
*30123 Venice, Italy*
*Tel: (041) 52 10 188, Fax: (041) 52 39 152*
*26 rooms, Double: Lire 240,000–420,000*
*Open all year, Credit cards: all major*
*No restaurant, breakfast only*
*Vaporetto stop: Accademia, also private dock*
*Region: Veneto, Michelin Map 429*

       *Hotel Descriptions*

At first glance the exterior of the Pensione Seguso appears quite bland: a rather boxy affair without much of the elaborate architectural enhancements so frequently evident in Venice. However, the inside of the pension radiates warmth and charm, with Oriental rugs setting off antique furniture and heirloom silver service. The hotel is located on the left bank of Venice—across the Grand Canal from the heart of the tourist area, about a 15-minute walk to St. Mark's Square (or only a few minutes by ferry from the Accademia boat stop). For several generations the hotel has been in the Seguso family who provide a home-like ambiance for the guest who does not demand luxury. In front there is a miniature terrace harboring a few tables set under umbrellas. Several of the bedrooms have views of the canal (although these rooms are the noisiest due to the canal traffic). Remember this is a simple pension, with most of the rooms sharing a bathroom: if you are looking for the amenities offered by a hotel, the Pensione Seguso would not be for you. However, the most pleasant surprise is that the value-conscious tourist can stay at the Pensione Seguso with breakfast and dinner included for what the price of a room alone would cost in most hotels in Venice. The Seguso has an elevator—handy if you have a problem with stairs.

*PENSIONE SEGUSO*
*Owners: Seguso family*
*Grand Canal Zattere, 779*
*30123 Venice, Italy*
*Tel: (041) 52 86 858, Fax: (041) 52 22 340*
*36 rooms, Double: from Lire 200,000*
 *(or from Lire 340,000– includes breakfast & dinner)*
*Open Mar to Nov, Credit cards: all major*
*Restaurant open daily for guests only*
*Vaporetto stop: Accademia (10-min walk) or Zattere (5-min walk)*
*Region: Veneto, Michelin Map 429*

The owner of one of the finest small hotels in France—whose opinion I value highly—recommended the Hotel Metropole (located just a few minutes' walk from Saint Mark's Square) as his favorite place to stay in Venice. Now, after being a guest, I can understand his choice. Other hotels might seem more glamorous or opulent, but none have more heart. On entering, I was immediately aware of an aura of hospitality that is usually encountered only in intimate, very small hotels—everyone seems to take personal responsibility that your stay will be a happy one. It appears that the owners, the Beggiato family, who personally manage the hotel, have imbued the staff with their own warmth of hospitality. Many employees have been with them since the hotel first opened in 1971, including the assistant manager, Gianni Derai, who seems to care about the hotel as if it were his own. The Beggiatos are passionate about antiques and have over 2,000 pieces displayed in the hotel, including a fascinating collection of very old corkscrews, small mother-of-pearl boxes, cradles, silver teapots, crucifixes, and intricate wrought-iron locks. All of the spacious bedrooms are individually decorated as in a private home and have fine antique furniture. Another great bonus of the Metropole is its romantic garden, a favorite place for lunch or dinner or to just sit quietly listening to the birds singing in the trees. Some of the bedrooms overlook this pretty garden while others have a beautiful view of the lagoon, as the Hotel Metropole has a marvelous waterfront setting.

*ROMANTIK HOTEL METROPOLE*
*Owners: Beggiato family*
*Riva degli Schiavoni, 4149*
*30122 Venice, Italy*
*Tel: (041) 52 05 044, Fax: (041) 52 23 679*
*E-mail: venice@hotelmetropole.com*
*72 rooms, Double: Lire 620,000–900,000*
*Open all year, Credit cards: all major*
*Restaurant open daily*
*Vaporetto stop: San Zaccaria, also private dock*
*Region: Veneto, Michelin Map 429*
*www.karenbrown.com/italyinns/hotelmetropole.html*

The Hotel Cipriani was founded by the late Giuseppe Cipriani, who during his lifetime became almost a legend in Venice. This beloved man, who founded the internationally famous Harry's Bar in Venice, had a dream of building a fabulous hotel within easy reach of St. Mark's Square and yet far enough away to guarantee seclusion and peace. He bought 3 acres on the island of Giudecca and with the financial assistance of some of his prestigious friends, such as Princess Briget of Prussia and the Earl of Iveagh (head of the Guinness brewing company in Dublin), he accomplished his dream—an elegant Venetian palace-style hotel. The Cipriani is the perfect hotel for those of you who must have a pool, for it is the only hotel with a pool in Venice. And what a pool—it is Olympic size and surrounded by beautiful gardens. The splendor continues inside where the lounges are tastefully decorated in whites and beiges and the bedrooms are large and elegant. In addition to the hotel rooms and suites there are seven super-deluxe apartments (some overlooking St. Mark's Square), which are located next to the hotel in the renovated Palazzo Vendramin. You truly have the best of all worlds at the Cipriani—you are at a superior resort yet only minutes from the heart of Venice in the private launch that waits to whisk you, any time of the day or night, to St. Mark's Square.

*HOTEL CIPRIANI*
*Manager: Dr. Natale Rusconi*
*Isola della Giudecca, 10*
*30133 Venice, Italy*
*Tel: (041) 52 07 744, Fax: (041) 52 03 930*
*E-mail: info@hotelcipriani.it*
*106 rooms, Double: Lire 1,300,000–2,040,000*
*Palazzo Vendramin & Palazzetto: Suite: Lire 2,900,000–6,500,000*
*Open all year, Credit cards: all major*
*Restaurant open daily*
*Vaporetto stop: Zitelle, also private dock*
*Region: Veneto, Michelin Map 429*
*www.karenbrown.com/italyinns/hotelcipriani.html*

The tiny island of Torcello is located about 50 minutes from Venice by boat. This lovely, sleepy little island is usually considered a short stop for the tour boats as they ply their way among the maze of little islands surrounding Venice. But for those who want to linger on Torcello, where they can be close to Venice yet feel out in the country, there is a deluxe inn owned by the Cipriani family. This small inn, the Locanda Cipriani Torcello, is well known to knowledgeable gourmets as a fantastic restaurant. Many arrive every day from Venice just to dine, and depart never knowing that this restaurant also has guestrooms upstairs. The inn is very simple, much more like a small farmhouse than a deluxe hotel. Inside there is a rustic, cozy dining room and outside a beautiful dining terrace surrounded by gardens brilliant in summer with all varieties of flowers. There are only a few bedrooms—all are suites. This is an expensive inn, but an elegant hideaway for relaxing and dining royally in a beautiful country setting. Many famous guests have already discovered this oasis—including Ernest Hemingway, who came here to write. I think you will share his belief that the Locanda Cipriani Torcello is a very special place. Note: The Locanda Cipriani closed for major renovations in 2000, but will be open again by the time of your visit and should be more charming than ever.

*LOCANDA CIPRIANI TORCELLO*
*Owner: Carla Cipriani*
*Manager: Bonifacio Brass*
*30012 Isola Torcello*
*Venice, Italy*
*Tel: (041) 73 01 50, Fax: (041) 73 54 33*
*5 suites: Lire 400,000\**
*\*Rate includes breakfast*
*Closed Nov 4 to Mar 15, Credit cards: all major*
*Restaurant closed Tuesdays*
*Island location, Vaporetto stop: Torcello*
*Region: Veneto, Michelin Map 429*

If the idea of being close to Venice and yet near a beach and casino appeals to you, then perhaps you should consider a hotel located on the Lido, a small island opposite St. Mark's Square. A 15-minute boat ride and a short taxi trip bring you to the Albergo Quattro Fontane, a charming inn that reminds me more of a French country home than an Italian villa. It has a white-stucco exterior with gabled roof, green shutters, and vines creeping both over the door and around some of the small balconies. To the left of the main building is a lovely courtyard whose privacy is established by another wing of the hotel, giving the garden a cozy, walled-in effect. Inside the hotel there is an ambiance of a country home with antiques cleverly used throughout the lounges. The beach is only a short distance away and the Albergo Quattro Fontane can make arrangements for you to reserve a private beach cabana when you arrive at the inn. The cost per day will vary, depending both upon the location and the comparative luxury of the cabana you choose. The beach is wide and the water inviting and clear, although the sand is not as fine and white as we have seen on some of the beaches in southern Italy. It is quite an experience to sample the interesting hierarchy of the Italian beach system.

*ALBERGO QUATTRO FONTANE*
*Manager: Bente Bevilacqua*
*Via 4 Fontane*
*30126 Lido of Venice*
*Venice, Italy*
*Tel: (041) 52 60 22 7, Fax: (041) 52 60 72 6*
*E-mail: info@quattrofontane.com*
*68 rooms, Double: Lire 460,000–580,000*
*Open Apr to mid-Nov, Credit cards: all major*
*Restaurant open daily*
*Vaporetto stop: Lido*
*Region: Veneto, Michelin Map 429*
*www.karenbrown.com/italyinns/quattrofontane.html*

The Hotel Gabbia d'Oro, ideally located in the heart of Verona, is truly a gem that captures the romance of this fascinating city. From the moment you step inside you are surrounded by a relaxed, understated elegance. Although this is a deluxe hotel, there is no hint of stiff formality—your welcome is genuinely warm and friendly in this superbly managed small hotel. Just off the spacious reception area is a cozy lounge with massive beamed ceilings, ancient stone walls, fine antiques, Persian carpet, and handsome old prints in gold frames. Beyond the lobby is an intimate bar where wood paneling—richly mellowed with the patina of age—sets off to perfection chairs upholstered in cherry-red fabric. There is also a charming, sun-filled inner courtyard, called *L'Orangerie*, where you can savor a cup of tea or sip a glass of champagne while relaxing after a day of sightseeing or while enjoying a well-chosen assortment of reading material such as books on travel, fashion, interiors, and flowers. The guestrooms continue the ambiance of loving care. All are individually decorated, reflecting exquisite taste: antiques abound and handsome color-coordinating fabrics are used throughout. Nothing has been spared to make each room beautiful. The standard bedrooms are very pretty, but if you want to splurge, opt for one of the junior suites, which are more spacious. It is such a pleasure to see a hotel that reflects so beautifully the authentic rich heritage of the original building.

*HOTEL GABBIA D'ORO*
*Manager: Camilla Balzarro*
*Corso Porta Borsari, 4/A*
*37121 Verona, Italy*
*Tel: (045) 80 03 060, Fax: (045) 59 02 93*
*E-mail: gabbiadoro@easynet.it*
*27 rooms, Double: Lire 550,000–680,000*
*Suite: Lire 980,000–1,350,000*
*Open all year, Credit cards: all major*
*No restaurant, breakfast only*
*In the heart of Verona, Region: Veneto, Michelin Map 429*
*www.karenbrown.com/italyinns/gabbiadoro.html*

The entrance to the Hotel Victoria is starkly modern—almost with a museum-like quality. The white walls, white ceiling, white floors, and an enormous skylight are softened by green plants. At first glance I was disappointed since I had heard so many glowing reports of the merits of this small hotel. However, the mood begins to change as you enter the reception area with its Oriental carpets and by the time you arrive in the lounge area, there is a definite move toward an antique ambiance. Here you find original heavy ancient wooden beams and one of the original stone walls exposed, leather chairs, and some lovely antique tables. The bedrooms are extremely modern and beautifully functional with good reading lights, comfortable chairs, and excellent bathrooms. The Victoria actually dates back centuries and the new hotel is built within the shell of an ancient building. The architect incorporated some of the archaeologically interesting finds of the site into a museum in the basement level. When the hotel is not full and all of the tables are not needed, special "windows" open up on the floor of the bar and coffee lounge and the museum below is lit so that you can study the artifacts as you enjoy an aperitif or your breakfast. *NOTE:* Hotel Victoria will offer a 20% discount to guests who advise when booking that they are "Karen Brown" readers. (Discount does not apply during opera season or during fairs.)

*HOTEL VICTORIA*
*Owner: Signor Andrea Tamaurini*
*Manager: Signora Giusy Loro*
*Via Adua, 8*
*37121 Verona, Italy*
*Tel: (045) 59 05 66, Fax: (045) 59 01 55*
*E-mail: hotel.victoria@ifinet.it*
*66 rooms, Double: Lire 350,000–450,000*
*Suite: Lire 530,000–750,000*
*Open all year, Credit cards: all major*
*No restaurant, breakfast only, In the heart of Verona*
*Region: Veneto, Michelin Map 429*
*www.karenbrown.com/italyinns/hotelvictoria.html*

With great finesse and determination, Lucia and Paolo, an editor and art collector, managed to purchase Villa Campestri, a magnificent Renaissance villa—no easy feat, considering the 400-acre property had been in one family for 700 years. The pale-yellow villa with handsome lawns and surrounding cypress woods commands a spectacular view over the immense valley and Mugello mountain range. A swimming pool among the trees enjoys this same view. This is the area north of Florence known for its concentration of Medici villas. The guestrooms in the villa have been restored to their original splendor, with high Florentine woodworked ceilings, carefully selected antiques, and delightful blue-and-white-tiled bathrooms. The honeymoon suite features a grand gold-crowned red canopy bed. A sitting room adorned with rich paintings leads to the elegant, stencil-painted dining rooms where original combinations of fresh local produce, cited in several noted restaurant guides, are served with great attention to detail, accompanied by an excellent selection of wines. Equally characteristic rooms are located in the side wing and small independent house. In the vicinity are a golf club, tennis courts, and riding stables. Villa Campestri offers refined and romantic accommodations with the professional and cordial hospitality given by daughter, Viola. *Directions*: Exit at Barberino di Mugello from the A1 autostrada and follow signs for San Piero A Sieve, then Cardetole, then Sagginale, and finally up the road on the right to Vicchio—35 km from Florence.

*VILLA CAMPESTRI*
*Owners: Lucia & Paolo Pasquali*
*Localita: Campestri 19/22*
*50039 Vicchio di Mugello (FI), Italy*
*Tel: (055) 84 90 107, Fax: (055) 84 90 108*
*E-mail: villa.campestri@villacampestri.it*
*21 rooms, Double: Lire 280,000–350,000*
*Open Mar to Nov, Credit cards: all major*
*Restaurant for guests only*
*35 km NE of Florence*
*Region: Tuscany, Michelin Map 429/430*
*www.karenbrown.com/italyinns/villacampestri.html*

Valle d'Aosta

*Milan*

Piedmont

Lombardy

Trentino-
Alto Adige

Friuli-
Venezia
Giulia

Veneto

*Venice*

Emila-Romagna

*Genoa*

Liguria

*Florence*

Tuscany

Marches

CORSICA
(France)

Umbria

Abruzzo

*ROME*

Lazio

Molise

*Bari*

Campania

*Naples*

Basilicata

Apulia

Sardinia

Calabria

*Cagliari*

*Palermo*

Sicily

*Regions of Italy*

325

# Hotels by Region

**Abruzzo**

Civitella del Tronto, Hotel Zunica

**Apulia**

Alberobello, Hotel dei Trulli
Marina di Pulsano, Tenuta del Barco
Monopoli, Il Melograno
Savelletri di Fasano, Masseria San Domenico

**Basilicata**

Maratea, La Locanda delle Donne Monache
Maratea–Acquafredda, Villa Cheta Elite
Maratea–Fiumicello, Santavenere Hotel

**Calabria**

Cittadella del Capo, Palazzo del Capo
Tropea–Parghelia, Porto Pirgos

**Campania**

Amalfi, Hotel Santa Caterina
Capri
    Casa Morgano
    Grand Hotel Quisisana
    Hotel Luna
    Hotel Punta Tragara

Capri (continued)
    La Scalinatella
    Villa Brunella
Positano
    Albergo Casa Albertina
    Buca di Bacco
    Hotel Palazzo Murat
    Hotel Villa Franca
    Il San Pietro di Positano
    Le Sirenuse Hotel
    Romantik Hotel Poseidon
Ravello
    Hotel Palumbo
    Marmorata Hotel
    Palazzo Sasso
    Villa Cimbrone
    Villa Maria
Santa Maria di Castellabate, Hotel Villa Sirio
Sorrento, Grand Hotel Excelsior Vittoria

**Emilia-Romagna**

Bologna, Hotel Corona d'Oro 1890
Brisighella, Relais Torre Pratesi
Castel Guelfo, Locanda Solarola
Montegridolfo, Albergo Palazzo Viviani
Ravenna, Albergo Cappello
Soragna, Locanda del Lupo

## Friuli-Venezia Giulia

Rivarotta, Villa Luppis
San Floriano del Collio, Romantik Golf Hotel

## Lazio

Anguillara Sabazio, Country Relais I Due Laghi
Bracciano, Hotel Villa Clementina
Farnese–Voltone, Il Voltone
Grottaferrata, Park Hotel Villa Grazioli
Ladispoli–Palo Laziale, La Posta Vecchia
Poggio Mirteto, Hotel Borgo Paraelios
Ponza (Isola di), Gennarino A Mare
Rome
    Albergo del Sole
    Hotel Gregoriana
    Hotel Hassler
    Hotel Lord Byron
    Hotel Majestic Roma
    La Residenza
    Romantik Hotel Barocco
    The Inn at the Spanish Steps
Tivoli, Hotel Sirene
Tivoli–Villa Adriana, Hotel Restaurant Adriano

## Liguria

Camogli, Hotel Cenobio dei Dogi
Chiavari a Leivi, Ca'Peo
Finale Ligure, Hotel Punta Est

Levanto, Hotel Stella Maris
Portofino
    Hotel Eden
    Hotel Splendido
    Splendido Mare
Sestri Levante, Hotel Helvetia
Tellaro, Locanda Miranda

## Lombardy

Argegno–Lake Como, Albergo Villa Belvedere
Bellagio–Lake Como
    Grand Hotel Villa Serbelloni
    Hotel Florence
    La Pergola
Cernobbio–Lake Como, Villa d'Este
Gardone Riviera–Lake Garda, Villa Fiordaliso
Gargnano-Villa–Lake Garda, Baia d'Oro
Limone sul Garda–Lake Garda, Hotel Le Palme
Luino, Camin Hotel Luino
Maleo, Albergo del Sole
Milan
    Antica Locanda dei Mercanti
    Four Seasons Hotel Milano
    Grand Hotel et de Milan
    Hotel de la Ville
Milan–Vizzola Ticino, Hotel Villa Malpensa
Pescatori–Lake Maggiore, Hotel Verbano

## Lombardy (continued)

Sirmione–Lake Garda
    Albergo Sirmione
    Hotel Grifone
    Villa Cortine Palace Hotel
Valsolda–Lake Lugano, Stella d'Italia

## Piedmont

Cannero Riviera, Cannero Lakeside Hotel
Cioccaro di Penango, Locanda del Sant'Uffizio
Sauze d'Oulx, Il Capricorno

## Sardinia

Sardinia–Oliena, Hotel Su Gologone
Sardinia–Porto Cervo, Hotel Pitrizza
Sardinia–Porto Conte, Hotel El Faro
Sardinia–Santa Margherita di Pula, Is Morus Relais

## Sicily

Sicily–Agrigento
    Foresteria Baglio della Luna
    Villa Athena
Sicily–Erice, Hotel Moderno
Sicily–Gangivecchio, Tenuta Gangivecchio
Sicily–Marina di Ragusa, Eremo della Giubiliana
Sicily–Palermo
    Centrale Palace Hotel
    Villa Igiea Grand Hotel

Sicily–Syracuse, Grand Hotel Siracusa
Sicily–Taormina
    Grand Hotel Timeo
    Hotel Belvedere
    Villa Sant'Andrea

## Trentino-Alto Adige

Bressanone (Brixen), Hotel Elephant
Castelrotto (Kastelruth), Hotel Cavallino d'Oro
Corvara, Romantik Hotel La Perla
Fiè (Völs), Romantik Hotel Turm
Merano
    Hotel Castel Labers
    Hotel Fragsburg
Pergine, Castel Pergine
Rasun di Sopra, Ansitz Heufler Hotel
Sesto (Sexten), Berghotel Tirol
Tires–San Cipriano, Pensione Stefaner

## Tuscany

Campiglia Marittima, Castello di Magona
Carmignano–Artimino, Paggeria Medicea
Castellina in Chianti
    Locanda Le Piazze
    Romantik Hotel Tenuta di Ricavo
Castiglion Fiorentino, Relais San Pietro
Cetona, La Frateria di Padre Eligio

**Tuscany (continued)**

Cortona
    Hotel San Michele
    Il Falconiere Relais e Ristorante
    (Montanare), Locanda del Molino
Elba–Ottone, Hotel Villa Ottone
Florence
    Grand Hotel Villa Cora
    Hotel Continental
    Hotel Helvetia and Bristol
    Hotel Il Guelfo Bianco
    Hotel Lungarno
    Hotel Regency
    Mario's
    Torre di Bellosguardo
    Villa Montartino
Florence–Candeli, Hotel Villa La Massa
Florence–Fiesole
    Hotel Villa Fiesole
    Pensione Bencista
    Villa San Michele
Gaiole in Chianti, L'Ultimo Mulino
Lucca, Locanda L'Elisa
Montebenichi, Castelletto di Montebenichi
Montefiridolfi, Il Borghetto Country Inn
Montefollonico
    La Chiusa
    Locanda La Costa
Monticchiello, L'Olmo
Orbetello, San Biagio

Panzano in Chianti, Villa Le Barone
Petrignano, Alla Corte del Sole
Portico di Romagna, Albergo Al Vecchio Convento
Porto Ercole, Il Pellicano
Porto Santo Stefano, Hotel Torre di Cala Piccola
Radda in Chianti, Relais Fattoria Vignale
Reggello–Vaggio, Villa Rigacci
San Gimignano
    Hotel L'Antico Pozzo
    La Cisterna
    La Collegiata
San Gusmè, Hotel Villa Arceno
San Leonino, Hotel Belvedere di San Leonino
San Sano, Hotel Residence San Sano
Scansano, Antico Casale di Scansano
Siena, Hotel Antica Torre
Sinalunga, Locanda dell'Amorosa
Sovicille–Pretale, Borgo Pretale
Vicchio di Mugello, Villa Campestri

**Umbria**

Armenzano, Hotel "Le Silve di Armenzano"
Assisi
    Hotel Subasio
    Hotel Umbra
    Il Palazzo
    La Fortezza
Bevagna, L'Orto degli Angeli
Canalicchio di Collazone, Relais Il Canalicchio

## Umbria (continued)

Colle San Paolo, Hotel Villa di Montesolare
Gubbio, Relais Ducale
Montefalco, Villa Pambuffetti
Orvieto, La Badia
Ronti, Palazzo Terranova
Solomeo, Locanda Solomeo
Spoleto
     Hotel Gattapone
     Hotel San Luca
Spoleto–Monteluco, Eremo delle Grazie
Torgiano, Le Tre Vaselle
Umbertide, Borgo di Basti Creti

## Valle d'Aosta

Champoluc, Villa Anna Maria
Cogne–Valmontey, Hotel Petit Dahu

## Veneto

Asolo
     Albergo al Sole
     Hotel Duse
     Villa Cipriani
Cortina d'Ampezzo
     Baita Fraina
     Hotel de la Poste
     Hotel Menardi
Follina, Romantik Hotel Villa Abbazia

Gargagnago, La Foresteria Serègo Alighieri
Mira, Romantik Hotel Villa Margherita
Pedemonte, Hotel Villa del Quar
San Viglio–Lake Garda, Locanda San Viglio
Scorzè, Villa Soranzo Conestabile
Venice
     Hotel Concordia
     Hotel Flora
     Hotel Gritti Palace
     Hotel La Fenice et Des Artistes
     Hotel Lisbona
     Locanda Ai Santi Apostoli
     Londra Palace
     Pensione Accademia
     Pensione Seguso
     Romantik Hotel Metropole
Venice–Isola della Giudecca, Hotel Cipriani
Venice–Isola Torcello, Locanda Cipriani Torcello
Venice–Lido, Albergo Quattro Fontane
Verona
     Hotel Gabbia d'Oro
     Hotel Victoria

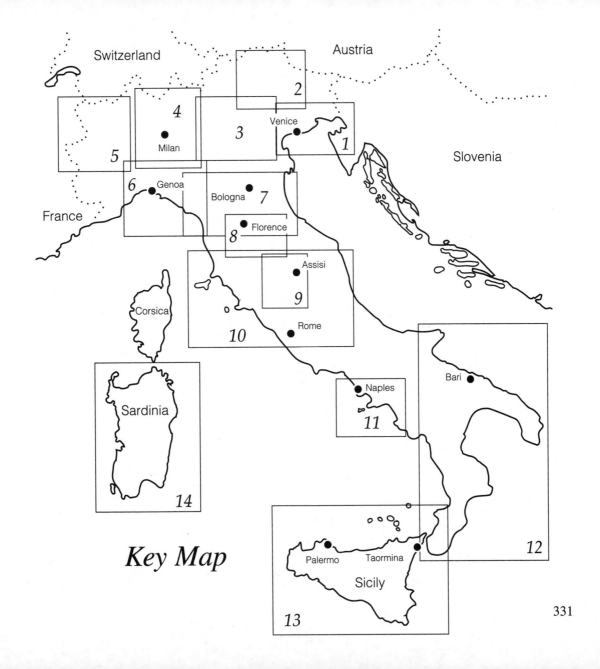

Switzerland

Austria

*2*

*4*

Milan

*5*

*3*

Venice

*1*

Slovenia

*6*

Genoa

Bologna

*7*

France

*8*

Florence

Corsica

Assisi

*9*

*10*

Rome

Bari

Sardinia

Naples

*11*

*12*

*14*

*Key Map*

Palermo

Taormina

Sicily

*13*

331

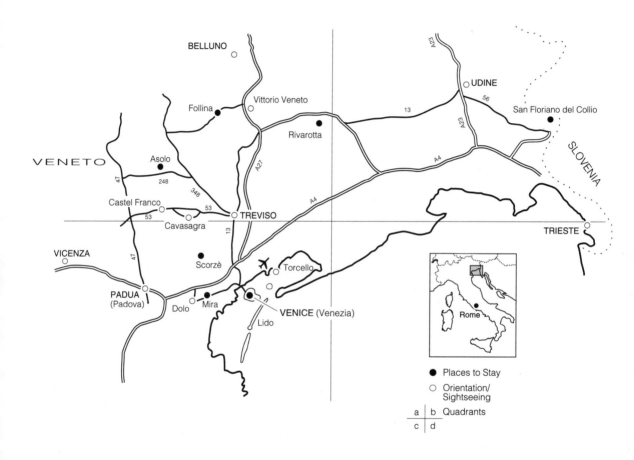

BELLUNO

UDINE

A23

Follina

Vittorio Veneto

San Floriano del Collio

13

Rivarotta

56

A23

SLOVENIA

VENETO

A4

Asolo

248

A27

348

A4

Castel Franco

53

53

TREVISO

TRIESTE

Cavasagra

13

VICENZA

Scorzè

47

Torcello

PADUA
(Padova)

Dolo   Mira

VENICE (Venezia)

Lido

Rome

● Places to Stay

○ Orientation/
  Sightseeing

| a | b | Quadrants |
|---|---|-----------|
| c | d |           |

*Map 1*

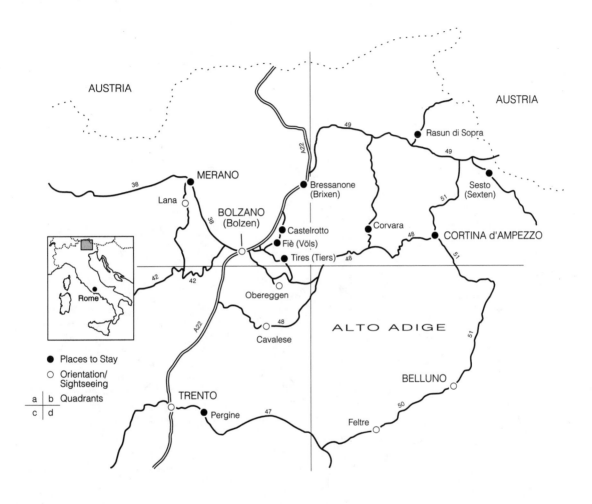

AUSTRIA

AUSTRIA

38

MERANO

Lana ○

Rasun di Sopra

49

49

Bressanone
(Brixen)

BOLZANO
(Bolzen)

Castelrotto

Fiè (Völs)

Tires (Tiers)

Corvara

51

Sesto
(Sexten)

CORTINA d'AMPEZZO

48

51

Rome

42

42

Obereggen ○

48

Cavalese

ALTO ADIGE

51

● Places to Stay

○ Orientation/
  Sightseeing

| a | b | Quadrants |
| c | d |

TRENTO

Pergine

47

BELLUNO

50

Feltre

*Map 2*

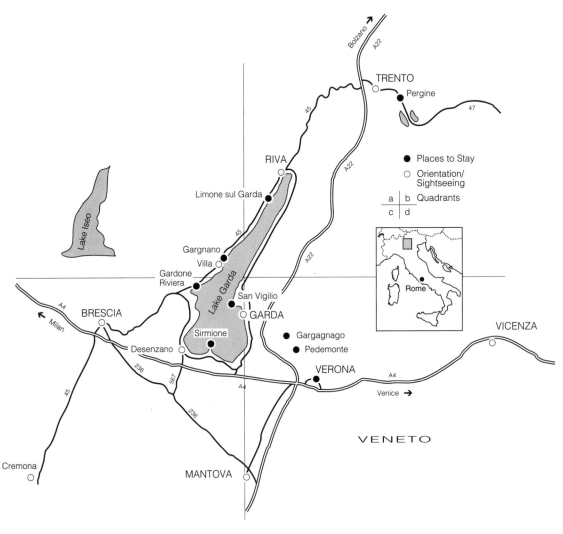

● Places to Stay

○ Orientation/
Sightseeing

| a | b | Quadrants |
|---|---|-----------|
| c | d | |

*Map 3*

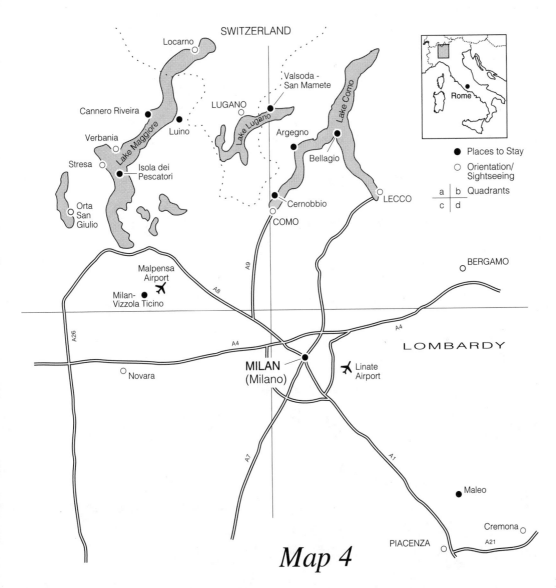

Map 4

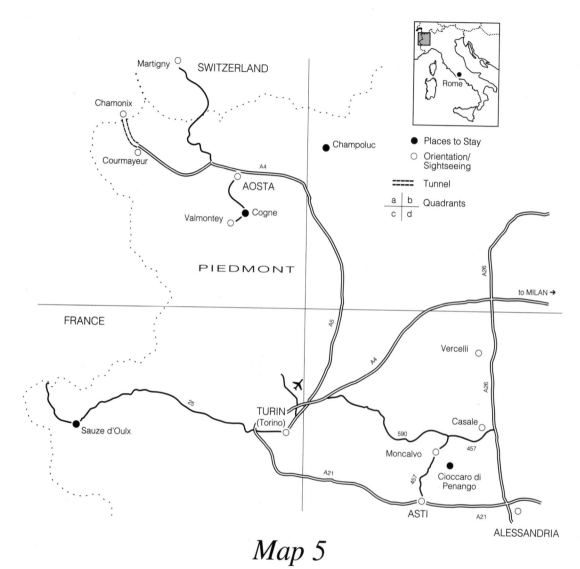

Martigny ○   SWITZERLAND

Chamonix ○

Courmayeur ○

A4

○ AOSTA

Valmontey ○   ● Cogne

PIEDMONT

FRANCE

● Champoluc

● Places to Stay

○ Orientation/
Sightseeing

════ Tunnel

| a | b |
|---|---|
| c | d |

Quadrants

Rome

A26

to MILAN →

A5

A4

Vercelli ○

A26

Casale ○

Moncalvo ○

TURIN
(Torino) ●

590

457

● Cioccaro di
Penango

457

Sauze d'Oulx ●

25

A21

ASTI ○

A21 ○

ALESSANDRIA

*Map 5*

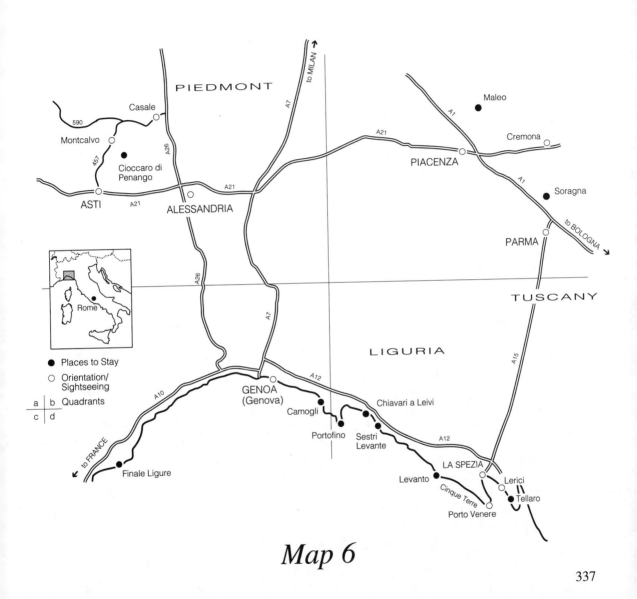

PIEDMONT

to MILAN

Casale

590

Montcalvo

457

Cioccaro di
Penango

ASTI

A21

ALESSANDRIA

A26

A7

Maleo

A1

A21

PIACENZA

Cremona

A1

Soragna

to BOLOGNA

PARMA

Rome

TUSCANY

● Places to Stay

○ Orientation/
   Sightseeing

a | b   Quadrants
c | d

LIGURIA

A15

A26

A7

A10

GENOA
(Genova)

A12

Chiavari a Leivi

Camogli

Portofino

Sestri
Levante

A12

to FRANCE

Finale Ligure

Levanto

Cinque Terre

LA SPEZIA

Lerici

Tellaro

Porto Venere

*Map 6*

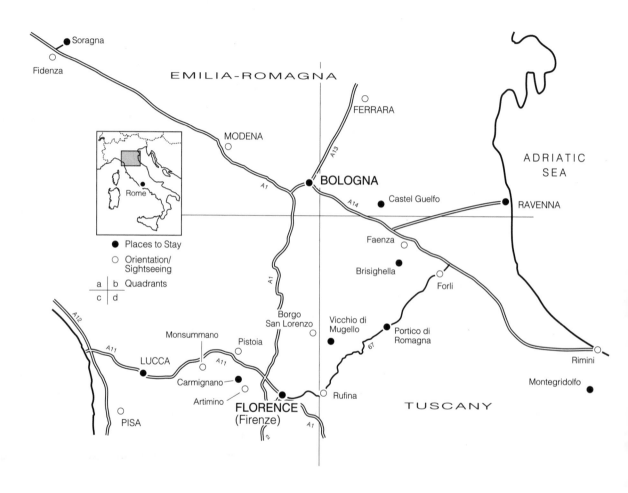

*Map 7*

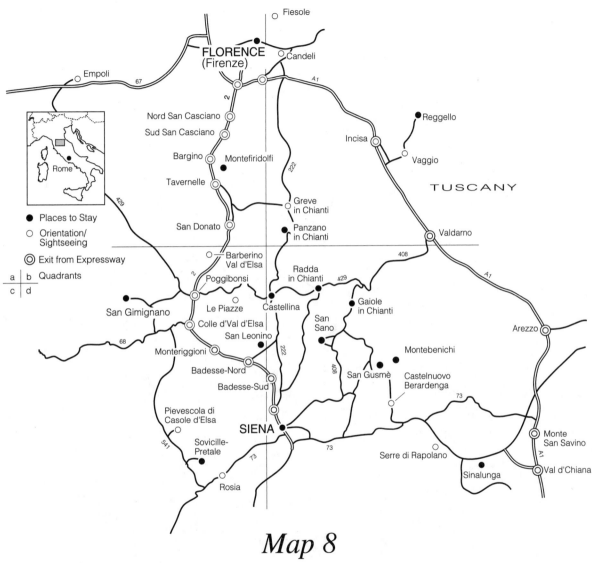

Fiesole

FLORENCE
(Firenze)

Candeli

Empoli                    67

Reggello

Nord San Casciano                                    Incisa

Sud San Casciano                                              Vaggio

Bargino      Montefiridolfi                    TUSCANY

Tavernelle

Greve
in Chianti

San Donato                    Panzano
in Chianti                    Valdarno

Barberino
Val d'Elsa                    408

Radda
in Chianti

Poggibonsi                    429

Le Piazze                    Gaiole
in Chianti

San Gimignano                    Castellina

Colle d'Val d'Elsa        San
Sano                    Arezzo

San Leonino

68                    Montebenichi

Monteriggioni

Badesse-Nord                    San Gusmè        Castelnuovo
Berardenga

Badesse-Sud                    Monte
San Savino

Pievescola di
Casole d'Elsa

SIENA                    73                    Val d'Chiana

Sovicille-
Pretale                    73        73                    Serre di Rapolano

Rosia                    Sinalunga

● Places to Stay

○ Orientation/
Sightseeing

◎ Exit from Expressway

a | b
——  Quadrants
c | d

Rome

*Map 8*

to Florence

73

Fossombrone

TUSCANY

AREZZO

Polvano

Citta dei Costello

Ronti

GUBBIO

Monte
Savino

73

Castiglion Fiorentino

Spedalicchio

Umbertide

UMBRIA

SIENA

326

A1

Val
d'Chiana
Bettolle

CORTONA

Montanare

15

Petrignano

Lake
Trasimeno

15

Pianello

Sinalunga

Montefellonico

Pienza

A1

Montepulciano

Chiusi
Chianciano

Panicale

PERUGIA

ASSISI

Armenzano

Monticchiello

3

Cetona

220

Colle
San Paolo

SPINA

Torgiano

Spello

Foligno

A1

Fabro

Bevegna

Montefalco

Trevi

2

Orvieto
exit

TODI

SPOLETO

ORVIETO

Lake Corbara

Monteluco

Rome

to Rome

A1

3

● Places to Stay

○ Orientation/
  Sightseeing

◎ Exit from Expressway

Lake
Bolsena

TERNI

| a | b | Quadrants |
| c | d | |

*Map 9*

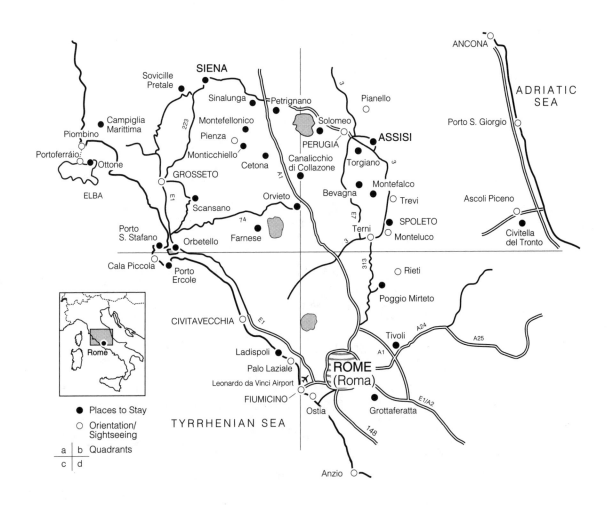

ANCONA

ADRIATIC
SEA

SIENA

Sovicille
Pretale

Sinalunga

Petrignano

Pianello

Solomeo

Porto S. Giorgio

Campiglia
Marittima

Montefellonico

Piombino

Pienza

PERUGIA

ASSISI

Portoferráio

Ottone

Monticchiello

Cetona

Canalicchio
di Collazone

Torgiano

ELBA

GROSSETO

223

Orvieto

Montefalco

Ascoli Piceno

Scansano

E1

Bevagna

Trevi

SPOLETO

74

Terni

Monteluco

Civitella
del Tronto

Porto
S. Stafano

Orbetello

Farnese

A1

E7

3

Cala Piccola

Porto
Ercole

313

Rieti

Poggio Mirteto

Rome

CIVITAVECCHIA

E1

Tivoli

A24

A25

Ladispoli

A1

Palo Laziale

ROME
(Roma)

Leonardo da Vinci Airport

E1/A2

FIUMICINO

Ostia

Grottaferatta

● Places to Stay

○ Orientation/
  Sightseeing

TYRRHENIAN SEA

148

| a | b | Quadrants
| c | d |

Anzio

*Map 10*

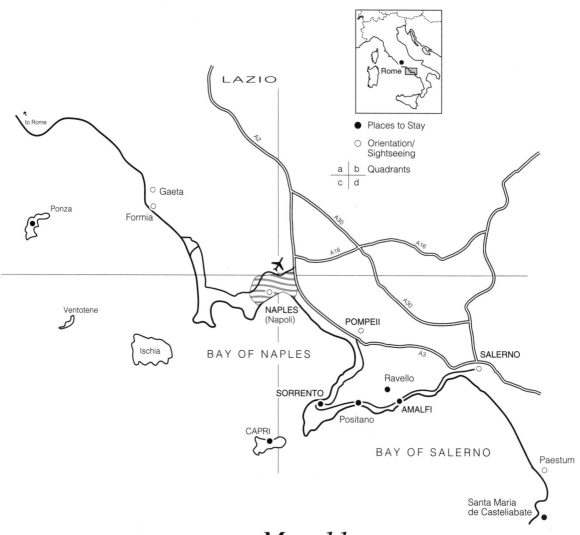

to Rome

LAZIO

Rome

● Places to Stay

○ Orientation/
   Sightseeing

| a | b | Quadrants |
|---|---|-----------|
| c | d |           |

A2

○ Gaeta

Ponza

Formia ○

A30

A16                    A16

Ventotene

NAPLES
(Napoli)

POMPEII
○

A30

Ischia

BAY OF NAPLES

A3                    SALERNO

Ravello
●

SORRENTO                    AMALFI

Positano

CAPRI

BAY OF SALERNO

Paestum
○

Santa Maria
de Casteliabate ●

*Map 11*

342

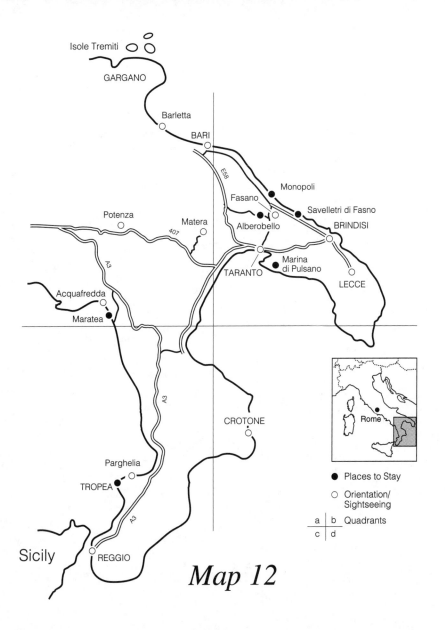

Isole Tremiti

GARGANO

Barletta

BARI

E58

Monopoli

Fasano

Savelletri di Fasno

Potenza

Matera

Alberobello

BRINDISI

407

Marina
di Pulsano

TARANTO

LECCE

Acquafredda

A3

Maratea

CROTONE

Parghelia

A3

TROPEA

Sicily

A3

REGGIO

*Map 12*

Rome

● Places to Stay

○ Orientation/
Sightseeing

| a | b | Quadrants |
|---|---|---|
| c | d | |

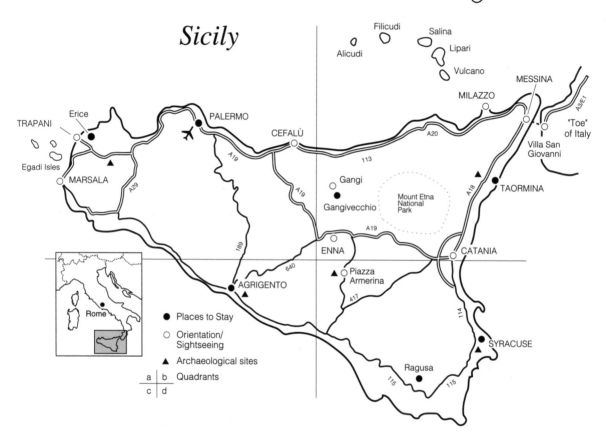

Sicily

Stromboli

Filicudi

Salina

Alicudi

Lipari

Vulcano

MESSINA

MILAZZO

"Toe" of Italy

Villa San Giovanni

Erice

TRAPANI

PALERMO

CEFALÙ

A20

A3/E1

A19

113

Egadi Isles

A18

TAORMINA

MARSALA

A19

Gangi

Gangivecchio

Mount Etna National Park

A29

A19

A19

640

189

A19

ENNA

CATANIA

AGRIGENTO

Piazza Armerina

417

114

Rome

● Places to Stay

○ Orientation/ Sightseeing

▲ Archaeological sites

SYRACUSE

Ragusa

115

115

| a | b | Quadrants |
| c | d | |

Map 13

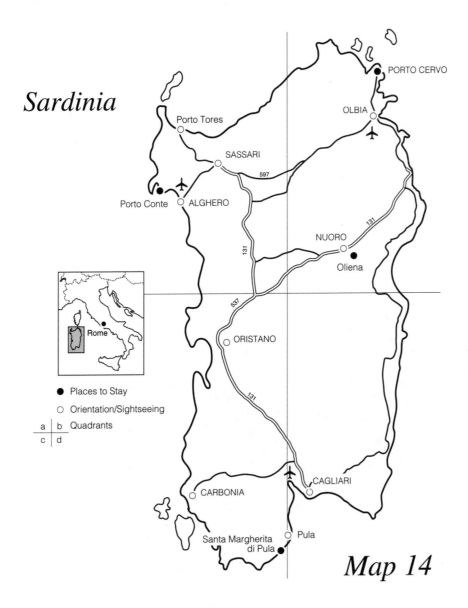

*Sardinia*

PORTO CERVO

Porto Tores

OLBIA

SASSARI

597

Porto Conte
ALGHERO

131

NUORO

131

Oliena

Rome

537

131

ORISTANO

● Places to Stay

○ Orientation/Sightseeing

| a | b | Quadrants |
| c | d | |

CARBONIA

CAGLIARI

Santa Margherita
di Pula

Pula

*Map 14*

345

346

# *Index*

# W

Enhance Your Guides

Online

# www.karenbrown.com

- Hotel News
- Color Photos
- New Discoveries
- Currency Converter
- Corrections & Edits
- Property of the Month
- Postcards from the Road
- Links to Hotels & B&Bs

## Visit Karen's Market

books, maps, itineraries
and travel accessories
selected with our
KB travelers in mind.

# Become a Karen Brown Preferred Reader

Name _____

Street _____

Town _____

State _____ Zip _____ Country _____

Tel _____ Fax _____

E-mail _____

We'd love to welcome you as a Karen Brown Preferred Reader. Send us your name and address and you will be entered in our monthly drawing to receive a free set of Karen Brown guides. As a preferred reader, you will receive special promotions and be the first to know when new editions of Karen Brown guides go to press.

Please send to: Karen Brown's Guides, Post Office Box 70, San Mateo, California 94401, USA
tel: (650) 342-9117, fax: (650) 342-9153, e-mail: karen@karenbrown.com, website: www: karenbrown.com

## SHARE YOUR COMMENTS AND DISCOVERIES WITH US.

Please share comments on properties that you have visited. We welcome accolades, as well as criticisms.

Also, we'd love to hear about any hotel or bed & breakfast you discover. Tell us what you liked about the property and, if possible, please include a brochure or photographs. We regret we cannot return photos.

Owner _____  Hotel or B&B _____

Address _____  Town _____  Country _____

Comments on places that are in the book and/or recommendations for your own *New Discoveries*.

Your name _____  Street _____

Town _____  State _____  Zip _____  Country _____

Tel _____  E-mail _____  Date _____

Do we have your permission to electronically publish your comments on our website?  Yes _____  No _____

If yes, would you like to remain anonymous? Yes ___No ___, or may we use your name? Yes___ No___

Please send report to: Karen Brown's Guides, Post Office Box 70, San Mateo, California 94401, USA
tel: (650) 342-9117, fax: (650) 342-9153, e-mail: karen@karenbrown.com, www.karenbrown.com

## SHARE YOUR COMMENTS AND DISCOVERIES WITH US

Please share comments on properties that you have visited. We welcome accolades, as well as criticisms.

Also, we'd love to hear about any hotel or bed & breakfast you discover. Tell us what you liked about the property and, if possible, please include a brochure or photographs. We regret we cannot return photos.

Owner _____ Hotel or B&B _____

Address _____ Town _____ Country _____

Comments on places that are in the book and/or recommendations for your own *New Discoveries*.

Your name _____ Street _____

Town _____ State _____ Zip _____ Country _____

Tel _____ E-mail _____ Date _____

Do we have your permission to electronically publish your comments on our website? Yes _____ No _____

If yes, would you like to remain anonymous? Yes ___No ___, or may we use your name? Yes___ No___

Please send report to: Karen Brown's Guides, Post Office Box 70, San Mateo, California 94401, USA
tel: (650) 342-9117, fax: (650) 342-9153, e-mail: karen@karenbrown.com, www.karenbrown.com

Need a dual voltage hair dryer, a wrinkle-free blazer, quick-dry clothes, a computer adapter plug? TRAVELSMITH has them all, along with an enticing array of everything a Karen Brown traveler needs.

Karen Brown recommends TRAVELSMITH as an excellent source for travel clothing and gear. We were pleased to find quality products needed for our own research travels in their catalog—items not always easy to find. For a free catalog call TRAVELSMITH at 800-950-1600.

When placing your order, be sure to identify yourself as a Karen Brown Traveler with the code TKBX1 and you will receive a 10% discount.* You can link to TRAVELSMITH through our website *www.karenbrown.com.*

*offer valid till December 2001

# auto ⊛ europe.

## *Karen Brown's*

### Preferred Car Rental Service Provider

### When Traveling to Europe
for

International Car Rental Services
Chauffeur & Transfer Services
Prestige & Sports Cars
Motor Home Rentals

### 800-223-5555

*Be sure to identify yourself as a Karen Brown Traveler.*
*For special offers and discounts use your*
*Karen Brown ID number 99006187.*

# ANY OF THE ACCOMMODATIONS IN THIS GUIDE CAN BE RESERVED THROUGH NICOLE FRANCHINI'S TRAVEL SERVICE, HIDDEN TREASURES OF ITALY.

Reservations provide additional services such as:

- **Personalized itinerary planning**
- **Concert and museum ticket reservation**
- **Private guides, car rental and chauffeured transfers**
- **Special interest itineraries (golf programs, food and wine tours, cooking classes, organized dinners in private historical villas, private garden visits, chartered sailing itineraries to islands).**

Complete wedding/honeymoon planning. Personalized consultation and arrangements for civil or religious wedding ceremonies and reception in the city of your choice. From a private romantic ceremony for two, to a complete wedding in the most enchanting historical places in Italy.

Full pre-payment by check or Mastercard/Visa. Service fees apply.

HIDDEN TREASURES OF ITALY, INC.
55 East Washington Street
Suite 1807
Chicago, IL 60602, USA
U.S. Toll Free Tel: (888) 419-6700

U.S. Tel. (312) 460-8219
Fax: (312) 460-8238
e-mail: info@htitaly.com
www.htitaly.com

# HIDDEN TREASURES OF ITALY

ALSO PRESENTS A SPECIAL **"LIMITED COLLECTION"** OF PERSONALLY SELECTED VILLAS AVAILABLE FOR HOLIDAYS, WEDDINGS AND PERSONALIZED PROGRAMS.

THE HIGHEST EXPRESSION OF QUALITY, SERVICE AND HOSPITALITY IN THE MOST CHARMING LOCATIONS.

HIDDEN TREASURES OF ITALY

**www.htitaly.com**

# KB Travel Service

❖ **KB Travel Service** offers travel planning assistance using itineraries designed by *Karen Brown* and published in her guidebooks. We will customize any itinerary to fit your personal interests.

❖ We will plan your itinerary with you, help you decide how long to stay and what to do once you arrive, and work out the details.

❖ We will book your airline tickets and your rental car, arrange rail travel, reserve accommodations recommended in *Karen Brown's Guides,* and supply you with point-to-point information and consultation.

Contact us to start planning your travel!

800.782.2128 ext. 328 or e-mail: info@kbtravelservice.com

*Service fees do apply*

**KB Travel Service**
16 East Third Avenue
San Mateo, CA 94401 USA
www.kbtravelservice.com

Independently owned and operated by Town & Country Travel
CST 2001543-10

# Seal Cove Inn

## *Located in the San Francisco Bay Area*

Karen Brown Herbert (best known as author of the Karen Brown's guides) and her husband, Rick, have put 22 years of experience into reality and opened their own superb hideaway, Seal Cove Inn. Spectacularly set amongst wild flowers and bordered by towering cypress trees, Seal Cove Inn looks out to the distant ocean over acres of county park: an oasis where you can enjoy secluded beaches, explore tidepools, watch frolicking seals, and follow the tree-lined path that traces the windswept ocean bluffs. Country antiques, original watercolors, flower-laden cradles, rich fabrics, and the gentle ticking of grandfather clocks create the perfect ambiance for a foggy day in front of the crackling log fire. Each bedroom is its own haven with a cozy sitting area before a wood-burning fireplace and doors opening onto a private balcony or patio with views to the park and ocean. Moss Beach is a 35-minute drive south of San Francisco, 6 miles north of the picturesque town of Half Moon Bay, and a few minutes from Princeton harbor with its colorful fishing boats and restaurants. Seal Cove Inn makes a perfect base for whale-watching, salmon-fishing excursions, day trips to San Francisco, exploring the coast, or, best of all, just a romantic interlude by the sea, time to relax and be pampered. Karen and Rick look forward to the pleasure of welcoming you to their coastal hideaway.

*Seal Cove Inn • 221 Cypress Avenue • Moss Beach • California • 94038 • USA*
*tel: (650) 728-4114, fax: (650) 728-4116, e-mail: sealcove@coastside.net, website: sealcoveinn.com*

KAREN BROWN wrote her first travel guide in 1976. Her personalized travel series has grown to fourteen titles which Karen and her small staff work diligently to keep updated. Karen, her husband, Rick, and their children, Alexandra and Richard, live in Moss Beach, a small town on the coast south of San Francisco. They settled here in 1991 when they opened Seal Cove Inn. Karen is frequently traveling, but when she is home, in her role as innkeeper, enjoys welcoming Karen Brown readers.

CLARE BROWN, CTC, was a travel consultant for many years, specializing in planning itineraries to Europe using charming small hotels in the countryside. The focus of her job remains unchanged, but now her expertise is available to a larger audience—the readers of her daughter Karen's country inn guides. When Clare and her husband, Bill, are not traveling, they live either in Hillsborough, California, or at their home in Vail, Colorado, where family and friends frequently join them for skiing.

JUNE BROWN'S love of travel was inspired by the *National Geographic* magazines that she read as a girl in her dentist's office—so far she has visited over 40 countries. June hails from Sheffield, England and lived in Zambia and Canada before moving to northern California where she lives in San Mateo with her husband, Tony, their daughter Clare, their German Shepherd, and a Siamese cat.

BARBARA TAPP, the talented artist who produces all of the hotel sketches and delightful illustrations in this guide, was raised in Australia where she studied in Sydney at the School of Interior Design. Although Barbara continues with freelance projects, she devotes much of her time to illustrating the Karen Brown guides. Barbara lives in Kensington, California, with her husband, Richard, their two sons, Jonothan and Alexander, and daughter, Georgia.

JANN POLLARD, the artist responsible for the beautiful painting on the cover of this guide, has studied art since childhood, and is well-known for her outstanding impressionistic-style watercolors which she has exhibited in numerous juried shows, winning many awards. Jann travels frequently to Europe (using Karen Brown's guides) where she loves to paint historical buildings. Jann lives in Burlingame, California, with her husband, Gene.

# Travel Your Dreams • Order your Karen Brown Guides Today

Please ask in your local bookstore for Karen Brown's Guides. If the books you want are unavailable, you may order directly from the publisher. Books will be shipped immediately.

_____ *Austria: Charming Inns & Itineraries* $19.95

_____ *California: Charming Inns & Itineraries* $19.95

_____ *England: Charming Bed & Breakfasts* $18.95

_____ *England, Wales & Scotland: Charming Hotels & Itineraries* $19.95

_____ *France: Charming Bed & Breakfasts* $18.95

_____ *France: Charming Inns & Itineraries* $19.95

_____ *Germany: Charming Inns & Itineraries* $19.95

_____ *Ireland: Charming Inns & Itineraries* $19.95

_____ *Italy: Charming Bed & Breakfasts* $18.95

_____ *Italy: Charming Inns & Itineraries* $19.95

_____ *New England: Charming Inns & Itineraries* $19.95

_____ *Portugal: Charming Inns & Itineraries* $19.95

_____ *Spain: Charming Inns & Itineraries* $19.95

_____ *Switzerland: Charming Inns & Itineraries* $19.95

Name _____ Street _____

Town _____ State_____ Zip _____ Tel _____

Credit Card (MasterCard or Visa) _____ Expires: _____

For orders in the USA, add $4 for the first book and $1 for each additional book for shipment. California residents add 8.25% sales tax. Overseas orders add $10 per book for airmail shipment. Indicate number of copies of each title; fax or mail form with check or credit card information to:

KAREN BROWN'S GUIDES
Post Office Box 70 • San Mateo • California • 94401 • USA
tel: (650) 342-9117, fax: (650) 342-9153, e-mail: karen@karenbrown.com
You can also order directly from our website at www.karenbrown.com.

# Notes